11/23

D0568118

EXPLORING THE OLD TESTAMENT

Volume 1

The Pentateuch

Gordon Wenham studied theology at Cambridge, London (King's College), Jerusalem (Ecole Biblique) and Harvard University (USA). He lectured at Queen's University, Belfast (1970–81) before moving to Cheltenham, where he is professor of Old Testament at the University of Gloucestershire. He has written a thesis on Deuteronomy and commentaries on Genesis, Leviticus and Numbers as well as numerous articles in scholarly journals. He chairs the Tyndale Fellowship Old Testament Study Group. He is married and has four children. His hobbies include gardening, cycling and Jewish affairs.

Exploring the Old Testament

The Pentateuch by Gordon Wenham

The Historical Books by Philip Satterthwaite and Gordon McConville

The Psalms and Wisdom Literature by Ernest Lucas

The Prophets by Gordon McConville

Exploring the New Testament

The Gospels and Acts by David Wenham and Steve Walton

The Letters and Revelation by Howard Marshall, Stephen Travis and Ian Paul

OLD
TESTAMENT

Exploring the
Old Testament

A Guide to the Pentateuch

GORDON J. WENHAM

Volume
One

InterVarsity Press
Downers Grove, Illinois

InterVarsity Press
P.O. Box 1400, Downers Grove, IL 60515-1426
World Wide Web: www.ivpress.com
E-mail: email@ivpress.com

InterVarsity Press® is the book-publishing division of InterVarsity Christian Fellowship/USA®, a student movement active on campus at hundreds of universities, colleges and schools of nursing in the United States of America, and a member movement of the International Fellowship of Evangelical Students. For information about local and regional activities, write Public Relations Dept., InterVarsity Christian Fellowship/USA, 6400 Schroeder Rd., P.O. Box 7895, Madison, WI 53707-7895, or visit the IVCF website at <www.intervarsity.org>.

Cover photograph: National Gallery Budapest/SuperStock

ISBN 978-0-8308-2541-7

Printed in the United States of America ∞

g **green press INITIATIVE** *InterVarsity Press is committed to protecting the environment and to the responsible use of natural resources. As a member of Green Press Initiative we use recycled paper whenever possible. To learn more about the Green Press Initiative, visit <www.greenpressinitiative.org>.*

Library of Congress Cataloging-in-Publication Data has been requested.

P	29	28	27	26	25	24	23	22	21	20	19	18	17	16	15	14	13	12	11	10	9	8	7	6	5	4	3	2	1
Y	33	32	31	30	29	28	27	26	25	24	23	22	21	20	19	18	17	16	15	14	13	12	11	10	09	08			

Contents

THE PENTATEUCH

List of Illustrations   vii
Key to Panels   viii
Preface   xi
Acknowledgements   xii
Introduction   xiii
Abbreviations   xv

1 **What Is the Pentateuch? Basic Features**   1
   Name   1
   Genre   2
   Biography of Moses   2
   National History   3
   Torah or Law   4
   Why Five Books?   5
   When Did the Pentateuch Become Part
      of the Bible?   6
   Further Reading   7

2 **Genesis 1—11**   9
   Ancient Near Eastern Parallels to
      Genesis 1—11   9
   Genesis' Transformation of Oriental Origin
      Stories   15
   The Organization of Genesis 1—11   18
   The New Testament Use of Genesis 1—11   33
   Further Reading   34

3 **Genesis 12—50**   35
   The Genre of Genesis 12—50   36
   11:27—25:11: The Story of Abraham   37
   25:12–18: Genealogy of Ishmael   45
   25:19—35:29: The Story of Jacob and Esau   45
   36:1—37:1: Genealogy of Esau   51

37:2—50:26: The Story of Joseph and His
   Brothers   51
The New Testament Use of Genesis 12—50   55
Further Reading   56

4 **Exodus**   57
   Structure   58
   Slavery in Egypt and Liberation   58
   The Law-giving   67
   The Tabernacle   74
   The New Testament and the Book of Exodus   79
   Further Reading   79

5 **Leviticus**   81
   Structure   81
   The Problems of Reading Leviticus   82
      Visualization   82
      Significance   83
      Interpretation   84
   1:1—7:38: Laws on Sacrifice   84
   8:1—10:20: Institution of the Priesthood   89
   11:1—16:34: Uncleanness and Its Treatment   91
   17:1—27:34: Prescriptions for Practical
      Holiness   95
   The New Testament and Leviticus   99
   Further Reading   100

6 **Numbers**   103
   Structure   103
   The Contents of Numbers   105
   Numbers and the New Testament   121
   Further Reading   121

7   **Deuteronomy**   123
    Structure   125
    Deuteronomy and the New Testament   142
    Further Reading   143

8   **Theme of the Pentateuch**   145
    Martin Noth on the Themes of the Pentateuch   145
    Gerhard von Rad and the Pentateuch   147
    David Clines on the Theme of the Pentateuch   150
    Reassessment   153
    Further Reading   157

9   **Composition of the Pentateuch**   159
    The Traditional Ascription of the Pentateuch
        to Moses   159
    The Documentary Hypothesis   160
    The Identification of the Sources   165
    Twentieth-century Adjustments to the
        Documentary Hypothesis   171
    The Collapse of the Consensus since 1975   172

    The Trend towards Unitary Readings   173
    The Dating of the Sources   176
    Further Reading   183

10 **Rhetoric of the Pentateuch**   187
    Guarded Optimism – a Twelfth-century
        Setting   188
    Celebration and Protest – a Tenth-century
        Setting   189
    Reassurance to the Dispirited – a
        Seventh-century setting   191
    Hope in Difficult Times – A Fifth-century
        Setting   193
    Further Reading   195

11 **Epilogue**   197

    Glossary   199

    Index   203

ILLUSTRATIONS

MAPS

1 Abraham's wanderings	42
2 Exodus route	65
3 Borders of Canaan	119

FIGURES

1 Ziggurat	17
2 Adam's family tree	46
3 The tabernacle	75
4 Cleanness rules	92
5 Arrangement of material in Exodus in relation to Numbers	104
6 Israel in camp	105
7 Israel on the march	106
8 Scalloped loincloth	111
9 Phylactery	133
10 The documentary hypothesis	167

TABLES

Parallels between the Sumerian flood story and Genesis 1—9	11
Internal titles in the book of Genesis	18
Creation	19
Genealogies of Adam to Noah	25
Creation before and after the flood	30
Structure of Genesis 12—50	35
Arrangement of the story of Jacob	46
Arrangement of the story of Joseph	51
The plagues	61
Sacrifices: An overview	87
Cleanness rules	92
Spectrum of conditions from holy to unclean	96
Grades of uncleanness	96
Festivals	98
Sacrifices: An overview (completed)	101
Structure of Numbers	104
Two halves of Numbers	104
Parallels between Exodus and Numbers	109
Scenes in the Balaam story	115
Further parallels between Exodus and Numbers	116
Animal sacrifices	117
Deuteronomy's structure as a cross between a law code and a treaty	125
Structure of the second sermon	129
Deuteronomy's application of the Ten Commandments	133
Astruc's analysis of Genesis 1—11	164
Identification of sources	166
Documentary hypothesis	166
Dating of sources	167
Characteristics of different eras and sources	170
Deuteronomy in parallel with Hittite and Assyrian treaties	180

KEY TO PANELS

This key to the panels helps locate the special and suggested exercises that occur throughout the volume. It should be noted that the panels are not exhaustive treatments of topics, and are meant to be read and used in their contexts.

'WHAT DO YOU THINK?' PANELS

Rewriting the story of human origins	11
The definition of myth	13
The Protevangelium	23
Hardening the heart	62
The Ten Commandments in today's society	70
The jubilee today	99
The structure of Numbers	104
Why were later complaints treated more harshly?	110
The biblical definition of murder	120
Reflecting on Noth's themes	147
Claims of Mosaic authorship	160
Is Whybray right?	175

'DIGGING DEEPER' PANELS

The Sumerian King List opening lines	12
Retelling modern cosmology theologically	17
Significant days in Genesis 1	20
Genesis and ecology	20
Adam and Cain: Deeds, words and character	22
The symbolism of Eve	23
Did Methuselah really live 969 years?	26
Find the palistrophe	28
Was there a universal flood?	30
Noah's drunkenness: Does Genesis think it sinful?	32
Parallels between the patriarchs	37
Are the patriarchal stories historical?	38
Changing promises	40
The Akedah or sacrifice of Isaac	44
Ancient marriage customs	48
Judah's speech	54
The name of God	60
The Passover	64
Slavery and the *lex talionis*	72
What did the cherubim look like?	76
Structure of the laws	85
Making sense of sacrifice	86
Clean and unclean	91
Clarifying the order of ceremonies on the Day of Atonement	95
Ancient versions of the priestly blessing	108
Parallels in complaint stories	109
The spies and the golden calf	111
Archaeology and the tassels	112
The bronze snake in the Timnah temple	113
Balaam and his donkey	114
Balaam outside the Bible	115

Festivals and their importance 117

The New Testament's appeal to Numbers 121

The Ten Commandments and ancient treaties 126

Spin and the spies 127

The love of God in Deuteronomy 130

Use of Deuteronomy in Jewish worship 132

The chosen place of worship in Deuteronomy 134

Deuteronomy's humanitarianism 135

War in Deuteronomy 137

Story and fulfilment of promises 152

Source analysis of Genesis 1—11 163

Joseph and his brothers, Genesis 37 174

Settings for the Pentateuch 195

OTHER PANELS

The religion of the patriarchs 49

Egypt in the Joseph story 53

Further reflection on the census results 106

PREFACE

Exploring the Old Testament is designed to help the beginning student understand the writings of the Old Testament. It serves the purpose of an introduction, but its unique format is devised to make the volumes accessible to the modern reader. *EOT* engages with the reader, by interspersing interactive panels with the main text. These panels ask for responses, suggest lines of thought, give further information, or indicate ways in which particular topics might be followed up in more depth. This design aims to make the volumes useful either for independent study or as a class text.

EOT aims to show the relevance of Old Testament study both to theology and to modern life. Its four authors, each writing in areas in which they have previously published extensively, believe that the Old Testament has foundational significance for theology and Christian belief and practice.

For that reason *EOT* expressly aims to incorporate modern approaches to interpreting the text. While the traditional historical questions are given their due place, newer approaches such as canonical and rhetorical criticism are represented. It is hoped that this will enable the student to see the potential applications of the books of the Old Testament to modern life.

EOT is a companion series to *Exploring the New Testament*.

Gordon McConville
Series editor

ACKNOWLEDGEMENTS

I should like to thank Ruth McCurry, Gordon McConville and Alan Millard for their advice and encouragement and my son Christopher for the maps and graphics.

INTRODUCTION

The first five books of the Bible, often called the Pentateuch, are fundamental to the faith of both Christians and Jews. These books contain the familiar stories of creation, the fall and the flood. They tell of the origins of the human race and of the Jewish people. They include laws as basic as the Ten Commandments and as complex as the regulations for food and sacrifices. These books relate the call of Israel to be God's chosen people, yet hold out the prospect of universal salvation for all mankind. So profound has been the influence of these books on Western culture that their ideas are embedded in our language and ideology at point after point.

Yet anyone picking up a Bible and starting to read Genesis for the first time will soon be surprised, puzzled and sometimes shocked, for despite the Pentateuch's foundational role in our culture, its ideas often seem utterly alien to the modern reader. Its approach to chronology, history, ethics and God challenge the modern world view at so many points that readers may be tempted to stop reading

very quickly. But this would be a great mistake. The Pentateuch is a fascinating world, which deserves to be explored carefully and sympathetically. And this is what this volume tries to do.

Exploring the Old Testament is the general title of this series, and this first volume will try to guide you through the Pentateuch so that you can appreciate what it was trying to say to its first readers and why it should still be of interest to people living in the twenty-first century. I shall introduce you to the social world of the Bible, to its marriage customs, national festivals, welfare systems and legal ideals. I shall endeavour to illuminate the relationship between Israel and the surrounding cultures, the subtle mix of dependence and originality that characterizes the Pentateuch's use of ancient Near Eastern ideas. We shall look at some of the literary techniques used in the Pentateuch, its love of symmetrical patterns and its rhetorical devices. But pre-eminently the Pentateuch speaks of God and his relationship to Israel mediated by Moses, so in exploring the book we shall try to come to terms with its theology, its ideas about God, its religious practices, its concepts of faith, obedience and loyalty.

But a guide to the Pentateuch needs to be more than a description of what is there: it needs to explain something of the history of the study of the Pentateuch, of how scholars have come to understand it in the way they now do. It therefore contains, at various points, summaries of current scholarly debates, e.g. on patriarchal religion, or notes on recent archaeological discoveries. The later chapters of the book contain a more extended discussion of the composition of the Pentateuch, an issue that has been more fully debated by biblical scholars than any other topic. My treatment does not pretend to be comprehensive, just to give the first-time reader some bearings in a most complicated discussion.

So how is this guide organized? Its opening chapters take you through the Pentateuch book by book explaining the contents and ideas of each book chapter by chapter, trying to show how the parts cohere as part of a larger whole. Frequently this running narrative is interrupted by diagrams, tables, maps or boxes headed 'Digging deeper'. In them you will find short discussions on particular topics, or issues to be researched or reflected on. Often they pose questions without giving an answer. These digressions are important: they are designed to make you think about significant issues, e.g. slavery or famine relief, or make you try out the principles

of literary criticism for yourself. I want you to get out of the tourist bus and explore the terrain yourself, before you move on to the next issue. When you have completed the suggested exercise, read on in the main text and you may find what I think about the issue I raised in the 'Digging deeper' box.

Overseas travel often prompts thoughtful tourists to reflect on their own culture and to realize their own peculiarities. Reading the Pentateuch should have a similar effect, and sometimes I have tried to encourage this by asking reader-orientated questions in these 'What do you think?' boxes. In these cases I have usually avoided giving my opinion later in the text, as I do not want to impose my personal convictions on the reader.

In the next chapters, on Theme, Composition and Rhetorical Function of the Pentateuch, I address issues that relate to all five books. Here I attempt to describe the major scholarly approaches to the original message, processes of composition and function of the Pentateuch. Of necessity this involves much summarizing of secondary literature in a rather descriptive way, but I have again tried to introduce interactive elements, challenging readers to try to reproduce the results of source analysis for themselves and to examine their own critical assumptions or those of the scholars who have argued for particular views.

Finally let me point out that a guidebook is no substitute for visiting the place itself!

This *Exploring the Old Testament* series is designed to encourage the reading of the Bible, not replace it! I simply hope this volume will make the Pentateuch easier to grasp, and help you to appreciate its abiding power, beauty and relevance, and to share my enthusiasm for reading it.

ABBREVIATIONS

ABD	*Anchor Bible Dictionary*
BA	*Biblical Archaeologist*
ESV	English Standard Version
JBL	*Journal of Biblical Literature*
JJS	*Journal of Jewish Studies*
JSOT	*Journal for the Study of the Old Testament*
JSOT Press	Journal for the Study of the Old Testament Press
NIV	New International Version
NRSV	New Revised Standard Version
RSV	Revised Standard Version
SBL Diss	Society of Biblical Literature Dissertation Series
VT	*Vetus Testamentum*
WTJ	*Westminster Theological Journal*
ZAW	*Zeitschrift für die alttestamentliche Wissenschaft*

Chapter 1

WHAT IS THE PENTATEUCH? BASIC FEATURES

The Pentateuch, the first five books of the Bible, has always been regarded as one of the most significant parts of Scripture. It offers an explanation of the world and its inhabitants. It explains the origins of sin and traces its consequences. It introduces the idea of a chosen people through whom the world will be redeemed. In the law it sets out a pattern for the ideal society and in the Ten Commandments expresses principles of behaviour that have commanded almost universal respect. Thus traditionally these opening books have been regarded both by Christians and Jews as the most important and authoritative part of the Old Testament.

Yet for modern readers these key books are often viewed as the most problematic, historically, ethically and theologically. But it is this clash between tradition and modern thinking that has led to such continuing interest in these books. An introduction to the Pentateuch cannot pretend to solve the modern reader's problems, but we hope it will lead to an understanding of the debates and the reasons behind different approaches to resolving these issues.

NAME

The word Pentateuch, Greek for 'five books', draws attention to the most obvious feature of this part of the Bible. It is essentially a long narrative, which according to its own chronology covers some 2700 years of world history concluding with the death of Moses. But this period is very unequally covered. Genesis with 50 chapters and 1534 verses covers some 2300 years. Then Exodus to Numbers 14 covers the events at Sinai, just over a year in chronological time, in 81 chapters and 2617 verses. The remaining chapters of Numbers (22 with 739 verses) deal with the 40 years of wanderings in the wilderness, and the last book Deuteronomy, focusing on the last day or so of Moses' life, comprises some 34 chapters with 955 verses.

This unevenness in the representation of chronological time in the narrative helps us to see the writer's chief interest, namely

1

the law-giving at Sinai and its reinterpretation by Moses just before he died. So it is quite apt that Jews term the Pentateuch the Torah, which is usually translated 'law' in English. Genesis provides the background to the law-giving, Exodus to Numbers is largely taken up with the proclamation of the law, while Deuteronomy offers a most authoritative commentary on the law by Israel's greatest prophet Moses.

GENRE

But should the whole Pentateuch be described as 'law' when so much of it is narrative? It is essentially a history of the world from creation to the death of Moses with a number of digressions dealing mainly with the law. Would it be better to call it a biography of Moses (van Seters 1999), or a national history (van Seters 1999; Whybray 1995)? This issue of genre is important for it gives a clue to the author's understanding of his work and how he hoped his readers would understand it. So these alternatives need to be explored a little more carefully.

BIOGRAPHY OF MOSES

Probably the most obvious description of Exodus to Deuteronomy is a biography of Moses. It tells of his birth to a Levite family, his adoption by an Egyptian princess, and his upbringing in the Egyptian court. It tells how he was forced to flee from Egypt, and became a shepherd in the wilderness of Midian. There, at the burning bush, he

encountered God, who sent him back to rescue his fellow Israelites from Egyptian slavery. The drama heightens with Moses demanding that the Pharaoh release the Israelites, and the Pharaoh refusing despite the ever-graver plagues that his obstinacy brought on the Egyptians. But eventually Israel is released and Moses leads them triumphantly through the Red Sea to Mount Sinai, where the law is given and the covenant between God and Israel is sealed. In both law-giving and covenant making Moses plays a central role as mediator between God and Israel. He receives the Ten Commandments and all the other rules and regulations. Then when the people break the covenant by making the golden calf, it is Moses' intercession that turns back God's anger so that the nation survives and is allowed to proceed towards the promised land of Canaan. He does the same again, when the spies bring back a discouraging report about the difficulty of conquering the land and the people wish to return to Egypt: Moses intercedes for the people and ensures that at least their children will enter the land. Finally, like the patriarchs before him when they knew they were about to die, Moses summons the whole nation, and in three speeches and two poems he gives his last will and testament to the nation. Then he dies, and is buried in an unmarked grave in Transjordan.

Thus many features of Exodus to Deuteronomy are well explained if these books are seen as a biography of Moses. However, it is not so obvious that the whole Pentateuch fits this definition: Genesis seems rather loosely related to the life of Moses. One would not have expected so much background material as Genesis provides to have been included if the whole Pentateuch were intended to be a biography of Moses. Some features of the patriarchs' careers do seem to foreshadow Moses'. For example Abraham's exodus from Egypt is described in terms that resemble the later exodus (Gen. 12:20—13:1). Moses' great role as a prophetic intercessor is foreshadowed by Abraham (Gen. 18:23–33; 20:7 cf. Exod. 33:12–16; Num. 14:13–19). Jacob's career as a shepherd, his encounter with his future wife by a well, and his deathbed blessing (Gen. 29; 49) all parallel episodes in Moses' life (Exod. 2:16—3:6; Deut. 33). But in the context of the whole of Genesis these features seem to be marginal to its chief interests. There are many aspects of the book that would suggest that Genesis at least is most interested in the origin of the people of Israel and the 12 tribes, and in the promise of the land of Canaan.

NATIONAL HISTORY

For these reasons van Seters, while holding that an early form of Exodus to Numbers may have been a biography of Moses, prefers to see the current Pentateuch as the first part of a national history of Israel: the second part consists of the next section of the Hebrew Bible from the book of Joshua to 2 Kings. (He believes that the second part of this history was actually written before the first.) The two parts of this national history thus trace Israel's history from the call of Abraham to the death of Moses: the second runs from the conquest of the land under Joshua's leadership to the fall of Jerusalem and the people's exile from the land.

Van Seters draws attention to the work of Herodotus, the Greek historian, as providing a fitting analogy to the Pentateuch as a national history. Interestingly, Herodotus' near-contemporaries Hecataeus and Hellanicus linked their national histories to primeval events, such as the flood, just as Genesis 1—11 does. Somewhat later in time (c. 300 BC) but closer in space the Babyloniaka of Berossus and the Aegyptiaka of Manetho do something similar. It has therefore been conjectured that both Greek and Hebrew works ultimately derive their pattern from Mesopotamian forerunners.

It is undoubtedly the case that there are strong Mesopotamian parallels to Genesis 1—11, as we shall see in the next chapter. There are also Mesopotamian historical works that span up to eight centuries, but they do not link the eras they relate to primeval times. This is one reason why Blenkinsopp (1992) and Whybray (1995) think the Pentateuch is unique. It is also unlike the Greek histories in recounting events from an impersonal divine perspective, as opposed to the very personal style of Herodotus, who clearly informs the reader at the outset that he is telling the story. Finally the enormous quantity of law and other ethical material sets the Pentateuch apart from Greek historical works.

TORAH OR LAW

The difficulties of defining the Pentateuch as either a biography of Moses or as a national history make it worth re-examining the traditional term for the Pentateuch as the law, which is of course very common in the New Testament (e.g. Luke 24:44) and the term used in the Hebrew Bible for the first five books. On the face of it 'law' seems a good description of Exodus 20 to the end of Deuteronomy, at least if one ignores the narrative framework of the laws, but it seems somewhat awkward to describe the stories of Genesis as law, or the account of Moses' early life and the exodus from Egypt.

However, the Hebrew word *torah*, conventionally translated 'law' is a much broader idea than its English translation conveys. *Torah* derives from the verb *yarah* to 'teach' or 'instruct', so we would be wiser to render *torah* as 'instruction' rather than 'law'. And Genesis of course is full of instruction, about the nature of God, the history of the world and Israel. It is also instructive in giving examples of behaviour that should be imitated and mistakes that should be avoided. The same is true of the early chapters of Exodus, which demonstrate the folly of the greatest of earthly kings pitting himself against almighty God. Likewise Israel's mistakes in the wilderness are surely recorded, to remind them both of God's mercies in the past and of the danger of making the same mistakes again in the future (Deut. 1:19–45; 9:6—10:11). Obviously all the laws and ritual legislation could well be termed 'instruction' too: these laws are not restrictions hemming people in from doing what they like, rather they are God's wise advice, which if followed, will lead to a happy and prosperous society. As Deuteronomy puts it: 'Keep them and do them: for that will be your wisdom and your understanding in the sight of the peoples, who, when they hear all these statutes, will say, "Surely this great nation is a wise and understanding people"' (Deut. 4:6).

For these reasons I think there is merit in retaining the old Hebrew term *torah* to describe the Pentateuch, translating it or at least understanding it as 'instruction' rather than 'law'. This instruction though is more than merely imparting information. It is not purveying historical facts for facts' sake or laws for laws' sake; rather it is seeking to persuade its hearers to obey. It instructs in order to persuade: 'that it may go well with you, and with your children after you' (Deut. 4:40).

However, persuasive instruction is not unique to the first five books of the Bible. The Book of Proverbs aims to instruct and to persuade, as do the prophets; but their poetic form distinguishes them from the Pentateuch. Instruction through narrative is the hallmark of most of the historical books of the Old Testament, from Joshua to Esther, so that in a broad sense these books too could be called *torah* 'instruction'. To capture the uniqueness of the Pentateuch, it would probably therefore be best to define it as *torah* 'instruction' in the form of a biography of Moses.

WHY FIVE BOOKS?

Whether understood as a biography of Moses, national history or instruction Genesis to Deuteronomy constitute a consecutive coherent narrative, so why and when was it split up into five separate books? Chapter divisions were the inventions of Stephen Langton, an Archbishop of Canterbury about AD 1200; and verse numbers were introduced in the sixteenth century, although the division into verses goes back at least a thousand years earlier. Other subdivisions of the text, which are not apparent in English translations, only in the Hebrew original, are earlier still and are designed to divide the text into manageable sections for reading in synagogue worship. But the origin of the division into five books is lost in the mists of time, and appears to go back well into pre-Christian times.

The division into five books and their names was simply taken for granted in the first century AD. Matthew, who portrays Jesus as the second Moses, presents his teaching in five large blocks, which are often seen as reflecting the five books of the law. The first-century Jewish writers Josephus and Philo know the fivefold division and mention some of their names. Other texts from the second and third centuries BC, such as Ecclesiasticus and the letter of Aristeas, also seem to presuppose the division into five books.

But the most interesting evidence comes from the book of the Psalms. The Psalter, like the Pentateuch, is divided into five books. But, as has been realized fairly recently, this is no superficial feature of the Psalms but is fundamental to the editor's understanding of the Psalms. The psalms about the law stick out by the position, e.g. Psalm 1, or their length, Psalm 119. Psalm 1 is an invitation to the reader to meditate on the law day and night to ensure his own prosperity; the law envisaged is not just the five books of Moses, but the five books of the Psalms. Here we have a high claim for the value of the psalms in their own right, but this claim rests on the unquestioned premise of the significance of the law. It also of course presupposes that the Pentateuch existed in five books, an arrangement that the Psalter is imitating.

If we knew when the Psalter was arranged in its present form, we could say that the fivefold division of the Pentateuch must be earlier still. Unfortunately it is impossible to be dogmatic about this. There is nothing in the Psalms that looks as though it comes any later than the exilic, or perhaps early post-exilic period. In this case the Psalms could have been arranged in five books no later than the fifth century BC. On the other hand the Psalms are found in the last part of the Hebrew Bible, whose canon may not have been closed till the second century BC or even the first century AD. This would allow us to suppose that the Psalms were arranged in five books somewhat later than the fifth century. So in turn the Pentateuch might have been divided into five books later too. Nevertheless the evidence does suggest the division reaches well back into the Old Testament period.

But why divide the Pentateuch into five books at all? Modern synagogue scrolls contain the whole Pentateuch in a single parchment scroll, so why were the books originally separate? Part of the reason may have been the writing material used. According to Haran, parchment made from animal skin did not come into use among the Jews until post-exilic times; earlier, as the tale of King Jehoiakim slicing up the scroll of Jeremiah suggests, literary works were written on papyrus (Jer. 36). This meant works had to be much shorter, as papyrus was not so strong and supple as parchment. Genesis seems to have been close to the practical limit, for there are few books in the Old Testament that are much longer.

In the standard printed Hebrew Bible Genesis takes 85 pages, Exodus 72, Leviticus 51, Numbers 74, and Deuteronomy 71. Ancient scrolls would similarly have varied in length. It is easy to see why Genesis was made into a separate scroll, as it serves as an introduction to the other books. Deuteronomy too stands apart as Moses' farewell to his people. But Exodus to Numbers do form a consecutive story interspersed with law, which had to be split up just to make their length manageable. But this division does not seem to be arbitrary, for both Exodus and Numbers are about the same length, with the somewhat shorter Leviticus sandwiched in between. It may be that this arrangement with Leviticus at the heart of the Pentateuch draws attention to the importance of its laws on sacrifice and uncleanness, which, as we shall see, are fundamental to the message of the Pentateuch.

WHEN DID THE PENTATEUCH BECOME PART OF THE BIBLE?

Canonization, or the process by which books of the Bible were first recognized as inspired and authoritative and then incorporated into the collection of holy books which constitute the Bible, has been a topic of long and heated debate. However, it is generally agreed that the Pentateuch was the first part of the Bible to be accepted as canonical by the Jews, that the second main division of the Hebrew Bible, the Prophets, came next, and that finally the other books, the Writings, were canonized. Most of the debate centres round the final stage of the canonization of the Writings: there is much wider agreement that the Pentateuch was recognized as canonical in the fifth century BC about the time of Ezra. Not only does Ezra read and interpret the law publicly to all the people (Neh. 8—9), but the books of Ezra and Nehemiah are peppered with phrases such as 'as it is written in the law of Moses' (Ezra 3:2; Neh. 8:14 etc.) which attest the canonical status of the Pentateuch. There are hints in earlier times that the law was considered authoritative. The book of Amos (eighth century BC) repeatedly alludes to the legal requirements and threats in the Pentateuch, and in Josiah's reign a book of the law was found in the temple whose public reading caused great consternation in the royal court. Usually this law book is identified with Deuteronomy or part of it, but while its contents may be uncertain the writer of Kings is in no doubt about its authority (2 Kings 22—23).

Within the Pentateuch itself there are hints that it is supposed to be understood canonically from its inception. Exodus 24:3–4 mentions that Moses wrote down all the words that God told him and that the people promised to obey it. Deuteronomy insists that its words must not be added to or changed (4:2), must be read to the people periodically and that it must be stored beside the ark (31:10–13, 26). This shows that it is viewed as inspired and authoritative, in other words as canonical. It may be that this concept of canonicity has been adapted from earlier oriental texts, for often law codes and international treaties were regarded in this way. The laws of Hammurabi (c. 1750 BC) declare that they are not to be changed but must be kept in the temple in Babylon. Similarly ancient Near Eastern treaties had to be stored in the temple near the image of the god and read out annually to the vassal. For these reasons it seems likely that the Pentateuch was viewed as canonical from the time it was composed, whether that was in the fifth century or sometime earlier.

FURTHER READING

GENERAL INTRODUCTIONS

T. D. Alexander *From Paradise to the Promised Land*. Carlisle: Paternoster Press, 2002.

J. Blenkinsopp *The Pentateuch: An Introduction to the First Five Books of the Bible*. London: SCM Press, 1992.

J. van Seters *The Pentateuch: A Social-Science Commentary*. Sheffield: Sheffield Academic Press, 1999.

R. N. Whybray *Introduction to the Pentateuch*. Grand Rapids: Eerdmans, 1995.

DISCUSSION OF PARTICULAR ISSUES

R. T. Beckwith *The Old Testament Canon of the New Testament Church*. London: SPCK, 1985.

M. Haran 'Book-Scrolls in Israel in Pre-Exilic Times' *JJS* 33, 1982, pp. 161–173.

M. Haran 'Book-Size and the Device of Catch-Lines in the Biblical Canon' *JJS* 36, 1985, pp. 1–11.

G. H. Wilson *The Editing of the Hebrew Psalter*. SBL Diss 76. Chico: Scholars Press, 1985.

Chapter 2

GENESIS 1—11

Next to the parables of Jesus the stories of Genesis 1—11 must be the most familiar part of the Bible. Nearly everyone has heard of Adam and Eve, the Flood, and the tower of Babel. Yet at the same time it is the most contentious: some people dismiss it as myth or fairy tale, while others hold it to be good science and accurate history. And as far as the New Testament and early Christian writers were concerned this was the part of the Old Testament that was most influential in the formulation of Christian doctrine. Here the stakes are high and tempers rise: even mild-mannered scholars have been known to damn opposing interpreters of these chapters angrily. So I shall try to tread carefully and I hope readers will be charitable.

At the heart of the debate is the question of genre: that is, what kind of literature are we dealing with here? In trying to answer this question, we need to enquire how Genesis 1—11 relates to the rest of the book, and whether there are any parallels to this material inside or outside the Bible.

I shall take these issues in reverse order. First, we shall compare Genesis' account of world origins with other texts discovered in the Middle East to see what light this sheds on the nature of Genesis 1—11. Then we shall review the contents of Genesis 1—11 to see both how it is similar to and how it differs from the stories told by other peoples from that era and area. Finally we shall discuss the relationship of Genesis 1—11 to the rest of the book, where the author's main concerns are most evident. By this means I hope we shall come to a better understanding of what the writer of Genesis was trying to say to his readers when he put pen to paper some 3000 years ago. Indirectly this should shed light on the issues that so perplex modern readers, when they approach Genesis conditioned by a scientific and historical mindset whose assumptions differ from those of past ages.

ANCIENT NEAR EASTERN PARALLELS TO GENESIS 1—11

It was in 1872 that George Smith, a curator in the British Museum, discovered the first close parallel to Genesis 1—11. Translating a cuneiform tablet found in the Assyrian library of Ashurbanipal (seventh century BC) at Nineveh, he realized he had an account of a world-wide flood that in many respects resembled the story told in Genesis. Subsequently it was recognized that the flood story formed part of the Gilgamesh epic, a tale of a great king who dropped out of his royal role to travel the world in a quest for immortality. The Gilgamesh epic was probably composed in about 1700 BC and then revised in about 1200 BC to produce the best-known standard version of the epic. Scholars think that the flood story was probably borrowed by the author of the Gilgamesh epic from another source, who then used it to enhance his own tale.

A possible source for the flood story is the Atrahasis epic, another Old Babylonian classic, which covers the history of the world from the creation of man to the new order established after the flood. It begins when the minor gods lived on earth excavating the rivers and canals and growing food for the great gods. But after 3600 years the minor gods became tired of their work and went on strike. They besieged the great god Enlil in his palace, who eventually caved in to their demands! Another great god Ea and the mother goddess Nintu then created seven human couples, seven men and seven women, to do the work of the minor gods.

But the creation of mankind led to problems for the great gods. After 600 years the population had increased so much that their racket stopped the great gods sleeping! Enlil therefore decreed that a plague should blot them out. But a timely sacrifice to the plague god by Atrahasis, or 'Extra-wise' stopped the plague. But then the population grew again, and twice more Enlil tried to check it by drought and famine. But once again sacrifices to the right gods saved the situation.

Eventually Enlil persuaded all his fellow gods to back his plan to destroy mankind by sending a flood. However, the god Ea disagreed with this proposal and secretly tipped off Atrahasis to build an ark for his family, friends and animals to escape in. The flood was indeed catastrophic, wiping out all living creatures and scaring the gods by its ferocity. But Atrahasis and his crew survived. The ark eventually landed on a mountain and those inside disembarked.

Pious Atrahasis offered a sacrifice as soon as he landed. Immediately the gods crowded round the sacrifice anxious to enjoy the barbecue. They were very hungry! Destroying mankind in a flood meant that all sacrifices had stopped and the gods had had nothing to eat. A little late Enlil, the most powerful god, turned up at the sacrifice and was shocked and angry to find some human beings had escaped. He calmed down when the other gods explained it was Ea's fault, and he granted Atrahasis eternal life, the only man to achieve this.

However, to stop the population explosion ever getting out of hand again Enlil had the mother goddess redesign man a little. From now on some women would suffer from infertility, babies would often be stillborn or die very young, and yet other women would enter religious orders and never have children. Finally it seems likely that from then on death would now come to everyone in old age: up to this time people died only from disease or if they were killed by someone.

Another text from about the same period as the Atrahasis epic is the Sumerian flood story. It too tells of the creation of mankind and culminates with the story of the great flood. Unfortunately many parts of the Sumerian story are lost, but as reconstructed it parallels Genesis 1—9 quite strikingly.

There are enough similarities in the storylines of Genesis and the Sumerian

What do you think?
REWRITING THE STORY OF HUMAN ORIGINS

Read the story of creation in Genesis 2 and the flood in Genesis 6—9 and compare it with the account above. What similarities and differences do you notice? How does Genesis change the story? What do these changes tell us about the writer's attitude?

If you have access to other texts read the whole Babylonian version. Note that in Gilgamesh tablet 11 Atrahasis is usually called Ut-Napishtim ('He found life').

flood story to show that both are dependent on a common understanding of what took place at the dawn of human history. However, we shall see that the spin

PARALLELS BETWEEN THE SUMERIAN FLOOD STORY AND GENESIS 1—9

Sumerian Flood Story	Contents	Genesis
Lines 1–36	Creation of man and animals; man's sad plight, no irrigation canals, no clothes, no fear of animals including snakes	Gen. 1 Gen. 2—3
37–50	Goddess Nintur's plan to end human nomadism	Gen. 4:1–16
51–85	Failure of Nintur's plan	
86–100	Establishment of kingship; building of first cities, including Eridu Establishment of worship	Gen. 4:17–18 Gen. 4:26
101–34	List of antediluvian kings Man's noise	Gen. 5 Gen. 6:1–8
135–260	The flood	Gen. 6:9—9:29

the storytellers put on those events is quite different. But clearly both Genesis 1—11 and the Sumerian Flood Story have a similar character or genre: that is why the scholar who edited the Sumerian story entitled it 'the Eridu Genesis'.

A fourth ancient text that has some obvious similarities to Genesis is the Sumerian King List, which in an early

---

Digging deeper:
THE SUMERIAN KING LIST
OPENING LINES

When kingship was lowered from heaven, kingship was first in Eridu. In Eridu Alulim became king and ruled 28,800 years. Alalgar ruled 36,000 years. Two kings thus ruled it for 64,800 years.

(Six more kings in four other towns are mentioned)

These are five cities, eight kings ruled them for 241,000 years.

Then the Flood swept over the earth.

After the Flood had swept over the earth and when kingship was lowered again from heaven, kingship was first in Kish. In Kish, Ga..ur became king and ruled 1200 years ... Pala-kinatim ruled 900 years ... Kalibum ruled 960 years; Qalumum ruled 840 years; Zuqapip ruled 900 years; ...

Twenty-three kings thus ruled it for 24,510 years, 3 months, and 3½ days.

---

form dates to about 1900 BC. This king list mentions eight, nine or ten kings who reigned before the flood (ancient versions differ as to the number of antediluvian kings). Then it mentions that the flood came, and after that kingship was reintroduced and it lists the kings who reigned in different centres and for how long.

This King List resembles Genesis 5—11 in four respects. First, it presents history in list form, which parallels the genealogies in Genesis 5 and 11. Second, it divides early human history into three phases, pre-flood, flood and post-flood. Third, it claims that kings reigned much longer before the flood than afterwards, just as the pre-flood heroes in Genesis 5 live much longer than the post-flood heroes of Genesis 11. Fourth, the number of pre-flood kings (8, 9 or 10) is very similar to the ten generations from Adam to Noah listed in Genesis 5. Nevertheless, the names of the kings are quite different from the commoners listed in the Bible, so that we cannot suppose there was any borrowing by the Bible from the Sumerian list. But once again we have a piece of literature similar in genre and from the same general period and place as Genesis 1—11, so that we can appeal to one to clarify the nature of the other.

Having surveyed a number of ancient texts that are close in content and time to Genesis 1—11, we are in a better position to discuss the question of the genre of these chapters. Modern writers on Genesis often describe its opening chapters as 'myth'; though when their concept of

What do you think?
THE DEFINITION OF MYTH

A myth may be defined as a 'purely fictitious narrative usually involving supernatural persons etc and embodying popular ideas on natural phenomena etc.; fictitious person or thing.'
Concise Oxford Dictionary

Read Genesis 1—11. How far do you think it fits this definition of myth? How else might these chapters be characterized?

myth is unpacked, it may not correspond very closely to the dictionary definition. As the dictionary shows, the primary sense of myth is something fictitious or untrue. 'That's a complete myth' we say, if we want to rubbish someone else's views.

Though we may find aspects of these stories extraordinary, it seems quite clear that they are not entirely fictitious. Gilgamesh and Atrahasis were real kings to whom these stories became attached, perhaps a bit like King Arthur or Robin Hood. The Sumerian King List not only involves real places, but some of the later kings have left inscriptions proving they existed.

Furthermore, it has been observed that these ancient oriental texts are akin to history in that they set events in a chain of cause and effect. The kindly goddess Nintur sees primitive man's wretched state, so she provides him with cities to live and kings to organize society. This works so well that the human population grows, which in turn disturbs the peace of the

gods. They react by sending plague, famine and flood. Jacobsen comments: 'This arrangement along a line of time as cause and effect is striking, for it is very much the way a historian arranges his data' (Jacobsen 1981, p. 528).

The obvious interest in chronology in the Sumerian and biblical texts is also striking. Both give precise lengths of reign or life spans of the people they mention. The numbers are admittedly incredibly large, but the interest in chronology is more characteristic of historiography and chronicles than folktales or myth. The latter are usually unconcerned with time: they float outside time. Often they begin 'Once upon a time,' and end with 'they lived happily ever after'. For this reason Jacobsen believes these ancient stories should be classified as mytho-historical accounts.

Despite drawing attention to the history-like features of these texts, Jacobsen still describes them as mytho-historical, i.e. he regards them as myths told as though they were history. Modern definitions of myth often rest on two features: that they are stories about the gods and that they explain aspects of present life. How far is this true of the stories we have been considering?

It is striking that modern scholars have not called any of the Mesopotamian texts we have been considering myths. Rather they are called epics (Gilgamesh, Atrahasis), Flood Story or King List, for gods are hardly mentioned in the King List and in the others it is the human characters who are the focus of the narrative. Genesis 1—11 is similar: though God is of course active, his actions are all related to man. Nothing is said about his interactions with other spiritual beings. Thus modern commentators tend to avoid describing Genesis 1—11 as myth. If the only reason for calling Genesis 1—11 a myth is because God is present in the story, one would have to call the whole Bible a myth, which few would wish to do.

It is certainly true that part of the function of these stories is to explain features of life in the writer's time. The Atrahasis Epic explains why some women are infertile, the Gilgamesh Epic why human beings are mortal, while Genesis justifies the origin of the Sabbath and explains why snakes bite and weeds grow. But these are features of modern origin stories too: how many times have we been told that a certain human or animal characteristic is explicable in terms of our evolutionary development! Indeed much history writing tends to explain the present by telling us what went on in the past. All the time we trace the successes or problems of our era back to what our ancestors did. So although the types of explanation in the ancient texts offered for present phenomena may differ from modern explanations, that does not justify the term myth being applied to them.

Even the incredible aspects of the stories are a poor reason for calling them myths. Modern stories of origin include elements that are in some ways even more astonishing than Methuselah living 969 years or the snake speaking. The idea that the whole cosmos came from an initial big hot bang of microscopic size blows the imagination. Elements in the theory of evolution, such as the origin of life or the eye, are also very difficult to ascribe to mere chance. But we accept these ideas because many eminent scientists affirm them. Doubtless there was a similar intellectual consensus in the ancient orient about their theories of origin, which these stories reflect. We do them an injustice if we call them myths, just because we find it difficult to believe all they affirm.

A careful reading of Genesis 1—11 gives us an insight into how the Israelites must have understood them. Genesis is built round a chain of genealogies. The first major one begins with Adam and ends ten generations later with Noah (Gen. 5). The next important one consists of ten generations from Shem to Abraham (Gen. 11:10–26). The stories about Abraham and his descendants must have been understood as historical: they deal with typical family problems, which every Israelite could identify with and indeed was expected to identify with because Abraham, Isaac and Jacob were his ancestors. But the genealogies show that this chain of historical individuals stretches back to the beginning of history.

Nevertheless, the first three chapters of Genesis do suggest that they are dealing with a different world from the present. Chapter 1, as we shall see below, is an overture to the whole book. The main storyline begins in 2:4, but the situation described in chapter 2 changes dramatically in chapter 3. The curses on the land, man,

14

woman and the snake describe life as it was for an Israelite in Bible times. Crops were hard to grow, women suffered pain in childbirth, and snakes bit humans. But chapter 2 describes a world without these woes: a garden with abundant fruit, no inhibitions spoiling male-female relationships, and no conflict between mankind and the animal kingdom. In other words chapter 2 is set in an era quite distinct from the historical period. What is more, chapter 3 ends with Adam and Eve being expelled from paradise and unable to return because of the cherubim wielding a flaming sword. In other words the garden of Eden is now somehow beyond the grasp of human beings.

Rogerson has well summed up how the first readers viewed these chapters. 'For Israelites … the narratives of Genesis 1—11 were factually true, but Israelites did not expect to experience the things they describe. Adam and Eve were accepted as real human beings, but any Israelite woman who claimed that she had had a conversation with a snake would have been dismissed as a crank' (Rogerson 1991, p. 54). Today's readers still have a problem in defining them. The German term *Urgeschichte*, that is Protohistory, is one option. Another possibility is 'Origin Story', the ancient equivalent of Darwin's *Origin of Species* or Hawking's *A Brief History of Time*.

GENESIS' TRANSFORMATION OF ORIENTAL ORIGIN STORIES

Comparison of Genesis 1—11 with other ancient Near Eastern origin stories not only clarifies its genre but sheds great light on their theological purpose. So far we have concentrated on the similarities between Genesis and these other stories from Mesopotamia to clarify their genre, but it is even more instructive for an understanding of Genesis to see how it differs from these earlier accounts.

There are quite a number of differences that are probably not very significant. For example, in the Gilgamesh account of the flood, Atrahasis (Ut-Napishtim) builds a seven-decked cube as an ark, whereas Noah's is more like a supertanker. In Gilgamesh the destructive phase of the flood lasts seven days, whereas in Genesis it lasts 40. After the flood Atrahasis sends out a dove, a swallow and a raven, whereas Noah sends out a raven and a dove. There are many other differences of this sort between the biblical and other versions. This makes it virtually certain that the author of Genesis did not know these other texts in the versions we possess. Rather, these stories circulated in the ancient world in different versions, oral and written. Most people then knew the story of the flood even though they had not read or heard the Atrahasis or Gilgamesh epics, just as people today know about evolution without having read Darwin.

What we have in Genesis is a major *theological* reinterpretation of traditional origin stories. Throughout the ancient Near East people believed in a multitude of gods and goddesses: they were polytheists. This is reflected in all the Mesopotamian tales we have considered.

15

But in Genesis there is but one supreme God, who creates everything and controls everything. The Atrahasis epic tells of the lesser gods going on strike against the higher gods, and the higher gods are divided among themselves: that is why Ea (Enki) tips off Atrahasis about the flood. We read of the gods cowering like dogs at the flood they have released, whereas at the height of the flood 'God remembered Noah' and immediately the waters start to subside. Whereas the Babylonian gods cannot control the flood, the God of Genesis can. The biblical insistence on the unity and sovereignty of the one God is clearest in Genesis 1. There he speaks and, stage by stage, the world is brought into existence. In oriental thought the sun and the moon were important gods, but Genesis affirms they were simply created by God on the fourth day.

Strikingly different is Genesis' portrayal of God's attitude to man from that in the other texts. According to the Atrahasis epic mankind was created as an afterthought to break the strike called by the lesser gods and to supply food to the gods through the offering of sacrifice. But in Genesis 1 the creation of man constitutes the climax of the creation story: created in God's image human beings are God's representatives on earth. Far from man supplying God with food, it is God who supplies man with food.

As far as the Babylonian world-view was concerned one of the big problems with humanity was its fertility. The population explosion disturbed the rest of the gods: three times they tried to control it by plague, drought and famine before they resorted to the flood. Then after the flood they resorted to disrupting the reproductive process by making some women infertile, letting children die young and assigning other women to celibacy. Genesis has a very different perspective. From the start God blesses mankind and encourages procreation with the words 'Be fruitful and multiply' (Gen. 1:28). After the flood the same command is given to Noah, not once but three times (8:17; 9:1, 7).

When it comes to morality the Babylonian deities do not appear to be paragons of virtue. They squabble among themselves, and are not averse to deceiving each other or humans. The flood as we have seen was sent not because of human sin as in Genesis, but simply because there were too many people around. Atrahasis escaped because he worshipped Ea, who did not approve of the flood, whereas Noah escaped because of his exemplary behaviour. 'Noah was a righteous man, blameless in his generation' (6:9).

Thus as Genesis retells familiar oriental stories about the origins of the world, it dramatically transforms them theologically. Polytheism is replaced by monotheism, divine weakness by almighty power. Human beings are no longer seen as a sideline but central to the divine purpose. God looks after man by supplying him with food, not the other way round. Finally, the God of Genesis is very concerned about human sin: it was this that prompted him to send the flood, not population growth.

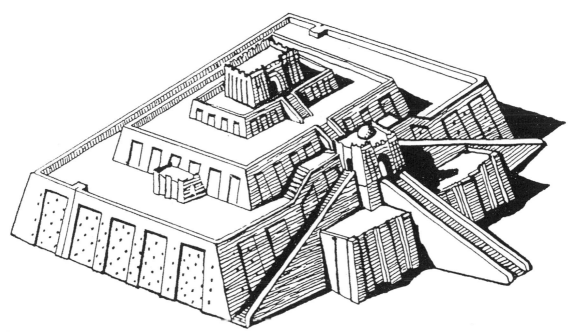

Figure 1: **ZIGGURAT**
Taken from p. 109 of the *New Bible Dictionary*, Downers Grove: IVP, 1996.

But there is more to Genesis' retelling of tradition than a piecemeal rejection of certain theological ideas: Genesis has a quite different view of the direction of history. For example, the Sumerian flood story 'takes throughout an affirmative and optimistic view of existence: it believes in progress. Things were not nearly as good to begin with as they have become since … In the biblical account it is the other way around. Things began as perfect from God's hand and grew then steadily worse through man's sinfulness until God finally had to do away with all mankind except for the pious Noah who would beget a new and better stock' (Jacobsen 1981, p. 529).

This challenge to the optimism of the Babylonian world reaches its climax in the tower of Babel (Babylon) story in Genesis

Digging deeper:
RETELLING MODERN COSMOLOGY THEOLOGICALLY

The ancient Near East told its story of origins by explaining what happened in the past as the result of the action of numerous gods. Genesis explains everything by reference to the will of one supreme and moral God.

Today's stories of origins, such as the big-bang cosmology and the theory of evolution, see all change as caused by scientific law and chance. How would you retell these stories bringing God into the picture? What sort of a God emerges if you posit that he controlled all that happened in the formation of our universe and still is in charge today?

11. Babel in Akkadian means 'Gate of God': the Babylonians held not only that Babylon was the centre of civilization but that its Ziggurat temple was the gateway to heaven, indeed that its top reached the heaven. Genesis ridicules this idea suggesting that Babel means 'confusion' or 'folly'. And so far from the temple touching heaven, God had to come down from heaven to be able to see it!

THE ORGANIZATION OF GENESIS 1—11

The arrangement of Genesis into chapters is quite a late development (see previous chapter) and sometimes these chapter divisions do not occur at the right places. The book itself has its own system of internal titles or headings, usually translated 'These are the generations/descendants of'. There are ten of these titles, one of which (36:1) is duplicated in 36:9. Sometimes this title introduces a long narrative, at others a short genealogy. The table below sets out the data.

Except in 5:1 the Hebrew phraseology of these titles is the same. The person named in the title is the senior figure in the narrative that follows. From the named person his descendants come and usually fill the stage of the ensuing section. This is clearest in the case of Isaac. He is alive throughout Genesis 25—35 and notionally at least head of the family, but his sons Jacob and Esau are the main actors in the story. Similarly from Genesis 37 to 50 Jacob is head of the family, but the main drama revolves around his sons. Probably

INTERNAL TITLES IN THE BOOK OF GENESIS

	Title	Subsequent Content
2:4	These are the generations of the heavens and the earth	The story of Adam and his descendants 2:4—4:26
5:1	This is the book of the generations of Adam	Genealogy from Adam to Noah 5:1—6:8
6:9	These are the generations of Noah	Story of flood 6:9—9:29
10:1	These are the generations of the sons of Noah	Table of nations descended from Noah 10:1—11:9
11:10	These are the generations of Shem	Genealogy from Shem to Abraham 11:10–26
11:27	These are the generations of Terah	Story of Abraham 11:27—25:11
25:12	These are the generations of Ishmael	Genealogy of Ishmael 25:12–18
25:19	These are the generations of Isaac	Story of Jacob and Esau 25:19—35:29
36:1, 9	These are the generations of Esau	Genealogy of Esau 36:1—37:1
37:2	These are the generations of Jacob	Story of Joseph and his brothers 37:2—50:26

the aptest translation of the titles would be: 'This is the family history of Noah/Sons of Noah/Shem/Terah/Ishmael/Isaac/Esau/Jacob.'

The distribution of titles shows that Genesis 2—50 falls into two main sections: 2:4—11:26 and 11:27—50:26. Both sections contain three narrative sections and two genealogies. This is significant, for it shows that essentially the first section anticipates the second, so that we cannot really understand the opening chapters without understanding the later chapters and *vice versa*. It enhances the case we made earlier for holding that the readers of Genesis would have regarded the people mentioned in Genesis 1—11 as just as real as those in chapter 12 onwards. It also shows that to understand the opening chapters of Genesis, we must read them not simply as commenting on and modifying ancient oriental ideas, but also introducing the main plot in chapters 12—50.

Conspicuously outside the scheme of titles is the first chapter of Genesis (more exactly 1:1—2:3). This account of creation in six days followed by the first Sabbath is an introduction to the whole book. It stands as 'a majestic festive overture' to Genesis, indeed to the whole Bible. Like an overture to an opera it introduces tunes and motifs that will be important in the following work. Here key ideas about God and his relationship with man that will be important in the succeeding chapters are introduced for the first time. These ideas are refined and developed in the next ten chapters, so that 2:4 to 11:26

constitute as it were a second exposition to the book, with the main storyline taking off in 11:27 with the birth of Abraham.

1:1—2:3: The first exposition

In its very first words Genesis asserts God's absolute power. 'In the beginning God created heaven and earth' i.e. everything. But to start with the earth was shrouded in darkness and covered with water.

As soon as God speaks this dark chaos is turned to order. On the first day he says: 'Let there be light'; and there was light. On the third: 'Let the dry land appear.' And it was so. God's acts of creation in the second half of the week echo those in the first half, so that there is a correspondence between the first three days and the second three days.

CREATION

Day 1 Light	Day 4 Sun, moon and stars
Day 2 Sky	Day 5 Birds (and fish)
Day 3 Land and plants	Day 6 Animals and man; plants for food

Day 7 Sabbath

This structuring of Genesis into a week of seven days is only one of a series of recurring formulae that run through this chapter, such as 'And God said', 'And it was so', 'God saw that it was good' or 'God blessed'. But though these formulae recur, they are not repeated mechanically, so that on some days a formula may appear once, on others twice, and sometimes it is

19

omitted. This creates a rich and interesting tapestry subtly indicating which acts of creation are most significant.

Digging deeper:
SIGNIFICANT DAYS IN GENESIS I

Which days of creation are described at most length? Which days mention God speaking twice 'and God said' and have the approval formula 'God saw that it was good' twice? How would you explain this?

Genesis 1 thus presents God as a God of power and order. He only has to speak and it happens. This is quite unlike other accounts of creation from the ancient orient, such as Enuma Elish, where the gods fight to achieve supremacy over each other and creation. The God introduced in Genesis 1 is absolutely sovereign. He created the sun and the moon: they were not rival deities as was often believed. It is this God who can do what he says, who makes the promises to the patriarchs that are central to the whole Pentateuch.

Genesis 1 not only asserts the sovereign power of God the creator, it affirms the centrality of mankind in the divine plan. Unlike the Atrahasis epic where man's creation is an afterthought of the hungry gods, the whole of Genesis 1 builds towards the action on the sixth day. The creation of the land and plants on the third day and the creation of the sun and moon on the fourth, which are so important for human life, are described more fully than other days. It is only when man has been

made that 'God saw all that he had made, and behold, it was very good.'

The creation of man is heralded by the divine invitation to the angels or other members of the Trinity, 'Let us make man in our image', in other words to make a creature who will be God's representative on earth. Other oriental peoples believed that kings were made in the divine image, but Genesis affirms that every human being is made in God's image. 'So God created man in his own image … male and female he created them' (Gen. 1:27). Again contradicting the Atrahasis epic, God blessed them and said to them, 'Be fruitful and multiply'.

Digging deeper:
GENESIS AND ECOLOGY

God's first commands to the human race 'Be fruitful and multiply, and fill the earth and subdue it; and have dominion over the fish of the sea and over the birds of the air and over every living thing', have sometimes been taken as sanctioning unbridled exploitation of the rest of creation. But this is to forget that humanity is made in God's image to be his representative on earth, that is, to act in a godlike way in caring for the earth and the other creatures in it. Kings in ancient times were expected to rule their people in a way that benefited their subjects and in particular kings had a duty to look after the poor and weak members of their realm. It is this language that Genesis is echoing here. Or to put it another way, humanity is expected to manage the earth for God in a way that pleases him.

The creation of man in God's image may be the climax of creation, but it is not the goal of creation. That is the seventh day, the day when 'God rested from all his work that he had done in creation' (Gen. 2:3). By implication man, who is made in God's image, should also rest on the seventh day. In other words Genesis, like the Ten Commandments (Exod. 20:11), traces the origin of the Sabbath back to creation. It is also, as Jesus says, made for man's benefit (Mark 2:27).

This opening chapter of Genesis is most important for understanding some of the writer's fundamental principles. Here he sets out ideas that are assumed in the rest of the book, such as the unity and power of God, his concern for human welfare, and the lifestyle that is best for human beings. It portrays a world of harmony, in which animals do not attack each other or men attack animals, for all are vegetarian (1:29–30). Rather, mankind as God's image bearer represents him on earth and manages the world for the benefit of all. These same ideals are visible in chapter 2, but then they break down in chapter 3 following. But they are not forgotten: they are still the yardstick by which the writer evaluates action and the ideals which one day he hopes will be realized in the promised land (see Gen. 49; Deut. 33).

2:4—11:26: The second exposition

Genesis 2—11 consists of five distinct sections, each headed by the title 'These are the generations', or as the title would be better translated 'This is the family history of'. They constitute a second exposition, for they elaborate the basic principles set out in the first chapter of the book.

2:4—4:26	The history of heaven and earth
5:1—6:8	The family history of Adam
6:9—9:29	The family history of Noah
10:1—11:9	The family history of Noah's sons
11:10–26	The family history of Shem

The longest of these family histories is the middle one, the story of the flood and its aftermath. Its fullness is a mark of its importance in the story. Just as in Mesopotamian accounts the flood divides world history into two eras, in Genesis the flood is seen as a great act of decreation: the world returns to its original state as described in Genesis 1:2, with water covering the surface of the earth. Nearly everything created in Genesis 1 disappears, land, plants, animals and man. The only survivors are to be found in the ark. But decreation is followed by recreation. When 'God remembered Noah' (Gen. 8:1), the wind blew (cf. Gen. 1:2) and everything started to reappear: outside the ark the land and the plants again became visible and, when Noah and the animals disembarked, the animal world started to be replenished. Noah himself is seen as a second Adam figure. He, like Adam, is viewed as the ancestor of all mankind, and like Adam he was told to be fruitful and multiply. Like Adam he cultivated fruit trees, in Noah's case vines. Adam ate a forbidden fruit, but Noah consumed too much wine, dishonoured himself and was further shamed by his son. So in a sense mankind fell again. Thus this central section is not only structurally important, but it is theologically significant too.

Each section is not only headed by its own title but typically concludes with a trailer for the next section, a few verses that sum up or introduce the next section. Thus 4:25–26 is a trailer for the genealogy of Adam in chapter 5. Genesis 6:5–8 sums up God's reasons for sending the flood, the topic of the next three chapters. Noah's blessing and curse of his sons in 9:25–27 explains the table of nations in chapter 10. Finally the birth of Abram in 11:26 introduces the Abraham stories, which begin in 11:27.

2:4—4:26

This section, called in the Hebrew 'the history of the heaven and earth', consists of two parts:

2:4—3:24   The Garden of Eden
4:1–26   Cain and his descendants

These two parts are not just linked by sequence: Cain is Adam's son, but he also sins in worse ways than his father Adam. The second part about Cain deliberately echoes the first part about Adam to show how much more Cain has degenerated than his father.

Digging deeper:
ADAM AND CAIN: DEEDS, WORDS AND CHARACTER

Compare Adam's deeds and dialogue with God (Gen. 3:6–12) with Cain's (4:8–15). In what way does Cain appear to be a worse sinner than his father?

The Garden of Eden story falls into parts: 2:4–25 describes life in the garden before the act of disobedience, while chapter 3 describes the deed and its consequences culminating in expulsion from the garden. Chapter 2 takes up motifs already addressed in chapter 1 but discusses them in greater detail: chapter 1 gives a panoramic view on the whole of creation, but 2:4–25 zooms in with a close-up on the creation of man and woman. Chapter 1 ended with the creation of mankind in two sexes to rule the rest of creation and supplied by God with food. In reverse order these three topics, food, dominion and sexuality, are the central topics of chapters 2 to 3. First, reinforcing the message of chapter 1 that God feeds man, not man the gods, as Babylonians held, God's rich provision of fruit trees in the garden is noted (2:8–17). Second, man's rule over the animals is reaffirmed by them coming to Adam to be named (2:18–20). It should be noted that the animals are viewed as potential companions for Adam: there is no suggestion that they are a danger to him or that he will exploit them. Finally, God creates Eve from Adam's rib and introduces her to him in an archetypal wedding ceremony (2:21–25). This episode expresses in story-form some of the book's convictions about relations between the sexes, which are alluded to in 2:24–25.

The location of the garden is tantalizing. Because the Tigris and Euphrates are fed by the river of Eden it might be surmised that Eden was located somewhere in the North, where these rivers rise. But on the other hand 3:24 tells us that no one can enter the garden because it is guarded by the cherubim. This suggests that somehow the garden is real but inaccessible to man.

The symbolism of Eden is clearer than its location. Eden means 'delight', and it is portrayed like a beautiful paradise island with abundant water and delicious fruits. What is more, it had lots of gold and precious stones: even God enjoyed strolling through its leafy trees. Later in the Bible this imagery is used to describe the tent shrine called the tabernacle (Exod. 25—40) and the temple in Jerusalem. All the symbolism, such as water and gold, contributes to making the point that this garden and the later temple are where God dwells, the God who gives life to all creation.

Chapter 3 shows how all the pleasures of Eden were lost by the woman picking the only forbidden fruit and the man eating it. Immediately the intimacy between them (2:25) was shattered: guilt-ridden they hid in the trees and made clothes out of fig-leaves, and when challenged by God

blame each other for their sin (3:6–13). But the longer-term consequences are graver still. Harmony between man and the animals is replaced by perpetual conflict (3:15). The woman's role as wife and mother is to be marred by tension and painful childbirth (3:16), while the man's task as keeper of the garden is from now on to be characterized by hard frustrating toil, and eventual death (3:17–19). Whereas Babylonian tradition held universal death originated after the flood, Genesis traces it back to the first human couple. Finally, both were expelled from Eden, the dwelling place of God and source of life. In this way the threat 'in the day that you eat of it you shall surely die' (2:17) was carried out.

These punishments, or curses as the text calls them, describe the problems faced by ancient Israelites, and to a greater or lesser extent every human being. Life was precarious in Bible times for the average peasant farmer. Crops were hard to grow and prone to fail in times of drought, while wild animals including snakes endangered human life. Death, pain and conflicts between man and wife were not unknown either. These universal human problems are the more poignant after the idyllic way of life described in chapter 2, which remained the dream that the Old Testament hoped one day would again be realized (see Amos 9:13–15; Isa. 11:6–9).

However, chapter 4, the story of Cain and his descendants, paints a picture of further deterioration. For the first time in the OT the most important topic of sacrifice is raised. Whereas Abel offers the best of his flock, 'the firstborn', Cain merely offers some of his produce. Only the best is good enough in sacrifice, so not surprisingly Cain's was rejected. But instead of mending his ways, Cain killed his brother. Murder is bad enough, but to kill your own brother is worse still, for brothers are specially responsible for their mutual well-being. Cheekily Cain brushed off God's enquiry about Abel with what sounds like a joke: 'Am I my brother's keeper?' The LORD was not fooled and he sentenced Cain to a life of perpetual nomadism. As mentioned earlier, this looks like a reversal of Nintur's attempt to rescue primeval man from his original nomadic way of life.

Further points of contact with Sumerian traditions have already been noted in 4:17–18, 26 (see above, p. 11). Other traditions may lie behind 4:20–22, which list the inventors of various arts and crafts, who were descended from Cain.

Mesopotamian tradition told of seven sages who were sent by the god Ea to teach mankind the arts of civilization. Here they are merely human achievements shadowed by the violence of Cain and his even more vicious descendant Lamech (4:18, 23–24).

5:1—6:8

This section entitled in the Hebrew 'the book of the family history of Adam' consists of three sections:

5:1–32	Genealogy of Adam to Noah
6:1–4	'The sons of God' episode
6:5–8	Trailer for the flood

We have already noted that in certain respects the genealogy in Genesis 5 corresponds to the antediluvian section of the Sumerian King List, which lists eight, nine or ten kings who reigned before the flood. Genesis has ten generations from Adam to Noah.

Some commentators have supposed that this genealogy of Adam to Noah is a variant of the genealogy of Adam to Lamech in Genesis 4. They point out that some of the names are the same, Adam, Enoch and Lamech, and others are somewhat similar, e.g. Methushael and Methuselah, Irad and Jared. On closer inspection the two genealogies do not seem to be alternative versions of the same line.

First, it should be noted that the similar-looking names do not come in the same order. Second that the similar-looking names are actually more different in the Hebrew than in their English forms:

GENEALOGIES OF ADAM TO NOAH

Genesis 4	Additional Comments	Genesis 5	Additional Comments
Names		Names	
Adam		Adam	
Cain		Seth	
Enoch	Named a city	Enosh	
Irad		Kenan	
Mehujael		Mahalel	
Methushael		Jared	
Lamech	Had two wives	Enoch	Walked with God
		Methuselah	
		Lamech	Prayed for relief from the curse
		Noah	*Righteous*

Hebrew speakers would not have identified them. Finally, the identical names (Enoch and Lamech) are carefully distinguished in both lists by comments to prevent them being confused. This makes it plain that the writer of Genesis saw these genealogies as quite distinct. Later in Genesis the family history of the non-elect line (e.g. Ishmael (25:12–18) or Esau (36:1—37:1)) precedes that of the chosen line (e.g. Isaac (25:19—35:29) or Jacob (37:2—50:26). The arrangement here is similar: the genealogy of the wicked Cainites precedes that of the chosen Sethites, whose line contains saints like Enoch and Noah.

The four verses 6:1–4 about the sons of God marrying the daughters of men are probably the most problematic in the whole of Genesis. Much discussion is found in the commentaries about the identity of the sons of God and the nature of their sin. Four main interpretations have been advocated. 1) The sons of God are kings, who have large harems in their courts. 2) The sons of God are the sons of Seth who intermarried with the daughters of Cain (men). 3) The sons of God are the sons of Cain who married the daughters of Seth (men). Both explanations 2 and 3 see the problem as essentially godly humans (sons of God) marrying ungodly humans (daughters of men). The interpretations disagree whether the descendants of Cain or the descendants of Seth are the godly line. 4) The sons of God are spirits/angels/demons/minor gods who married human girls (daughters of men).

Extraordinary as the last suggestion seems to modern secular readers, it is the

Digging deeper:
DID METHUSELAH REALLY LIVE 969 YEARS?

The ages at which the men listed in Genesis died or even had their first child are astonishing to say the least. Since it is hard to take them literally, there have been a variety of attempts to explain these ages. Could their years have been much shorter, e.g. just a month? Though this would make their ages at death more reasonable, they would then have been rather young to father their children!

Another suggestion is that each figure represents a dynasty and that many generations have been omitted. This breaks down where it can be tested, i.e. at the beginning or end of the genealogy, where Seth is clearly the son of Adam and Noah is the immediate descendant of Lamech. Another possibility mooted is that the ages are related to astronomical periods, e.g. Enoch's 365 years correspond to the days in the solar year. Not all the figures are explicable so easily, nor is it clear why anyone should want to equate their ages to obscure astronomical data.

In the light of the Sumerian King List, which makes the first king reign 28,800 years and his seven successors another 30,000 years each approximately, the Genesis figures look quite modest! Indeed, according to the Lagash King List babies were kept in nappies till they were 100 years old. So the heroes of Genesis matured quite quickly to procreate their first child at 130 years (Adam) or 70 (Kenan)! It therefore seems likely that in antiquity it was believed people matured slowly and lived to a great age. We could see Genesis 5 as a step from the impossible figures of Mesopotamia towards reality.

However, this observation still does not explain the exact figures in either Sumerian or biblical texts. It has been suggested that many of these ages can be easily generated by formulae familiar to Babylonian mathematicians. They used a sexagesimal system, and liked calculating numbers using the factors of 60. Thus Adam's ages, 130 and 930, may be easily produced by manipulating factors of 60. $130 = 2 \times 60 + 10$ (factor of 60). $930 = 30^2 + 30$.

This is intriguing, but we are still left to wonder what was the point of generating such numbers. Could they just be a way of telling us that real people, who had names, lived, procreated and died a very long time ago?

For further discussion see Young (1988) and Wenham (1987, pp. 133–34).

interpretation that takes the key terms 'sons of the gods/God' and 'daughters of men' in their most natural sense. (For another picture of the divine council of which the sons of the gods were members see Job 1:6–12.) This meaning of the phrase 'sons of the gods' is known in Canaanite literature. It is also the understanding of the oldest Jewish writers, the New Testament (2 Peter 2:4; Jude 6, 7), and early Christian writers.

So much is relatively clear, but what practices are being referred to that provoked such a strong divine reaction? Clearly these 'marriages' between the sons of the gods and human girls were the last straw in God's eyes. Next came the flood. The one suggestion that makes sense here can be advanced only tentatively. The ancient world believed that from time to time 'divine beings', 'gods', mated with humans to produce supermen like Gilgamesh, whose father was a priest and whose mother was the goddess Ninsun. These creatures may be the Nephilim of 6:4. Furthermore, in the fertility cults of both Canaan and Babylon the practice of sacred prostitution was very important. Men went to the temple and had sexual intercourse with the god(dess). This was believed to promote fertility among ordinary women and good crops on the land. But it of course involved making girls into prostitutes. We therefore could read Genesis 6:1–4 as an outspoken attack on these ideas: far from sacred prostitution enhancing human and agricultural fertility it led to the flood and the near extinction of the race.

As already observed, 6:5–8 is a typical trailer with which major sections of Genesis end. While rounding off one section it introduces the theme of the next, which is the flood. The most damning judgement on human behaviour in the Bible (6:5) introduces God's decision to destroy mankind (6:7). Already here we see Genesis starting to contradict the usual oriental view that the gods destroyed man because he was too noisy: it was because of his incorrigible wickedness. The nature of this wickedness is explained further in 6:11–13. Finally at the last minute God's favourable attitude towards Noah is mentioned, but again it is Noah's blameless behaviour that allows him to escape, not capricious divine favouritism as in other accounts (6:9).

6:9—9:29

The family history of Noah is the longest of the five sections that make up the second exposition, and we have already discussed its relationship to other oriental flood stories, its probable dependence on oral tradition akin to but not identical with Mesopotamian versions, and its theological transformation of these accounts to show the uniqueness, morality and power of the one God. So here we shall focus on other issues, such as the structure of the narrative, the reason for the flood, and how the earth is protected from a similar future catastrophe.

The flood story is the central section of the five sections that make up the second exposition (Gen. 2:4—11:26) and carefully organized in its own right. As a result of the flood the old world is destroyed, but as the waters retreat the earth is recreated. Both the destruction and recreation echo the opening chapters of the book to make these points clear (e.g. 7:14 cf. 1:21–25; 9:6–7 cf. 1:27–28). Noah is seen as a second Adam, the second father of the human race.

The turning point in the story is 8:1 'But God remembered Noah'. When God remembers people in the Bible, he also acts (cf. Gen. 30:22). So now he sends a wind to make the waters retreat (cf. 1:2). The whole story is told symmetrically, for

27

the action is fairly symmetrical. Noah goes *into* the ark at the beginning of the story, and comes *out* at the end. The mountains are *covered* by water as the flood rises, and are *uncovered* as the waters fall. This arrangement of topics in which the second half reverses the order of the first half (ABBA) is called chiasmus, or when there are many more than four topics, a palistrophe. The flood story is probably the most elaborate palistrophe in the Bible, with up to 15 elements both sides of the key statement 'God remembered Noah', emphatically reminding us of the main point of the story, that God was in control of the flood and deliberately saved Noah.

Digging deeper:
FIND THE PALISTROPHE

See how many items in the flood story you can find that fit into a palistrophe, beginning at 6:10 and ending at 9:19. Names and numbers as well as actions may form part of the palistrophe.

Though the focus of the flood story is on salvation, God's rescue of Noah because he was righteous, the scale of destruction is horrific. This is so, even if 'the earth' does not mean the whole planet, but all the land visible from somewhere in the Middle East. Genesis is therefore at great pains to justify why God should have taken such drastic action. It was not that he could not stand the noise of human beings, as Mesopotamian stories said. It was much more serious. Genesis offers two main reasons for God sending the flood,

the perversity of human thought (6:5) and the violence of all creatures especially man (6:11–13). By prefacing the whole account with the story of the sons of the gods mating with human women, it implies yet a third reason, cult prostitution.

We have already discussed the last point, so just a little ought to be said about the others. Genesis 6:5 is the most shocking statement about human sinfulness in the whole Bible: 'Every intention of the thoughts of his [man's] heart was only evil continually.' In the Old Testament the heart is not just the seat of the emotions, but of the mind and the will. The thoughts that emanate from the heart may not be as bad as they could be, but according to this verse they tend always towards evil. (For Jesus' similar assessment cf. Mark 7:21–23.) No wonder God was disappointed with his creature, whom Genesis 1 sees as the climax of the creation. Disappointment is too mild a description: 'it grieved him to his heart.' This is the bitter indignation felt by Dinah's brothers when they were told of her rape, or David's grief over the death of Absalom, or a deserted wife (Genesis 34:7; 2 Samuel 19:2; Isaiah 54:6).

It was not just that human thought tended inexorably towards evil; it led to the earth being full of violence. Soon after Adam had been evicted from Eden, his son Cain murdered his brother out of jealousy. A few generations later Lamech promises seventy-sevenfold vengeance on anyone who attacks him. In this way Genesis traces violence back to the first days of human history. Furthermore it implies that before the flood human violence had spread to the animal kingdom, for 'all flesh', that is man and beast, 'had corrupted their way on the earth … for the earth is filled with violence through them'(Gen. 6:12–13). Genesis thus suggests God had three major reasons for sending the flood: misguided worship involving cult prostitution, the perversity of human thought, and universal violence. Noah, however, escaped because he was righteous, 'blameless in his generation' (6:9).

The flood itself is a great act of decreation. Not only is human and animal life destroyed, but the mountains and trees are covered, so that the earth returns to the watery chaos described in Genesis 1:2. Even the chronology of the flood, which is extraordinarily precise, seems to underline this reversal, for just as the original creation started on a Sunday and ended on a Friday, so did the first destructive phase of the flood, which lasted 40 days (Wenham 1987, pp. 180–81). But when God remembered Noah, a new process of creation begins. Whereas the original creation took six days, recreation takes nearly a year. As before, the wind blows, the dry land and plants appear, and the earth is repopulated by man and the animals. As before, they are both told to be fruitful and multiply.

But is the new creation identical with the old? Has the flood really purified the earth, or are the old problems of human perversity and violence going to rear their head again?

As soon as Noah has disembarked, the narrative addresses these very questions. Noah built an altar, offered sacrifice, and when God smelled it, he said: 'I will never again curse the ground because of man, for the intention of man's heart is evil from his youth' (8:21). The reason given here for *not* sending another flood is astonishingly similar to the reason given *for* sending the flood in the first place (6:5). How does one explain the divine U-turn? The slightly milder language in 8:21 is probably not significant: man's thought is still inveterately sinful 'from his youth'. The text ascribes God's change of heart to Noah's sacrifice 'When the LORD smelled the pleasing [better 'soothing'] aroma, he said in his heart …' Once again (cf. 4:3–6) Genesis makes a point about sacrifice through a narrative: here it illustrates how a righteous man's sacrifice can atone for the sins of others, in this case the sins of the whole human race (cf. Job 42:8).

But if man's thoughts are just as sinful as they were before, is not violence still likely to be a problem? This issue is addressed in 9:1–7. It begins with a very clear echo of 1:28: 'And God blessed Noah and his sons and said to them, "Be fruitful and multiply and fill the earth" ' (9:1). This underlines the parallel between the first creation described in Genesis 1 and the recreation of Genesis 8—9. But from this point on Genesis 9 deliberately contrasts the new post-flood situation and the original creation as the following table shows.

From this table it is clear that Genesis 1 envisages a world of harmony. Animals do not attack each other or human beings,

29

CREATION BEFORE AND AFTER THE FLOOD

Topic	Original Creation	New Creation after the Flood
Human–animal relationships	Under human control 1:28	In fear and dread of man 9:2
Permitted food	Only plants 1:29–30	Plants and meat without blood 9:3–4
Image of God	1:26–27 (No consequences stated)	Image of God means murder deserves exact retribution 9:5–6

Digging deeper:
WAS THERE A UNIVERSAL FLOOD?

Stories about a great flood are found among many peoples in many parts of the world. This has led archaeologists and historians of early man to search for traces of the flood in the ground. For many centuries it was believed that fossils were evidence for a universal flood, since they were found in so many places even on mountains. But as modern geology developed it became apparent that they were deposited millions of years before man existed.

With the discovery of the Gilgamesh epic archaeologists supposed that a flood in Mesopotamia, where the epic was told, might lie behind the story. In the early twentieth century traces of severe flooding were indeed found at several sites in southern Iraq dating from about 3000 BC. However, closer investigation showed that these floods were not simultaneous, but happened at different times. Nevertheless some people think a local flood in Mesopotamia could have been the basis of the story.

Another possibility is that the flood story reflects the heavy rains and flooding that marked the end of the last ice age about 10,000 BC. At that time the melting of the ice led to the oceans rising some 120 metres (400 feet), which would have led to vast tracts of land being inundated, perhaps an area equal to the continents of North and South America together!

Recently it has been discovered that the Black Sea basin was filled by a cataclysmic flood pouring in from the Mediterranean, when the land dam, situated where the straits of the Bosphorus are now, broke in about 5000 BC. In a very short time the villages around the shore of the sea were flooded and doubtless many died. Some may have escaped by boat.

Obviously none of these limited floods quite fits the traditional picture of a worldwide flood. Yet someone caught up in a flood might see water stretching as far as the eye could see and thus describe it in universal terms. But as we have suggested above, the theological significance of the flood is more important than its date or extent.

nor do humans kill each other or eat animals. But the experiences of Genesis 4—6 have shown that this is a forlorn hope, so chapter 9 lays down principles to stop violence getting out of hand again. Man's supremacy over the beasts is reasserted, but the benevolent management envisaged by 1:28 is replaced by fear and dread, terms more characteristic of war than peace. The primal vegetarianism of 1:29 is replaced by permission to eat meat, as long as the principle of life is respected by not consuming the blood of the animal (9:3–4). Finally the uniqueness of human life is to be protected by exact retribution: whoever or whatever kills a man must be put to death (9:5–6). This resort to the death penalty contrasts with the sevenfold or seventy-sevenfold vengeance demanded by Cain and Lamech (4:24). It expresses a central principle of Old Testament justice that the punishment should match the crime and aims to stop a blood feud developing in which the families of both sides keep on retaliating so that the initial death of one person leads to the death of many others.

The final episode (9:20–27) in the Noah story is surprising. It tells of Noah growing grapes, making wine, getting drunk and cursing his grandson Canaan for Ham's tactlessness. Does this episode really belong here, and what does it contribute to the plot of Genesis?

There are good reasons for holding that it is not a stray insertion into the book. First, in Greek myths grape-growing and wine-making are traced back to the time of the flood. Second, the Sodom and Gomorrah story, the next narrative in Genesis dealing with a universal act of judgement and the salvation of one family, also ends with the righteous man getting drunk and being abused by his children (19:30–38). Finally, this episode here acts as a trailer for the next major section, the table of nations in chapter 10. We have noted this pattern before in Genesis e.g. 4:25–26; 6:5–8.

It is the connection with chapter 10 that is the first clue to this episode's purpose in Genesis. It demonstrates the correctness of Shem and Japheth's behaviour over against Ham's impropriety. in the ancient world at least children were expected to cover up their parents' faults, not blab them abroad as Ham did. It was of course from Shem that Abraham and the Israelites were descended, but it was from Ham that Israel's traditional enemies came, peoples such as Egypt, Assyria and Babylon. But worst of all from Genesis' perspective were the Canaanites, the descendants of one of Ham's sons. Noah's curse on Canaan foreshadows the future subjugation of the Canaanites by the Israelites. In Noah's words 'Blessed be the LORD, the God of Shem; and let Canaan be his servant' (9:26). So just as Adam had three sons, two good (Abel and Seth) and one wicked (Cain), Noah has three sons, two good and one wicked. In both cases Genesis traces the parting of the ways, showing how the chosen line through Abraham can be traced back through Shem and Seth.

The parallels between Adam and Noah suggest another function of this story.

Noah like Adam is seen as the ancestor of the whole human race, everyone else having perished in the flood. After the flood he was, like Adam, told to be fruitful and multiply. At the beginning of the story we are told, 'Noah was a righteous man, blameless in his generation', OT terminology for a top-quality saint! Furthermore, in the flood story he is repeatedly said to obey God exactly (6:22; 7:5, 9, 16; 8:18). Yet sometime later he acts in a way that reminds us again of Adam, who ate of a forbidden fruit. Is Noah's over-consumption of the fruit of the vine a transgression akin to Adam's? Is this a second fall as it were? Opinions differ. One thing is clear: Ham's sin is obviously worse than his father's, just as Cain's murder was more serious than Adam's action. What is more, the situation deteriorates further in both cases, culminating in the punishment of the flood in the first case, and the dispersal of the nations, after they had tried to build the tower of Babel, in the second case.

Digging deeper:
NOAH'S DRUNKENNESS: DOES GENESIS THINK IT SINFUL?

The answer given to this question determines whether Genesis 9:20–27 should be read as a second fall like Adam's. Consider some other passages dealing with wine and other strong drinks. Is there a consistent attitude in them?

Compare Psalm 104:15; Deuteronomy 14:26; Isaiah 5:1–7 with Numbers 6:3–4; 1 Samuel 1:14; Proverbs 21:17; 23:20–21, 29–35; Isaiah 5:22.

10:1—11:9

The last major section consists of two very different pieces: the Table of Nations (10:1–32) and the Tower of Babel (11:1–9). On first reading they appear to offer contradictory explanations for the diversity of languages in the world, but they are both in the same part of Genesis headed by the title, 'These are the generations of the sons of Noah.'

The Table of Nations lists seventy nations known to the Israelites and by implication defines Israel's relationship to her neighbours. The sons of Japheth (vv. 2–5) seem to be the people on Israel's northern horizon, inhabitants of Turkey, the Greek islands, Cyprus and Crete. The sons of Ham (vv. 6–20) are a large group, covering peoples from Africa, Arabia, Mesopotamia as well as the indigenous inhabitants of Canaan (vv. 15–19), whose territory would be promised to Abraham. As already mentioned, Israel did not enjoy good relations with the descendants of Ham. The opposite is true of the sons of Shem (vv. 21–31). Not only did Israel trace its own line through Shem (11:10–26), but it seems to have enjoyed friendly relations with many of the Arabian and Aramaean groups related to Shem.

The Table of Nations regularly mentions that these different peoples spread out to their own territories and spoke their own languages without hinting that there was anything amiss (10:5, 20, 31, 32). But the Tower of Babel story puts a quite different spin on this dispersal. Babel is Babylon and in the local language meant 'Gate of God', in other words the entry to heaven.

Indeed the Babylonians claimed that their ziggurat, a sort of pyramid with a temple on top, had its foundations in the underworld while its top touched the heavens.

These pretensions are mercilessly sent up in this story. So far from its top reaching heaven, it was so low that God could hardly see it but had to come down to see what man was trying to do (11:5 cf. Isa. 40:22). The name Babel really means 'Confusion', and sounds like 'Folly'. According to one Sumerian story everyone would one day speak Sumerian, but Genesis says that God deliberately made people speak different languages so that they could not work together on godless projects that aimed to enter heaven. The derelict ziggurat in Babylon and the multiplicity of languages witness to God's judgement on human sin.

At many earlier points in Genesis we noted that it seemed to be criticizing Babylonian notions about the gods, the role of man, the flood and so on. Here in chapter 11 the attack on the pretensions of Babylon is open and blatant. It is not the greatest civilization, nor is it the closest to God: rather its buildings are a reminder that the human race cannot reach heaven on its own, but stands under divine judgement.

11:10–26

The genealogy of Shem links the protohistory of Genesis 1—11 to the stories of the patriarchs in chapters 12—50. Like the earlier genealogy of Adam via Seth it consists of ten generations and traces the chosen line from Shem to Abraham.

This time though the ages are considerably lower than in chapter 5, but still high by our standards. With this genealogy the second exposition of Genesis ends, and the main story is ready to unfold.

THE NEW TESTAMENT USE OF GENESIS 1—11

For the New Testament writers the opening chapters of Genesis are foundational to their theology. From John's imitation of Genesis 1:1 in the opening lines of his Gospel 'In the beginning was the Word and the Word was with God' to the reversal of the confusion of languages on the day of Pentecost (Acts 2), the New Testament draws on nearly every element in these opening chapters. Luke uses the genealogies to trace Jesus' line back to Adam to show that Jesus is the Son of God (Luke 3:23–38). Paul makes abundant use of the story of Adam and the fall to demonstrate that the obedience of Christ the second Adam saved mankind from the effects of the first Adam's disobedience (Rom. 5). Jesus cites the creation stories to demonstrate his view of marriage over against the Pharisees and uses the flood as a warning of future judgement (Matt. 19:3–12; 24:37–39). Finally the book of Revelation portrays the new Jerusalem descending from heaven to earth as a Garden of Eden, a place where God himself dwells and gives life to the nations (Rev. 21—22).

Early Christian writers continued to draw heavily on these chapters in their works.

Louth writes 'the early chapters of Genesis had arguably a greater influence on the development of Christian theology than did any other part of the Old Testament' (2001, p. xxxix). On the basis of these chapters they developed the insights of St Paul about Christ as the second Adam, the doctrine of creation, and particularly the implications of man being made in the image of God.

FURTHER READING

R. S. Hess and D. T. Tsumura *I Studied Inscriptions from before the Flood*. Winona Lake: Eisenbrauns, 1994. A collection of the most useful modern essays on these chapters including Jacobsen.

A. Louth *Genesis 1—11*. (Ancient Christian Commentary on Scripture.) Downers Grove: InterVarsity Press, 2001. Shows how Christian writers up to the eighth century understood Genesis.

G. von Rad *Genesis: A Commentary*. tr. by J. Bowden. London: SCM Press, 1972. The classic theological commentary.

J. Rogerson *Genesis 1—11*. Sheffield: Sheffield Academic Press, 1991. Manageable introduction to interpretative issues.

G. J. Wenham *Genesis 1—15*. Waco: Word Books, 1987.

C. Westermann *Genesis 1—11: A Commentary*. tr. by J. J. Scullion. London: SPCK, 1984. The authoritative German commentary, but it leaves Hebrew words untranslated.

NEAR EASTERN PARALLELS TO GENESIS 1—11 IN TRANSLATION

S. Dalley *Myths from Mesopotamia*. Oxford: Oxford University Press, 1989.

A. George *The Epic of Gilgamesh*. London: Penguin, 2000. Excellent introduction and translation.

A. Heidel *The Gilgamesh Epic and Old Testament Parallels*. Chicago: University of Chicago Press, 1949.

T. Jacobsen 'The Eridu Genesis' *JBL* 100, 1981, pp. 513–29. Reprinted in Hess and Tsumura, 1994, pp. 129–42.

J. B. Pritchard (ed.) *Ancient Near Eastern Texts relating to the Old Testament*. Princeton: Princeton University Press, 1955.

ON GENESIS 5

D. T. Bryan 'A Reevaluation of Gen 4 and 5 in the Light of Recent Studies in Genealogical Fluidity' *ZAW* 99, 1987, pp. 180–88.

D. W. Young 'On the Application of Numbers from Babylonian Mathematics to Biblical Life Spans and Epochs' *ZAW* 100, 1988, pp. 331–61.

D. W. Young 'The Influence of Babylonian Algebra on Longevity among the Antediluvians' *ZAW* 102, 1990, pp. 321–35.

ON GENESIS 6—9

W. A. van Gemeren 'The Sons of God in Genesis 6:1–4' *WTJ* 43, 1981, pp. 320–48.

R. L. Raikes 'The Physical Evidence for Noah's Flood' *Iraq* 28, 1966, pp. 52–63.

A. J. Tomasino 'History Repeats Itself: the "Fall" and Noah's Drunkenness' *VT* 42, 1992, pp. 128–30.

D. A. Young *The Biblical Flood*. Grand Rapids: Eerdmans, 1995.

On the Black Sea flood see www.nationalgeographic.com/blacksea

Chapter 3

GENESIS 12—50

With the call of Abraham in 12:1–3 the book of Genesis arrives at its focus of interest. The opening chapters of the book cover long stretches of time very quickly, but from chapter 12 the pace slackens and the narratives become much more detailed. Instead of relating events that affected the whole human race, the book now focuses on the life of one family, the descendants of Abraham. The sheer volume of material, more than 80 per cent of Genesis, devoted to this family shows where the interest really lies. Here are explained the origins of the nation of Israel, and more particularly of the 12 tribes that made up the nation. It tells too of the basis of the claim to the land of Canaan: the LORD had promised it to Abraham in a series of visions. For the writer of Genesis, the story he tells in chapters 12—50 is therefore of vital importance: it makes up the core of the book.

Like the second exposition in chapters 2—11, the core of Genesis consists of three major narratives separated by two short genealogies.

In the previous chapter we briefly considered the pattern of these headings and noted that the person mentioned in the title was head of the family during the period the title covers, though it is usually his sons who are the main actors in the

STRUCTURE OF GENESIS 12—50

Content	Heading	Reference
The story of Abraham	'These are the generations of Terah'	11:27—25:11
Genealogy of Ishmael	'These are the generations of Ishmael'	25:12–18
The story of Jacob and Esau	'These are the generations of Isaac'	25:19—35:29
Genealogy of Esau	'These are the generations of Esau'	36:1—37:1
The story of Joseph and his brothers	'These are the generations of Jacob'	37:2—50:26

story. Thus chapters 25—35 'the generations of Isaac' deals with the era between the death of Abraham (25:11) and the death of Isaac (35:29), in other words the latter years of Isaac. However, throughout this period Isaac was elderly and fairly inactive (see ch. 27) and most of the action takes place between his sons Jacob and Esau. A similar situation prevails in chapters 12—25, whose action mostly occurs before the death of Terah, but in these stories Abraham is the chief actor. Likewise chapters 37—50 tell of Jacob's later career, an era in which his sons make most of the running.

The stories of Abraham, Jacob and Esau, and Joseph and his brothers, thus constitute the three key narratives of Genesis. Not only do they all have a similar title, but many of the episodes within them seem to run in parallel. All have a divine revelation to the main actor near the beginning of the story, which foreshadows how the plot will develop. Abraham is told to leave home (12:1), Rebekah that she has two nations in her womb (25:23), while Joseph has dreams in which his family bow down to him (37:5–10). Each of the principal actors, Abraham, Jacob and Joseph, has to leave home. Each main story ends with a burial at the ancestral grave of Machpelah, near Hebron (25:9–10; 35:29; 50:13–14). There are quite a number of other parallels between the stories, which suggest that the writer wanted to point out the similarities between the careers of the patriarchs.

Theologians have often noticed parallels between the life of Jesus and people or events in the Old Testament. For example, Jesus was forced to flee to Egypt and then returned to his homeland, which Matthew compares to the exodus (Matt. 2:15 quoting Hos. 11:1). His 40 days of temptation in the wilderness are compared to Israel's 40 years in the wilderness. These parallels between different parts of Scripture are traditionally called typology. It is striking that we have the same phenomenon within the book of Genesis itself. We have noted already the parallels between Adam and Noah, but those between Abraham, Jacob and Joseph are even more striking. There are also parallels between the lives of these patriarchs and the subsequent history of Israel: in other words the patriarchs are not simply individuals in their own right but embodiments of the nation. Modern literary study pays close attention to such parallels, because they indicate what the writer was especially interested in and help to highlight the similarities and differences between different characters and show the development of the theme.

THE GENRE OF GENESIS 12—50

So far I have simply described these chapters of Genesis as narratives or the patriarchal stories. Can one be any more precise? Defining genre is important, if we are to interpret texts responsibly. We have suggested that the whole Pentateuch is *Torah*, 'instruction' in the form of a biography of Moses. Within this general definition, Genesis is essentially background to the main action, which begins in the book of Exodus. But we can try to be more precise about Genesis itself.

Simplest to define are the genealogies of Ishmael and Esau in 25:12–18 and 35:1—36:1. These are essentially tribal genealogies expanded with additional information as common in the Bible, cf. Genesis 4:17–24; 5:1–32. The major narratives in Genesis 12—50 are about the family life of the patriarchs, so older theories that these were originally stories about Canaanite gods or that the patriarchs are personified Israelite tribes have long been abandoned. These stories describe the joys and sorrows of family life in such a vivid way that we can still identify with them today. Births and deaths, quarrels and reconciliations, hopes delayed and hopes fulfilled, all bring these ancient families to life. It therefore seems reasonable to agree with Claus Westermann that 'The whole has the form of family history over three generations' (Westermann 1985, p. 28). While few

would quibble over this definition of the form of the material, some would doubt whether it should be taken as historical.

As with Genesis 1—11 a comparison with ancient Near Eastern storytelling is helpful. Apart from royal inscriptions, ancient stories about people fall into three main categories. First, there are biographies and occasional autobiographies, written close to the events described without extraordinary or miraculous embellishments. The Egyptian stories of Sinuhe and Wenamun are examples of this type of writing. Second, there are historical legends, such as the epic of Gilgamesh. These are based on historical figures, but they are written centuries after the hero and are full of fantastic deeds, clearly the product of storytellers' imaginations. Third, there are purely fictional stories, such as 'The Three Ox-Drivers of Adab'. It has been observed that the patriarchal stories fall somewhere between the first and second group of narratives. Their sober content and third-person style makes them resemble biographies. But their composition centuries after the lives of the heroes makes them more like legends, though they lack the fantasy elements characteristic of the legends. But whether we class these accounts as biography or legend, analogy with their Near Eastern counterparts would suggest we are dealing with real historical people, not make-believe figures.

11:27—25:11: THE STORY OF ABRAHAM

Like each major section of Genesis the story of Abraham begins with a heading,

Digging deeper:
ARE THE PATRIARCHAL STORIES HISTORICAL?

Traditionally Jews and Christians took the stories of the patriarchs at face value: that is, they assumed they were accurate, historical accounts about real people living in the land of Israel many centuries ago (e.g. John 8:39–58). But in the nineteenth century this came to be widely doubted by Old Testament scholars, so that the most famous of them, Julius Wellhausen, described the stories as a 'glorified mirage'! He held the stories were essentially fictional, reflecting the times and customs of a much later period.

In the twentieth century this scepticism gradually waned, as archaeologists discovered more about the ancient Near East and noted more and more parallels between the names, legal practices, and way of life of the patriarchs and the peoples of surrounding countries. These discoveries suggested that Genesis reflected life in the second millennium BC very accurately, so that it was reasonable to hold that the patriarchs were real historical individuals. John Bright in his standard *History of Israel* (1972) wrote: 'Abraham, Isaac, and Jacob were clan chiefs who actually lived between the twentieth and seventeenth centuries [BC] … The Bible's narrative accurately reflects the times to which it refers. But to what it tells of the lives of the patriarchs we can add nothing' (p. 92).

However, since 1972 debate has again broken out about the status of the narratives. There are those who fervently affirm that they are not historical at all: they are more like theological fiction projecting late ideas back into the past in an attempt to justify Israel's existence and its presence in the land.

Advocates of this stance have three main arguments. 1) The supposed parallels between Genesis and early second millennium texts are either illusory, or too general to prove an early date. Certain social customs and legal practices, e.g. marriage rites, changed little in 2000 years, so a parallel with Genesis proves very little. 2) Genesis was written many hundreds of years after the patriarchs lived, so it is unlikely to give accurate historical information about them. 3) Genesis, like many other biblical books, adopts an omniscient perspective, that is, it lets the reader into the secret thoughts of the actors in the story including God. Human historians cannot do this, so the biblical writers are essentially writing fiction.

Responses to this radical standpoint have tended to focus on the first point. Those who accept the historicity of the patriarchs make the following points. Though some of the alleged parallels between Genesis and other texts are worthless, many are not. And some of the parallels are only found between early texts and Genesis: the clearest pointers to the antiquity of the patriarchal traditions are 1) their names, which are not found later, 2) adoption customs and 3) lifestyle, all of which fit the second millennium better than other eras.

As for the late date of the composition of Genesis (itself a controversial issue, see Chapter 9, Composition), few would dispute that Genesis describes the patriarchal age from the perspective of a later period or that the writing of Genesis was preceded by a long era of oral storytelling. The issue at stake is whether the stories have been passed on relatively unchanged from generation to generation. Studies of bedouin practice have shown this is quite possible. 'Nomadic and semi-nomadic Arabs still relate in their tents the traditions, genealogies and stories of their tribes or families. Both adults and children hear the same stories again and again and whenever the narrator omits or adds something, they correct him at once' (de Vaux 1978, p. 182). Some tribes' oral history stretches back ten centuries.

Finally, the feature of omniscient storytelling can be viewed in quite a different light: it is a claim to inspiration, that God has shown the author what really happened and why. This is to make a very high claim about the authority of the narrative, but it does not prove it is unhistorical. It is an affirmation, whether justified or not, that God is behind the writing of the narrative. Thus the intention to write history is clear, even if some scholars think the biblical writer has not succeeded.

In the end neither side can muster a knock-out argument. Those who initially accept the historical reality of the patriarchs will not feel the sceptics have disproved it. On the other hand initial sceptics will not feel compelled by the counter arguments to admit the historicity of the patriarchal narratives. So the debate is likely to continue.

For further reading see the books by Alter (1981), Bright (1972), de Vaux (1978), Kitchen (1977), Millard and Wiseman (1980), Sternberg (1985), Thompson (1974) and van Seters (1975). For a compact summary see Wenham 1994, pp. xx–xxx.

'These are the generations of Terah'. As usual in the patriarchal narratives the person named in the heading is the father of the chief actor in the subsequent story: in this case Terah is the father of Abraham. Like the other two patriarchal stories, this one ends with a burial in the tomb of Machpelah (25:9–10; cf. 35:27–29; 50:13–14). It has been suggested that the story of Abraham is arranged like the flood story as a palistrophe with each episode in the first half of the story balanced by episodes in the second half. But it is not so obvious as it is in Genesis 6—9. However, it does seem that the first and last call of God to Abraham are meant to echo each other. On the first occasion the LORD commands him: 'Go from your country … to the land that I will show you' (12:1), and on the last 'Go to the land of Moriah … on one of the mountains of which I shall tell you' (22:2). These are some of the indications that the story of Abraham is not just a collection of tales about him but a carefully organized life of Abraham, albeit not so tightly knit as the subsequent lives of Jacob and Joseph.

After a quick sketch of Abraham's family background introducing his nephew Lot and his childless wife Sarah, the narrative rushes forward to the defining moment in Abraham's life, God's call to him to leave his homeland and family and move to an unspecified country that he would inherit. In our rootless and mobile Western culture we may easily miss what a drastic step this was. But in ancient society your family and tribe defined who you were: to break away was to lose your identity and security, for your extended family was your protection if anything went wrong. In Abraham's case he was being asked to leave the most sophisticated and affluent part of the Middle East, Ur of the Chaldees, in modern terms, southern Iraq, for the unknown 'land that I will show you'.

It was a momentous step for Abraham personally, but Genesis sees his call as a giant leap for mankind. In its exposition we read of two cycles of human failure. The first man Adam failed and that led eventually to the flood. The only righteous survivor of the flood and second father of the human race, Noah, also slipped and the whole race again fell under judgement at the tower of Babel. But now Abraham is promised: 'in you all the families of the earth shall be blessed.'

Genesis 12:1–3 are the first words God has spoken to man since the flood. Traditionally they are referred to as the call of Abraham, but they are much more than that: they sum up the theme of Genesis, if not the whole Pentateuch. In this call the LORD promises Abraham four things: 1) a land, 2) numerous descendants ('a great nation'), 3) blessing, that is protection and success, 4) blessing of the nations.

The storyline of Genesis, especially the Abraham story, is frequently punctuated by God speaking to the patriarchs. A casual reader could see these words as simply repetitious, but a careful inspection shows this is far from true. Each statement of the promises develops them in some way, either increasing their scope or

underlining their validity. It is also important to consider the circumstances in which they are given: there is a clear tendency for promises to be reaffirmed after an act of faith or obedience on the patriarch's part. For example, in chapter 13 after Abraham has generously offered his nephew Lot the choice of the land so as to defuse the dispute between their herdsmen, the LORD appears to Abraham and enlarges on the promises. Similarly the last and most dogmatic statement of the promise to Abraham comes after he has demonstrated his total commitment to God's demand in chapter 22.

Digging deeper:
CHANGING PROMISES

Compare the promises made to Abraham in Genesis. Take each aspect of the promise in turn, i.e. land, descendants, blessing, and notice how it is handled each time. What changes do you notice, either in the scope of the promises or in the definiteness in expression?

How do the promises relate to the contexts in which they occur?

Passages to consider 12:1–3, 7; 13:14–17; 15:1–16; 17:1–21; 18:10–15; 22:16–18.

Though God's words are obviously of central importance in Genesis, they are built into a narrative that is essentially about human action, so it is important to ask what the connection is between the promises and the plot. David Clines has defined the theme of the Pentateuch as 'the partial fulfilment – which implies also the partial non-fulfilment – of the promise … to the patriarchs' (Clines 1978, p. 29). In other words the events in Genesis all relate to the promises: sometimes things happen that show the promises being fulfilled, the patriarchs enjoy divine protection, children are born, or pieces of land are acquired. But at other times there are delays, or even setbacks, as for example when Jacob and all his descendants have to leave Canaan, the promised land, for Egypt. This is why Clines has defined the theme as the *partial* fulfilment of the promises. The problem of childlessness illustrates this very well. The first thing we learn about Sarah is that she is childless (11:30). Abraham is then promised descendants (12:2), but ten years pass and nothing happens (16:3), so they try for a child by surrogate marriage, which is successful. But another 14 years go by and still Sarah has no child (17:1). She is 89 and past the menopause (17:17; 18:11), but eventually after two specific promises (17:19; 18:10) she conceives and Isaac is born (21:1–2). Rebekah, Isaac's wife, had similar problems conceiving: she had to wait 20 years before her twins, Jacob and Esau, were born (25:20, 26). Finally Jacob's wife, Rachel, also had great difficulty conceiving: her sister Leah had seven children before Rachel bore Joseph (30:1–23). Modern readers of these stories tend to be so surprised by the ages of these parents, which like other figures in Genesis may have a symbolic dimension, that they fail to see the writer's interest in these stories. They show the promises being fulfilled, but painfully slowly. But

the persistent reader will see ever greater fulfilment as the story progresses. By the end of Genesis Jacob's extended family consists of seventy persons. By the beginning of Exodus they are so numerous that the Egyptians embark on genocide to protect themselves, while a few years later the Moabites, scared by their number, summon the most potent prophet in the Near East to curse Israel. But of course both attempts fail (Exod. 1; Num. 22—24).

The promises and their fulfilment explain how the plot of the Pentateuch subsequently develops. But why is Genesis 12—50 prefaced by the protohistory of Genesis 1—11? The promises to the patriarchs have been described as a 're-affirmation of the primal divine intentions for man' (Clines 1978, p. 29). In other words what God promised to Abraham is what he intended for the whole human race at the beginning. As Genesis portrays history, initially the whole human race, i.e. Adam and Eve, was in the Garden of Eden. There they enjoyed God's rich supply of all their needs, including land, food and fellowship. This is more or less what Abraham was promised in Genesis 12 and other places. Also, as soon as mankind was created in two sexes in 1:28, they were told, 'Be fruitful and multiply.' This corresponds to the promise to Abraham that he would have innumerable descendants. But as a result of Adam and Eve's disobedience, they were ejected from the garden, they forfeited God's presence and provision, and were told that every pregnancy would bring pain. With the call of Abraham, however, the ideals of

Genesis 1 and 2 are resurrected, and Abraham is assured that in him 'all the families of the earth shall be blessed' (12:3). The long-term vision of Genesis, if not the whole Old Testament, is that ultimately the reign of sin will be broken and the world will become what its Creator originally intended. In Abraham mankind sets out towards this goal.

But the path is far from straight: the key actors seem to meander towards it, not stride towards it. No sooner has Abraham reached Canaan and been told (12:7) that this is the land of promise, than he has to leave it for Egypt. Kicked out of Egypt, he returns to Canaan only to be in dispute with his nephew Lot over grazing rights (ch. 13). No sooner is this problem resolved than he has to go into battle against a coalition of northern kings, who

have taken Lot as one of their prisoners of war (ch. 14). Though Abraham is victorious, he realizes how tenuous his hold on the promised land is, if he has no children to succeed him (ch. 15), and it takes another six chapters before a true heir of Abraham is born (ch. 21).

These issues come to a head in chapter 15. Abraham gained nothing personally from his intervention on behalf of his nephew Lot and the king of Sodom, so the LORD assures him in 15:1 that his reward will be very great. But Abraham responds by pointing out that so far none of God's promises have materialized: he has not even a son, let alone the land of Canaan. So this leads into the first of two covenant ceremonies that are made with Abraham in chapters 15 and 17. In the first God appears to Abraham in a vision and in a

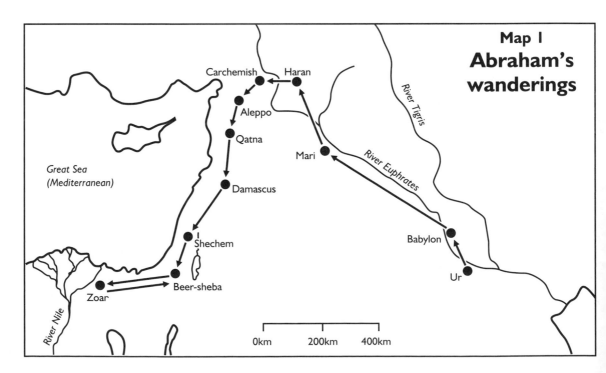

Map 1
Abraham's wanderings

vivid symbolic gesture promises him offspring as numerous as the stars of heaven and all the land of Canaan from the border with Egypt as far north as the river Euphrates.

The covenant made with Abraham in Genesis 15 is essentially a promise guaranteed by a remarkable sign: this makes it unlike most other covenants in the Pentateuch, which require some action by the human party as well as by God. On this occasion Abraham simply has to kill five animals traditionally used in sacrifice, split them, and lay them out in two lines. When birds of prey try to eat the pieces, Abraham drives them off. He then falls asleep, and he is assured that after four hundred years in a foreign land his descendants would inherit the land. Then a cauldron of fire passes between the animal pieces, and the promise is repeated. The precise significance of these acts is elusive, but they seem to foreshadow the exodus from Egypt and God's appearance in fire on Mount Sinai.

The next covenant has a different focus. It begins with the demand: 'Walk before me, and be blameless' (17:1). It involves changing Abram's name to Abraham, and Sarai's to Sarah and the introduction of the rite of circumcision as a mark of belonging to the covenant people. Here for the first time it is explicitly said that Sarah is going to have a child to be called Isaac: hitherto descendants have been promised to Abraham, but it has never been specifically said that Sarah would be their mother. Their new names, 'Father of a multitude' and 'Princess', are an

assurance that Isaac would indeed be born, and that Abraham would not simply become a great nation, but father of many nations. The imminence of Isaac's birth is confirmed in the next chapter by the LORD and two angels visiting Abraham and Sarah in their tent to tell them that it would happen 'this time next year' (18:10, 14). But the longer-term goal of Abraham fathering many nations depends on his obedience.

Abraham's first act of obedience is immediate: he and all the men of his household are circumcised. His second act of obedience is even more painful: he is asked to sacrifice his long-promised son Isaac. As if no words could do justice to Abraham's feelings, his response is told with the sparsest of detail. Conversation between Abraham and Isaac is minimal too. Only when Isaac is bound helpless on the altar and Abraham is about to slash his throat with a knife does the angel from heaven countermand the order to sacrifice. 'Abraham, Abraham! … Do not lay your hand on the boy or do anything to him, for now I know that you fear God, seeing you have not withheld your son, your only son, from me' (22:11–12). Then Abraham spots a ram, which he sacrifices instead of Isaac. Then the promises to Abraham are reaffirmed, not as a mere promise but in a solemn divine oath. Blessing, descendants, land and climactically 'in your offspring shall all the nations of the earth be blessed, because you have obeyed my voice' (22:18). It could be said that the original promises made in chapter 12 have now been turned into guarantees thanks to Abraham's faithful obedience.

Digging deeper:
THE AKEDAH OR SACRIFICE OF ISAAC

Within the book of Genesis and later Jewish and Christian theology the sacrifice of Isaac has been most significant. Literary critics marvel at the skill of the storyteller evoking the mood so powerfully with such economy of language.

Above we have sketched the importance of the episode for the confirmation of the promises to Abraham. It is also one of the passages in Genesis that explain the key principles of sacrifice. Cain and Abel's sacrifices show that only the pick of the flock should be offered in sacrifice (4:3–5). Noah's sacrifice shows how a righteous man's sacrifice can transform God's anger into goodwill (8:20–21; cf. 6:5–6). Abraham's sacrifice shows that when the worshipper is willing to offer his very life to God on the chosen mountain (2 Chron. 3:1 identifies Mount Moriah with the temple mount in Jerusalem), God will accept an animal instead and grant the worshipper even more blessing than he had before.

The New Testament sees the sacrifice of Isaac as a type of Christ's death on the cross (e.g. John 1:29; 3:16; Rom. 8:31–32; 1 Pet. 1:19–20) and Abraham's faith in this crisis as a model to imitate (Heb. 11:17–19; James 2:21–23).

Jews describe this episode as the Akedah (binding), and as a foreshadowing of their own call to suffer.

Look up the passages listed above. Do you see any parallels between this OT story and the sufferings of Christ in the NT?

What devices does the writer use to suggest the pain Abraham and Isaac suffered during this test of their obedience? Consider the use of repetition in the story, the dialogue between Abraham and his servants, and between him and Isaac. What remarks are ambiguous and can be taken in a variety of ways? What gaps are there in the story, i.e. items of information the reader has to supply?

In most episodes it is clear that Abraham is being presented as a model for his descendants to imitate. He unhesitatingly obeys God's commands in chapters 12, 17 and 22. He is anxious to resolve disputes amicably in chapters 13 and 21. He intercedes for the city of Sodom and for Abimelech and his household (chs 18, 20). He seeks no profit from others' misfortune (ch. 14), and he takes steps to ensure a decent burial for his wife and to find an appropriate bride for his son (chs 23, 24).

But from time to time Abraham behaves in ways that shock the reader. He twice pretends that Sarah is just his sister, so that she is abducted by the local king (chs 12 and 20). On another occasion he consents to surrogate marriage to provide himself with an heir (ch. 16). Jacob's behaviour is even more problematic. He deliberately tricks his brother out of his birthright and blessing, deceiving his old father in the process. He does nothing when his daughter Dinah is raped, except criticize his sons for their revenge. But does the writer of Genesis share our moral perspective?

It is difficult to know, for typically the biblical storytellers rarely make an explicit moral comment. It is therefore not surprising that some writers have supposed that ancient readers admired some of this deception: it showed how smart their forefathers were. However, there are clues that show the author's stance is different. The opening chapters of Genesis portray a world of harmony and contentment. Adam, Eve and the animals are portrayed as enjoying great peace with one another and with God in chapter 2. This is in such marked contrast with what follows that we must suppose that the opening chapters give us a glimpse of the writer's ideals. Indeed, Jacob's deception of his father has such long-range and tragic consequences that one must assume the writer was showing the folly of Jacob's behaviour. Abraham's economy with the truth does not seem to have had quite such dire consequences, but it does seem to slow down the conception of Isaac, which was the focus of Abraham's hope. But his life-story does end hopefully. After hard negotiations with the Hittites he buys with full legal title a field and a cave in which to bury Sarah. This field is his first substantial real estate in the land of promise. He also sends off his trusted servant to find a wife for Isaac. And he is remarkably successful in finding a girl who is at once from the right family, beautiful, energetic and willing. This means that the future of the chosen family is secure for another generation.

25:12–18: GENEALOGY OF ISHMAEL

It would be easy to overlook this short genealogy of Ishmael, Abraham's son

through his slave girl Hagar. Like Israel, Ishmael also seems to have formed a confederation of 12 tribes, which, in so far as they can be located, lived in Arabia. Although Ishmael was not the promised son, and therefore not an ancestor of Israel, he was a descendant of Abraham and therefore inherited some of the blessings. Genesis 16:12 had predicted that he would dwell over against all his kinsmen, and 21:18 that he would become a great nation. This genealogy (see 25:18) confirms these predictions. That these relatively minor predictions about the descendants of Ishmael have been fulfilled serves as an assurance that the major promises about Isaac's descendants will in due course be realized too. These form the subject matter of the next major section of Genesis. But as elsewhere in Genesis the genealogy of the minor characters who do not form part of the chosen line precedes the chosen line (Cain before Seth, Gen. 4—5; Japheth and Ham before Shem, Gen. 10—11; and Esau before Jacob, Gen. 36—37).

25:19—35:29: THE STORY OF JACOB AND ESAU

With the story of Jacob we reach the heart of Genesis. These chapters tell of the birth of the twins Jacob and Esau, their subsequent estrangement, Jacob's flight to Paddan-Aram, his marriage to Rachel and Leah, the birth of his 12 sons and his return to the promised land of Canaan.

Jacob's name is changed to Israel, which makes him the father of the nation, and his sons are the ancestors of the 12 tribes.

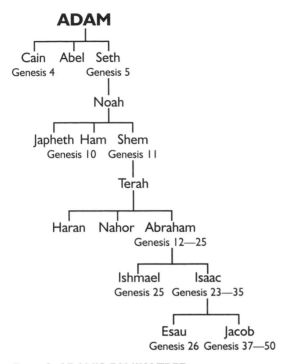

ADAM

Cain   Abel   Seth
Genesis 4   Genesis 5

Noah

Japheth   Ham   Shem
Genesis 10   Genesis 11

Terah

Haran   Nahor   Abraham
Genesis 12—25

Ishmael   Isaac
Genesis 25   Genesis 23—35

Esau   Jacob
Genesis 26   Genesis 37—50

Figure 2: **ADAM'S FAMILY TREE**

The story opens with the standard heading for each major section of Genesis, 'These are the generations of [Isaac]': here as elsewhere in the patriarchal stories it is the father of the main actors who is named in the title. Like the stories of Abraham and Joseph the story of Jacob closes with a burial in the ancestral grave (35:29). But as far as the storyline is concerned it does not end here, it continues through to chapter 50 where Jacob himself dies. Perhaps for reasons of symmetry the long biography of Jacob has been split into two equal parts by the insertion of Esau's genealogy in chapter 36.

We noted that the Abraham story seemed to be arranged palistrophically, that is, as a mirror-image pattern. This is even clearer in the Jacob story.

ARRANGEMENT OF THE STORY OF JACOB

25:19–34	First encounters of Jacob and Esau	A
26:1–33	Isaac and the Philistines	B
26:34—28:9	Jacob cheats Esau out of his blessing	C
28:10–22	Jacob meets God at Bethel	D
29:1–14	Jacob arrives at Laban's house	E
29:15–30	Jacob marries Rachel and Leah	F
29:31—30:24	Birth of Jacob's sons	G
30:25—31:1	Jacob outwits Laban	F'
31:2–55	Jacob leaves Laban	E'
32:1–2	Jacob meets angels of God at Mahanaim	D'
32:3—33:20	Jacob returns Esau's blessing	C'
34:1–31	Dinah and the Hivites	B'
35:1–29	Journey's end for Jacob and Esau	A'

Like the story of the flood the life of Jacob lends itself to palistrophic arrangement. Jacob leaves Canaan and returns, both times seeing angels (D/D'). He enters Laban's household and later escapes from it (E/E'). He is tricked by Laban into marrying both Leah and Rachel: he in turn tricks Laban to acquire the strongest animals in the flock (F/F'). Most striking is the way he illicitly acquires Esau's blessing and then returns it (C/C'). At first sight chapters 26 and 34 (B/B') have little in common, but they are both concerned with relations with the peoples of Canaan. Chapter 26 (B) shows Isaac living peaceably with the Philistines, the inhabitants of southern Canaan, whereas chapter 34 (B') shows Jacob's sons at war with the Hivites, who lived further north. Chapter 25 (A) telling of Jacob and Esau fighting each other in the womb finds its counterpart in their reunion to bury their father in chapter 35 (A').

At the centre of the pattern is the birth of Jacob's 12 sons, the fathers of the 12 tribes. This is the turning point in the narrative. More precisely it is 30:22, 'Then God remembered Rachel ... and opened her womb.' The flood story has a similar comment at its turning point, 'But God remembered Noah ... and God made a wind to blow over the earth and the waters subsided' (8:1). It is God's intervention that is decisive in both stories for reversing the period of judgement or estrangement. As soon as Rachel has given birth to Joseph, Jacob decides it is time to return to the home country (30:25–26).

Genesis 25:19–34 sets the tone for the whole Jacob story in several ways. First we see Rebekah's difficulty in becoming pregnant, a problem shared with Sarah before her and Rachel after her. Second, when she at last conceives, her pregnancy is so painful that she consults an oracle who declares: 'Two nations are in your womb ... the older shall serve the younger' (25:23). This announces the ultimate career of her two sons: one is to be the forefather of the nation of Israel, the other will be ancestor of the Edomites, who were Israel's often hostile neighbours south and east of the Dead Sea. But Esau the first born of the twins will be subject to the younger Jacob. With this cryptic announcement the plot of the ensuing Jacob story is summed up: in much the same way the Abraham and Joseph stories begin with a divine revelation of what is to follow (12:1–3; 37:5–10). Finally the story of the struggle between Esau and Jacob starts, first in the womb with them

fighting each other, then as they are born Jacob clutching Esau's heel, and somewhat later in life as young men with Esau selling his birthright to his opportunistic brother. Genesis 26:1–32 shows the great peace and prosperity that Isaac enjoyed, so much so that the people of the land wanted to make a covenant with him (26:12–13, 28–29). This serves as a backdrop to chapter 27, which shows Isaac's family torn apart by strife as both brothers struggle again to inherit the prosperity of their father. The proper procedure for a death-bed blessing is shown in Genesis 48—50 where Jacob summons all his sons for an appropriate final word. But Isaac breaches convention by inviting only Esau to be blessed. Incensed, Rebekah incites her favourite Jacob to sneak in and pretend to be Esau and thereby acquire the first-born's blessing. The writer of Genesis makes it clear that this deceit was condemned, not just by Isaac and Esau, but by God himself through the way that Jacob paid for his sin in the years ahead and by his penitence in returning the blessing to Esau in 33:11.

Nevertheless, despite suffering for his effrontery, Jacob does not forfeit divine protection. Fleeing his brother's wrath he falls asleep at Bethel, a place that was later to become a famous centre for worship. There in a dream he sees a ladder with God standing at the top, who assures him that he would inherit the promises first made to Abraham of land, descendants and blessing to the nations. But in a special adaptation to his own circumstances Jacob is assured, 'I am with

Digging deeper:
ANCIENT MARRIAGE CUSTOMS

Several stories in Genesis give us a good insight into the practices and conventions that surrounded marriage in Bible times. Which stories come to mind?

Our information from them can be supplemented by remarks from other biblical books, such as Exodus 22, Deuteronomy 22, and Judges 14, as well as other ancient collections of law (e.g. the Code of Hammurabi, 1750 BC) and numerous oriental wedding contracts.

These show that normally it was the parents of the bride and groom who arranged the marriage for the children: the latter might have been consulted, but what was essential was parental agreement. This was partly because marriage was entered into earlier: the couple would be in their teens usually. But more important was the financial consideration for the family. When the marriage was agreed, the groom's family had to pay a marriage present or bride price to the bride's family. This could well be equivalent to several years' wages. Then, on the occasion of the wedding, which usually lasted seven days, the father of the bride gave his daughter a dowry. This consisted of clothes, furniture and money. This dowry had to be preserved intact, in case the wife was divorced or widowed, so that she would have something to survive on. Because the giving of the dowry was so usual in Bible times it is not mentioned unless it contained something unusual, such as the city of Gezer that the Pharaoh of Egypt gave to his daughter when she married Solomon (1 Kings 9:16).

Now reread the stories of the marriages of Rebekah (ch. 24) and Rachel and Leah (ch. 29). How do they differ from the normal pattern just described? What do these differences suggest about the relationships between the various couples and their families?

What do the names given to Jacob's sons (29:32—30:24) tell us about the relationship between Jacob and his wives?

you and will keep you wherever you go, and will bring you back to this land' (28:15). The succeeding chapters show the fulfilment of this promise.

In chapter 29 he lands on his feet arriving in a foreign land, as he finds employment with his uncle and falls in love with his cousin Rachel. His delight is somewhat diminished when his uncle compels him to marry Rachel's ugly elder sister as well. Yet it is she, the unloved wife, who becomes the mother of six of the tribes. Her fertility is the source of great bitterness to Rachel, who, after various misconstrued attempts at motherhood, eventually has her prayers answered and gives birth to Joseph, whose sons Ephraim and Manasseh constituted two of the largest tribes.

As soon as Rachel has her first baby, Jacob decides it is time to return home. But that is not so easy for Laban does not want to

THE RELIGION OF THE PATRIARCHS

It is easy to read into Genesis ideas about the religious practices of the patriarchs from other parts of the Old Testament or from other cultures. But close reading of the stories suggests that in some ways their beliefs and practices differed from later times. Like later Israelites the patriarchs prayed, offered sacrifices, circumcised their children, avoided marrying Canaanites and so on.

But in other respects their understanding of God was subtly different. For many years it was held that the God of the patriarchs was the god of the clan, whose own name did not matter, and that the names of God used in Genesis, Yahweh (the LORD) and El Shaddai (God Almighty) were later additions to the text to show that the God known to Moses and later Israelites was the same as the patriarchal God.

But in recent times it has been noticed that in Genesis God is often referred to as El in patriarchal names (e.g. Ishmael, 16:11; Israel, 32:28) or place names (e.g. Bethel, 28:19; Peniel, 32:30). Sometimes El (33:20) or a compound form of the name 'El Elyon' (God Most High, 14:20; El Roi, 'God who sees me', 16:13; or El Shaddai, God Almighty, 17:1) are used to describe the God of the patriarchs.

It is now known that in the era of the patriarchs the Canaanites worshipped El as the leading god in their pantheon. He was known as the creator

God and king over all other gods. He was famed for his wisdom and mercy. Nothing could occur on earth without his permission. He had power over life and death, including the power to grant children. All this fits in with the picture of God in Genesis. It therefore seems likely that the patriarchs acknowledged El as their God.

Often though in Genesis the personal name of God is not El, but the LORD, which is Yahweh in Hebrew. However, Exodus 6:3 says: 'I appeared to Abraham, Isaac, and to Jacob, as God Almighty [i.e. El Shaddai], but by my name the LORD [i.e. Yahweh] I did not make myself known to them.' Various explanations of this remark have been offered. It could be saying that God's character (name = character) as Yahweh was unknown to the patriarchs. Or Exodus 6:3 could come from a different source from passages which call God Yahweh. But the easiest solution is to see the use of Yahweh in Genesis as making a theological point: the God who revealed himself to Moses with the name Yahweh was the same God whom the patriarchs knew by the name El Shaddai, God Almighty. The editor of Genesis, working after the new name had come into use, introduced it in the earlier stories to show the religious connections between the early period and the later eras.

For further discussion see the books by Alt (1968), Cross (1973), de Moor (1990), Moberly (1992), and Millard and Wiseman (1980).

lose his useful son-in-law or his daughters, let alone give Jacob the golden handshake a valued servant might expect when he left (Deut. 15:13–14). So Jacob negotiates a settlement, which Laban expects will cost him very little. He agrees to let Jacob have any lambs or goats of mixed colour, knowing that usually goats are all black and lambs pure white. However, Jacob finds a way of breeding his flocks that produces a high number of mottled sturdy sheep and goats for himself.

But this increases the tension between Laban's family and Jacob, so the latter decides to abscond in the middle of the busy sheep-shearing season. After a hot pursuit Laban eventually catches up with Jacob and there is a bitter and angry confrontation. In the end Laban accepts that he cannot change Jacob's mind and they make a covenant to respect each other's rights. Laban returns to the north and Jacob presses on to the south.

But is it out of the frying pan into the fire? Jacob is now approaching the territory of his brother Esau, who when last heard of was plotting to murder Jacob. Though angels meet him at Mahanaim, the tension palpably rises as they enter Esau's land. Jacob sets aside large parts of his flocks and herds to be given as gifts to Esau and sends them on ahead. He crosses his wives and children over the river Jabbok, which seems to represent the border with Esau's territory, and he is left alone on the northern bank of the river.
There Jacob finds himself fighting a 'man' all night. At dawn the 'man' wants to leave, but Jacob refuses to let him go

unless he gives him a blessing. So he does, changing his name from Jacob to Israel ('El [God] Strives'), which the narrator explains with a pun 'for you have striven with God and with men, and have prevailed' (32:28). The 'man' then blesses Jacob and leaves.

This brief episode is dark and mysterious, yet clearly of great significance for it explains the origin of the name Israel. It would be easy to see the 'man' as a personification of Jacob's fears, or as representing Esau, but the text views him as El, the high god of Canaan. For, as Jacob puts it 'I have seen God face to face, and yet my life has been delivered' (32:30). Why should the high God of Canaan be wrestling with Jacob, father of Israel? The text does not give answers to all the questions it provokes. It leaves us with a picture of Jacob a changed man. Not only has his name been changed from Jacob 'trickster' to Israel, 'God strives', but he has a limp to remind him of the encounter, and more important his character has changed. No longer does he dither at the prospect of meeting his brother, but he boldly puts himself at the head of the column going to meet Esau.

Esau too has been transformed. He runs forward to greet Jacob, hugging him and kissing him, the hatred of the past all forgotten. Jacob himself acknowledges his guilt as he urges Esau to accept all the animals he is presenting to him, because they are 'my blessing that is brought to you'. In other words he is giving back the blessing he had illicitly obtained in chapter

27. Such is the spirit of reconciliation that Esau presses Jacob to join him in his homeland of Seir in southern Transjordan, but Jacob sees it as his duty to return to Canaan to the land promised to him and his descendants.

Chapter 34, describing the rape of Dinah and the ensuing massacre of the Shechemites, is the most horrific chapter in Genesis. None of the participants emerges with credit. Jacob, whose own lack of concern for his daughter triggered her brothers' revenge, expresses his condemnation in 49:5–7. Yet once again God's promised protection is proved, as Jacob's family move south (35:5). With his arrival in Bethel Jacob has reached the point where his wanderings began, the spot where God had promised him, 'I will bring you back to this land' (28:15).

36:1—37:1: GENEALOGY OF ESAU

As is customary in Genesis a relatively short genealogy of those outside the line of promise is sandwiched between long narratives about the ancestors of the chosen people. Nevertheless, this genealogy of Esau is much longer than Ishmael's in 25:12–18. It is also unique in having a double heading, 'These are the generations of Esau' (36:1, 9). This has led some scholars to conclude that 36:9–43 is a later insertion into the text, possibly from the time of David when Edom was incorporated into his empire. It also acts as a reminder of the close connections between the kingdoms of Israel and Edom.

37:2—50:26: THE STORY OF JOSEPH AND HIS BROTHERS

The story of Joseph, as it is usually known, constitutes the second half of the life of Jacob, which began in 25:21. It closes with his burial in 50:14 and his son Joseph's death in 50:26. The heading, 'These are the generations of Jacob', better describes its contents than the usual scholarly title, the Joseph story, for though Joseph is the central character in these stories, he is by no means the only significant figure: Jacob, Judah, and the Pharaoh are also very prominent actors in the story.

It consists of the following episodes:

ARRANGEMENT OF THE STORY OF JOSEPH

37:2–36	Joseph is sold into Egypt	
38:1–30	Tamar and Joseph	
39:1–20	Joseph and Potiphar	A
39:21–40:23	Joseph in Prison	B
41:1–57	Joseph in the Palace	C
42:1–38	First visit of Joseph's family to Egypt	A'
43:1—45:28	Second visit of Joseph's family to Egypt	B'
46:1—47:31	Third visit of Joseph's family to Egypt	C'
48:1—50:26	The last days of Jacob and Joseph	

These chapters develop the theme of the Pentateuch showing the gradual fulfilment of the promises. Throughout, God protects his chosen people in remarkable ways and, through Joseph, Egypt and many of the surrounding nations are saved from starving in the worldwide famine. In this action the fulfilment of 'in your offspring shall all the nations of the earth be blessed' (22:18) is partially realized. But the land promise seems even more distant than ever by the end of the book, because all the descendants of Jacob are now living in Egypt. Only Joseph's dying words remind us that Egypt is neither his nor their final resting place (50:24–25).

Genesis 37:2–36 reminds us of the opening of the Jacob story (25:19–34). Once again we have brothers in the family at loggerheads from their earliest days. Once again we have divine revelation setting out the main course of the story: there through an oracle to Rebekah, here through two dreams of Joseph, which predict the rest of the family will bow down to him. Pairs of dreams are a feature of the Joseph story. The butler and baker imprisoned with Joseph have two dreams (40:5–19). Later the Pharaoh has two dreams predicting the coming famine (41:1–24). Their duplication is significant: 'the doubling of Pharaoh's dream means that the thing is fixed by God, and God will shortly bring it about' (41:32). What applies to Pharaoh's dreams doubtless applies to Joseph's as well.

The animosity between Joseph and his brothers, though fuelled by Jacob's favouritism, has deep roots in family history. Jacob never had much time for Leah or her children: he could not even be bothered to do anything when her daughter Dinah was raped. He cared only for Rachel and her boys Joseph and Benjamin. Now this hatred is perpetuated by the next generation. At the first opportunity the sons of Leah plot to kill Joseph, just as Esau had planned to kill Jacob. But in the end they decide they can make more out of him by selling him as a slave into Egypt and hurt their father just as much by pretending Joseph is dead. Jacob is quite taken in by their ruse, which involved using their brother's coat and killing a goat just as Jacob had deceived his father many years before (cf. 27:9–29) by killing a goat and wearing his brother's clothes. A leading light in this arrangement is Judah, Leah's fourth son.

Judah is the principal actor in the next episode (ch. 38), where once again he behaves without scruple and he in turn is tricked by unusual clothing and an agreement about a goat. Judah marries a Canaanite, a dubious move in itself (24:3; 28:1) and has three sons by her. The first died after marrying Tamar. As a widow she had a right under biblical law to marry her brother-in-law (Deut. 25:5–10), which she did. But he died. As there was a third brother, Tamar expected to marry him when he was old enough, but Judah did not allow this to happen, thus flouting accepted custom. But Tamar tricked Judah into making her pregnant. He declared she should be burnt in the fire as a flagrant prostitute (cf. Lev. 21:9). At the last minute she revealed who had made her pregnant, and Judah recanted declaring, 'She is more righteous than I' (38:26). This marks the beginning of Judah's repentance, which climaxes in his great plea for mercy in chapter 44.

With chapter 39 the focus switches back to Joseph and his three periods of employment in Egypt, first as head servant in Potiphar's household, second as deputy to the prison governor, and finally as deputy to the Pharaoh or vizier of Egypt. The three episodes have much in common, so in the table above they are labelled ABC to match the next three parallel episodes of his brothers' visits to Egypt, A'B'C'. The key remark that sums up the first three episodes is 'The LORD was with Joseph' (39:2, 3, 21, 23). Given Joseph's plight, sold as a slave into Egypt by jealous brothers, it is a surprising comment in the first place. It is astonishing when it recurs in 39:21, 23, when Joseph has just been thrown into prison falsely accused of raping his master's wife. But appearances are misleading in interpreting human action insists Genesis. Twice Joseph has to reassure his brothers that their evil deeds were turned to good by the power of God: 'you meant evil against me, but God meant it for good, to bring it about that many people should be kept alive' (50:20 cf. 45:5–8). Already, by the comment 'The LORD was with Joseph' the principle of God's overriding providence for good in the sufferings of Joseph is being asserted.

EGYPT IN THE JOSEPH STORY

The Joseph story is unique in the Old Testament in that it sets most of the action in Egypt as opposed to Canaan or Mesopotamia. The writer is astonishingly well informed about Egyptian customs, so that Egyptologists have concluded that he must have lived there. The names of people, Potiphar, Asenath, Zaphenath-Paneah, are typical Egyptian names. He knows about landholding practices (47:20–22) and investiture customs (41:41–44), about Semites rising to high office, about the importance of dreams in Egyptian thinking, about mummification, and the ideal span of life in Egypt of 110 years (50:26).

Because Egypt was a very conservative country, where ideas and practices changed very slowly, these observations do not readily yield chronological information about when Joseph lived or the story was written down. His name Joseph is a Semitic name typical of the early second millennium. In this period there were many Asiatic slaves in Egypt. For about a century (1650–1540 BC) Egypt was ruled by Semitic kings called the Hyksos, so it would be easy to suppose that Joseph rose to power during that era.

However, the story of Joseph was written up later, though scholars cannot agree how much later. Some features fit the Ramesside period (thirteenth century BC) best: for example some of the names, words like 'reed grass', and details of the investiture ceremony. This would put the original telling of the story roughly in the time of Moses. There are also features in it that suggest its present form was produced in Israel. For example, whereas in Egypt the grain is shrivelled by the south wind, in Israel the east wind (41:6) is to blame, and the title 'lord of all his house' (45:8) means prime minister in Hebrew but not in Egyptian. A possible period for writing is the time of Solomon, when Egypt–Israel relations were very close (1 Kings 3:1).

For further discussion see Hoffmeier 1996, pp. 77–106; de Vaux 1978, pp. 291–320; Wenham 1994, pp. xxv–xxviii.

Although there is no comment on God's presence with Joseph in the third episode (ch. 41), its truth is plain as he is released from prison, interprets Pharaoh's enigmatic dreams and is promoted to be vizier of Egypt.

The three accounts of Joseph's life in Egypt which climax in his appointment as vizier (chs 39—41) are followed by his brothers' three journeys to Egypt, which culminate in his reunion with his father Jacob (42:1–38; 43:1—45:28; 46:1—47:28). In the first two journeys all the old family tensions surface as the brothers go down to Egypt to buy corn, leaving the youngest, Benjamin, now the only surviving son of Rachel, at home with his elderly father Jacob. Joseph's demand that Benjamin be brought to Egypt if they want the release of Simeon from custody prompts much bitter debate back in Canaan before Jacob eventually relents and lets Benjamin go.

The arrest of Benjamin for stealing Joseph's cup precipitates a crisis: will the brothers sacrifice the second son of Rachel to save their own skin, or will they stand by him and by implication their father, though he did not really care about them, only about Joseph and now Benjamin. Judah's powerful and moving speech shows how they have changed. He identifies himself so closely with his father that he cannot bear to contemplate the effect Benjamin's non-return would have. At this point Joseph discloses who he really is and another great reconciliation ensues, akin to that between Jacob and Esau in chapter 33.

Digging deeper:
JUDAH'S SPEECH

Judah's appeal to Joseph (44:18–34) is generally recognized as the finest speech in the OT. Examine how Judah achieves his goal of persuading Joseph to release Benjamin. How does his account of events differ from what we have learned from earlier chapters in Genesis? What does he add? What does he leave out? What effect do these changes have? How does he describe his father's situation, and his relationship with Benjamin? What would Joseph have concluded about Judah's attitude from this speech?

The third journey involves transporting the elderly Jacob and the rest of the family to Egypt. Another emotional reunion between Jacob and Joseph follows, and the family is settled in the north-eastern part of the Nile Delta in the land of Goshen.

Chapters 48—50 record the last words of Jacob and Joseph. Hearing of Jacob's failing health, Joseph brings his two sons Manasseh and Ephraim to be blessed by their grandfather. But Jacob does more than bless them, he adopts them, thereby giving them a status equal to his sons. This explains why Ephraim and Manasseh are full tribes in Israel, indeed the two largest tribes in the north. Jacob gives precedence to Ephraim, although he was the younger boy. Joseph protests at this, but Jacob insists. It is a regular feature of Genesis that the younger child displaces the older: other examples include Cain and Abel in chapter 4, Perez and Zerah in chapter 38, and of course Jacob himself who supplanted Esau.

Chapter 49, the blessing of Jacob, could be described as the high point of Genesis. In it the dying Jacob reviews the past careers of his sons and their future prospects. It serves as a definitive statement of judgement on their past performance. His firstborn Reuben is condemned for his incestuous behaviour (35:22), and the next two sons Simeon and Levi for their brutal massacre at Shechem (ch. 34). The disgrace of the first three sons explains the rise of the fourth, Judah, whose future is painted in glowing colours (49:8–12). The only other son to excel in Jacob's blessings is Joseph (49:22–26). These blessings not only serve to explain the relative standing of the different tribes in the later history of Israel, they stand as a triumphant affirmation of the promise of the land. Jacob may be dying outside the promised land, in Egypt, but he pictures his sons dwelling in wealth and security within that land. In particular the prediction that 'the sceptre will not depart from Judah' reaffirms the promise made to Abraham that he would father kings (17:6, 16). Indeed, in a clear allusion to the Davidic dynasty and empire, Jacob goes on to predict a line of kings, to whom the nations will bring their tribute (49:10).

The final chapter tells of Jacob's burial in the land of Canaan in the patriarchal grave of Machpelah. It also records

Joseph's renewed pledge to forgive his brothers, who feared he might take advantage of his father's death to take revenge. Joseph's impassioned rejection of the idea shows how important the message of forgiveness and reconciliation is to the book of Genesis.

THE NEW TESTAMENT USE OF GENESIS 12—50

The New Testament sees the history of the Church as a continuation of the history of Israel: Israel is the olive tree into which Gentile believers have been grafted (Rom. 11:17–24). So the figures of Genesis are the earliest members of the Church, and their deeds should inspire later believers to imitate them. Most quoted is Genesis 15:6, 'He [Abraham] believed the Lord, and he counted it to him as righteousness,' which Paul uses to demonstrate the centrality of faith, and James to show that faith must issue in good deeds (Rom. 4:9, 22; Gal. 3:6; James 2:23).

But the most prolonged appeals to the examples of the patriarchs are to be found in Stephen's speech to the council, which ranges from the call of Abraham in Mesopotamia to Jacob's burial in Canaan (Acts 7:2–16), and in Hebrews 11. The latter's review of Genesis starts with Abel and ends with Joseph's last words insisting that in due time he should be buried in Canaan (Heb. 11:4–22). These were all people who, according to the author of Hebrews, lived by faith in the promises, who persisted in face of difficulty and persecution, just as he hopes his readers would too.

FURTHER READING

COMMENTARIES

R. W. L. Moberly *Genesis 12—50*. Sheffield: Sheffield Academic Press, 1992. Helpful introduction.

G. J. Wenham *Genesis 1—15, Genesis 16—50*. Dallas: Word Books, 1987, 1994.

C. Westermann *Genesis 12—36: A Commentary*. tr. by J. J. Scullion. London: SPCK, 1985. The authoritative German commentary. Also *Genesis 37—50*. 1986.

HISTORY AND THE PATRIARCHS

J. Bright *The History of Israel*. London: SCM Press, 1972. Though a little dated, still the most readable history of Israel.

J. K. Hoffmeier *Israel in Egypt*. Oxford: Oxford University Press, 1996. Good up-to-date discussion of evidence.

K. A. Kitchen *The Bible in Its World*. Exeter: Paternoster Press, 1977. A shrewd and learned Egyptologist reads the Bible.

A. R. Millard and D. J. Wiseman *Essays on the Patriarchal Narrative*. Leicester: IVP, 1980. Essays in reply to the sceptical views of van Seters and Thompson.

J. van Seters *Abraham in History and Tradition*. New Haven: Yale University Press, 1975. Influential critique of historicity of Genesis.

T. L. Thompson *The Historicity of the Patriarchal Narratives*. Berlin: de Gruyter, 1974. Despite the title a serious challenge to their historicity.

R. de Vaux *The Early History of Israel*. tr. by D. Smith. London: DLT, 1978. A masterly synthesis by the leading French Old Testament scholar of the twentieth century.

R. R. Wilson *Genealogy and History in the Biblical World*. New Haven: Yale University Press, 1977.

LITERARY AND THEOLOGICAL STUDIES

R. Alter *The Art of Biblical Narrative*. New York: Basic Books, 1981. Lively literary critic, who regards Bible narrative as historical fiction.

D. J. A. Clines *The Theme of the Pentateuch*. Sheffield: JSOT Press, 1978. A seminal study.

R. W. L. Moberly *The Old Testament of the Old Testament*. Minneapolis: Fortress Press, 1992. Important discussion of relationship of Genesis to other books of the Pentateuch.

M. Sternberg *The Poetics of Biblical Narrative*. Bloomington: Indiana University Press, 1985. Very important discussion of biblical writers' techniques.

PATRIARCHAL RELIGION

A. Alt 'The God of the Fathers', tr. by R. A. Wilson, in *Essays on Old Testament History and Religion*. Garden City: Anchor Books, 1968, pp. 1–100. Originally published in 1929 this essay was very influential.

F. M. Cross *Canaanite Myth and Hebrew Epic*. Cambridge, MA: Harvard University Press, 1973. Valuable discussion of patriarchal religion.

T. N. D. Mettinger *In Search of God: The Meaning and Message of the Divine Names*. tr. by F. H. Cryer. Philadelphia: Fortress Press, 1992.

J. C. de Moor *The Rise of Yahwism: The Roots of Israelite Monotheism*. Leuven: Leuven University Press, 1990. Sets Israelite religion against its Canaanite background.

Chapter 4

EXODUS

The book of Exodus takes its usual name from the central event it describes, the exodus (Greek for 'way out, exit') of the Israelites from Egypt under the leadership of Moses. Its alternative name, the second book of Moses, is even more appropriate, for Moses is the dominating human figure in the book from beginning to end. Exodus 2 tells of his birth, upbringing in the Egyptian court, and his first attempt to save his fellow countrymen from oppression. In chapter 3 he meets God at the burning bush, and from then on he is always prominent in the story, negotiating with the Pharaoh, leading the people across the Red Sea, receiving the Ten Commandments and numerous other laws, arranging the building of the tabernacle and having it erected. Out of the 770 references to Moses in the whole Old Testament about a third are found in the book of Exodus. Perhaps the most striking comment on Moses' role occurs in 14:31 just after the Israelites have escaped from the Egyptian army at the Red Sea, 'so the people feared the LORD, and they believed in the LORD and in his servant Moses.' The centrality of Moses to Exodus and the subsequent three books of the Pentateuch fully justifies it being viewed as *Torah* in the form of a biography of Moses (see Chapter 1, What is the Pentateuch?).

The books of Exodus to Numbers stand apart from the rest of the Pentateuch in the way that they focus on the life of Moses. Genesis illuminates the setting for Moses' career, while Deuteronomy offers Moses' own reflections on his achievements and his hopes and fears for the nation's future. But the books of Exodus to Numbers relate all the major events in his life, apart from the last few days before his death, with special attention being given to his mediation of the law. The two longest books, Exodus and Numbers, which mix law and narrative, flank the central book Leviticus, which is almost entirely law. But the introductions to each section of Leviticus, 'And the LORD said to Moses', and the episodes in chapters 8—10 and 24 remind the reader that Leviticus too is really a narrative about the giving of the law to *Moses*.

STRUCTURE

Unlike the book of Genesis Exodus has no titles for each new section: the narrative just runs on from episode to episode. Content, not form, must guide the definition of its parts.

Part 1   Slavery in Egypt and liberation
  1:1–22: Slavery and genocide
  2:1–22: Moses' birth and upbringing
  2:23—4:31: Moses' mission
  5:1—7:13: Negotiating with Pharaoh
  7:14—11:10: The plagues
  12:1—15:21: Exodus from Egypt
  15:22—18:27: Journey to Sinai

Part 2   The law-giving
  19:1—20:21: Revelation at Mount Sinai
  20:22—23:33: Laws and rules
  24:1–18: Making of the Covenant

Part 3   The tabernacle
  25:1—31:18: Directions for constructing the tabernacle
  32:1—34:35: Making the golden calf
  35:1—40:38: Construction of the tabernacle

SLAVERY IN EGYPT AND LIBERATION

1:1–22: Slavery and genocide

This chapter explains the background to Moses' birth. It begins with a flashback to the end of Genesis mentioning Jacob's family arriving in Egypt (1:1–6; cf. Gen. 46:8–27; 50:22–26) and the fulfilment of the promise of descendants (1:7 cf. Gen. 17:2, 6). But whereas in Joseph's day the Israelites were warmly welcomed and granted great privileges, a change of dynasty means that now they are feared and persecuted. This change is usually identified with the end of the Hyksos

dynasty, Semitic kings who ruled Egypt from about 1648 to 1540 BC. Whereas the Hyksos were foreigners like the Hebrews, the next ruling dynasties were Egyptian and did not like the immigrants, and put them to work building the store cities of Pithom (Tell el-Retabeh) and Rameses (Qantir) in the Goshen area (see map 2, p. 65).

As slavery does not stop the Israelite population growing, the Egyptians resort to infanticide. The refusal of the midwives to implement this policy leads the Pharaoh to insist that every Hebrew boy baby must be thrown in the river. This explains why Moses' mother has to hide him to keep him safe, and in the longer term why the death of the first-born of Egypt in the last plague had a certain justice about it: the Egyptians are punished by being made to suffer in the same way that they had made the Israelites suffer.

2:1–22: Moses' birth and upbringing

Swiftly the story moves from Moses' birth, his upbringing in the Egyptian court, to his escape from Egypt, from his marriage to a Midianite to the birth of his first son. The terminology of this chapter betrays its Egyptian background: many of the terms used seem to be borrowed from Egyptian, e.g. basket, bulrushes, pitch, reeds, river and even Moses' name. 'Mose' (child) is a familiar element in many royal names, e.g. Amenmose, Thutmose, so it is not surprising an Egyptian princess gives him this name. But as often in the Old Testament his name's significance, not its etymology, is explained. In Hebrew Mosheh (Moses) means 'drawer' and hints at his future role as the one who will 'draw' his people out of Egypt. The same point is made in the meeting-by-the-well scene (2:15–22). This has many similarities to the betrothal scenes of Isaac and Jacob, whose brides were also met by a well (Gen. 24; 29). The distinctive feature in the description of Moses' first encounter with his future bride is that he saved her and her sisters from the shepherds, who would otherwise have prevented them watering their flock. In so doing he foreshadows his saving role in rescuing his people from Egypt (Exod. 2:17, 19; cf. 3:8; 18:10). His future role is anticipated even more clearly in the second episode (2:11–15), where, having delivered one of his fellow-countrymen from Egyptian oppression, he then faces criticism for being a prince and a judge: such grumbles against his authority are common in the stories that follow (e.g. 5:21; 17:3; Num. 14:1–4; 16:1–11). Thus these few scenes from Moses' early life already anticipate his future career as saviour of a reluctant and ungrateful people of Israel.

2:23—4:31: Moses' mission defined

In 2:1–22 various aspects of Moses' subsequent role and career are foreshadowed, but from 2:23 on his mission is much more clearly defined. After an introductory comment about the suffering and prayers of the Israelites and God's recall of his covenant, the story moves immediately to Horeb, the mountain of God. There in the area where the law will be given at Sinai, God appears in fire at the burning bush. Moses is introduced to the idea of God's holiness, a concept of supreme importance in the

laws, and he is forced to acknowledge it by removing his sandals and hiding his face.

Then the LORD declares his plan to rescue his people from slavery and bring them to the land promised to their forefathers, which flows with milk and honey. Moses' task is to persuade Pharaoh to let the Israelites go and bring them to worship God 'on this mountain' (3:12). Moses then raises a series of objections to his mission, which God overrules one by one and at the same time clarifies his role.

First, the Israelites may not believe God has really revealed himself to Moses and test his credentials by asking what is God's name. The pentateuchal narrator has often used in Genesis the standard name of God, The LORD or Yahweh, but from this passage we learn that it was not known to the actors in the story before God appeared in the burning bush. There Moses learns that the God who had revealed himself to Abraham, Isaac and Jacob is called Yahweh, which means 'he will be' or 'he will cause to be', so he names himself 'I will be'. The God of the fathers is therefore the God of Moses, but more than that he is the self-subsistent one or the creator. Whatever the exact meaning of the name, it indicates God's total power and guarantees his ability to compel the Egyptians to let Israel go (3:13–22).

The second problem that Moses anticipates is that the Egyptians will not believe him. To answer their doubts he is given three signs to persuade them that God has spoken to him. His staff will turn into a serpent when thrown on the ground. The skin of his hand will peel off like snow when he puts it inside his cloak. Finally, when he pours water on the ground, it will turn to blood (4:1–9).

Digging deeper:
THE NAME OF GOD

The God of the Old Testament is generally called in English translations 'the LORD'. In this usage translators are following the practice of the oldest translation into Greek, the Septuagint, which originated in the third century BC. But the original Hebrew spelling of the word and this passage make it likely that originally the Hebrew name for God was Yahweh, which means 'he is' or 'he causes to be'. But for fear of breaking the third commandment by mistake (You shall not take the name of the LORD your God in vain, Exodus 20:7), Jews decided to stop using the word Yahweh and say Adonai (Lord) instead. That is why the Greek translation used the paraphrase 'the LORD'.

Yahweh, the LORD, is God's personal name, which distinguished him from all the other so-called gods of the ancient world, Baal, Ishtar, Hadad, Zeus, etc. But because the Israelites did not believe in these other gods, they could refer to Yahweh simply as God.

For a discussion of the use of Yahweh in Genesis, see panel on The religion of the patriarchs, p. 49.

Apparently convinced by these signs, Moses raises yet a third objection: he is no good at speaking. To deal with this, God appoints Aaron, Moses' brother, to speak on his behalf. Jethro, his father-in-law, encourages him to return to Egypt. The LORD again urges Moses to return to Egypt, but warns him that Pharaoh will be very reluctant to let the Israelites leave (4:10–23).

It therefore comes as a great shock to read in 4:24 'At a lodging place on the way the LORD met him and sought to put him to death.' Why should God try to kill Moses, when he is only obeying the divine instruction to go back to the Pharaoh? Similar questions arise in Genesis 32:24–30, when a 'man' wrestles with Jacob, although he was returning at God's behest to Canaan, and in Numbers 22:22–35, when the angel of the LORD, sword in hand, opposes Balaam on his mission to bless Israel. On all these occasions complete readiness to obey the will of God was essential, but Moses' failure to circumcise his son could have been a sign of his half-heartedness, for circumcision was a prerequisite for participation in the Passover, which preceded the exodus (12:48). Moses' mission was to lead his people out of Egypt in the exodus in fulfilment of the covenant promises made to the patriarchs, yet his own son was uncircumcised, even though Abraham had been warned that failure to circumcise would lead to the person dying suddenly (Gen. 17:14). Only the decisive action of Zipporah saves the family, and by implication the whole mission.

5:1—7:13: Negotiating with the Pharaoh
After meeting with Aaron and the people, Moses goes in to the Pharaoh and asks that the Israelites may go and hold a feast in the wilderness for three days. This was

of course much less than they wanted, but even this modest request is harshly rebuffed: indeed they are required to find their own straw to make bricks. This leads to bitter recrimination against Moses and Aaron, who are told that they have only made things worse.

This prompts the LORD to reaffirm his promises of deliverance in the most categoric terms. He is the LORD, whom the patriarchs knew as God Almighty. He will deliver them from slavery and bring them to the promised land. So Aaron and Moses return to Pharaoh and demonstrate their divine call by turning their staff into a serpent. But Pharaoh's advisers do the same with their staffs, and although Aaron's serpent eats up all the other serpents, Pharaoh refuses to give in and the exodus is no nearer to happening.

7:14—11:10: The plagues

The confrontation between Moses and the Pharaoh now rises to a dramatic climax. Indeed the struggle is not just between national representatives but between the gods of Egypt and the God of Israel. The Pharaoh was held to be divine and to be the guarantor of Egypt's welfare and security. But these disasters prove he is not in control and that he cannot protect his people. It is Moses and Aaron who declare what will happen and it is the LORD, the God of Israel, who effects it. The Pharaoh's initial truculence is tempered by his experiences, and after the seventh and eighth plagues, he contemplates letting Israel go, but then changes his mind. It is only the devastating last plague that forces him to capitulate, but even then he recants and as a consequence he and his army are lost in the Red Sea.

THE PLAGUES

Type of Plague	Warning	Time of Warning	Instruction	Agent	Reference
1 Blood	Yes	In the morning	Stand	Aaron	7:14–24
2 Frogs	Yes	not stated	Go in to Pharaoh	Aaron	8:1–16
3 Gnats	No	not stated	none	Aaron	8:16–19
4 Flies	Yes	In the morning	Present yourself	God	8:20–32
5 Livestock disease	Yes	not stated	Go in to Pharaoh	God	9:1–7
6 Boils	No	not stated	none	Moses	9:8–12
7 Hail	Yes	In the morning	Present yourself	Moses	9:13–35
8 Locusts	Yes	not stated	Go in to Pharaoh	Moses	10:1–20
9 Darkness	No	not stated	none	Moses	10:21–29
10 Death of first-born	Yes	not stated	none	God	11:1–10 12:29–32

The plagues are arranged in three groups of three and are followed by the tenth, which completes the series.

From the table on p. 61 it appears that plagues 1, 4 and 7 have a similar pattern of presentation: they include a warning to Pharaoh in the morning, the command to Moses to stand or present himself before Pharaoh (almost the same verb in Hebrew). Likewise plagues 2, 5 and 8 have a similar structure: a warning, but no mention of the time, a command to go in to Pharaoh. Plagues 3, 6 and 9 hit Egypt without warning. Plagues 1–3 are triggered by Aaron stretching out his hand, 6–9 by Moses' action, and 4, 5 and 10 by God himself.

These repeating formulae give a background unity to the narrative, while the tension is rising among the actors. As the plagues become more severe, Pharaoh pleads ever more pressingly that Moses will pray for their removal, promising each time that he will let Israel go. His rapid change of heart once the plague is removed thus becomes ever more blameworthy. Sometimes this change of heart is ascribed to the Pharaoh himself, who hardens his own heart (8:15, 32; 9:34). Sometimes it seems to be merely an observation 'Pharaoh's heart was hardened' (7:13, 22; 8:19; 9:35). Sometimes his change of heart is ascribed to God (9:12; 10:20, 27; 11:10). It is noticeable that after the earlier plagues, Pharaoh is said to have hardened his own heart, but after the later plagues God is said to have hardened Pharaoh's heart, as if to punish his original obstinacy with more obstinacy.

What do you think?
HARDENING THE HEART

The heart in biblical thinking is not seen as the organ that pumps blood round the body. Nor is it just our emotional side as opposed to our intellect or will. In the Bible the heart is regarded as the centre of one's being. People think and make decisions with the heart. The kidneys and the gut tend to be associated with feelings in the Bible. The heart in biblical terminology roughly equates to the mind and will.

So when Pharaoh is said to harden his heart, it means he is refusing to change his mind despite the evidence. He is becoming more stubborn and obstinate. More difficult to grasp is why God is sometimes said to harden the human heart. This idea occurs in the prophets as well, e.g. Isaiah 6:10, often quoted in the gospels (e.g. Matt. 13:14–15; Mark 4:12). It may be just a vivid way of saying that everything that happens is ultimately under God's control. If he allows people to become obstinate as a result of their own actions, one might say he makes them obstinate.

Some passages to consider: Genesis 6:5; Jeremiah 13:23; 17:9–10; Ezekiel 36:26; Mark 7:21–23; Romans 9:17–21; James 1:13–15.

The Bible sees the plagues as sent by God to persuade Pharaoh to let the Israelites go. They are announced in advance, and happen when Aaron or Moses stretch out their hand: they are thus evidence that God is in control, not Pharaoh. But though the plagues demonstrate God's active involvement, they are not unparalleled. Egypt was afflicted on other occasions with hail, sandstorms and locusts for example. But what has been suggested by Greta Hort (1957, 1958) is that many of the plagues may be seen as a chain of cataclysmic events over about six months triggered by freak weather conditions.

Heavy rainfall in the Nile catchment area leads to annual flooding in September. The first plague involved the water turning to blood and the fish dying, and Hort suggests this refers to the flagellates being washed down river, turning the water blood-red and killing the fish. This provided the basis for the next five plagues. The frogs left the river (plague 2). The damp conditions led to mosquitoes (plague 3) and dog flies (plague 4) breeding prolifically. The dead frogs were a source of anthrax spread by the flies to cattle (plague 5) and humans (plague 6). The next three plagues, hail, locusts and darkness, probably caused by a desert sandstorm, though of unusual destructiveness on this occasion, were well known hazards of Egyptian life. If the Egyptian royal advisers recognized a natural pattern behind the plagues, it is perhaps easier to see why the Pharaoh was tempted to ignore them, hoping that next year things would not be so bad. But when the last unprecedented plague struck and the first-born died, he decided to relent, at least for a while.

12:1—15:21: Exodus from Egypt
The execution of the final plague announced in chapter 11 does not follow immediately. Instead Moses instructs the Israelites how to celebrate the Passover, so that they do not suffer in the final plague.

When the Egyptian first-born die, the Israelites are summarily expelled from Egypt (12:29–42). But then the narrative is again suspended for a while for further instructions about celebrating the Passover, dedicating the first-born, and keeping the feast of unleavened bread (12:43—13:16). The story resumes properly in 13:17 recounting the departure from Egypt, the crossing of the Red Sea, and closing with the celebration Song of the Sea in chapter 15.

This mixture of materials poses a number of problems for commentators and historians, but the very mixture illustrates perfectly the character of the book of Exodus: it is *Torah*, that is religious instruction. It is designed to instruct its readers about the past, but also to teach them how to behave in the present. The Passover celebrates an event in the past, Israel's escape from slavery in Egypt, but it is also an annual festival, which must be kept in the approved manner if God is to continue to bless Israel. Thus while the storyline proceeds roughly chronologically detailing what happened when, it is interrupted from time to time with lengthy digressions on how the Passover must be celebrated for all time (12:14–27; 13:5–14). Some of the instructions, e.g. smearing the blood on the doorposts and lintels of the houses, seem to be unique to the first occasion in Egypt, but most of them seem to apply to future celebrations in the land of Canaan (12:19, 48–49; 13:5–14).

As far as the Old Testament is concerned, the Passover is the most important festival in the religious calendar, for it marks the founding moment in national history when Israel emerged as a separate nation. The month in which it fell is therefore declared the first month of the year, and all circumcised Israelites and their families were bound to keep it: anyone who did not was liable to die (12:2, 15, 19). Many of the Passover customs commemorate the circumstances of the exodus from Egypt, particularly the eating of lamb and unleavened bread (12:3–4, 39).

After the digression about the future celebrations of the Passover in the promised land (13:1–16), the main narrative resumes with a mention that Moses took Joseph's bones with him (13:19; cf. Gen. 50:25) and some brief details of their route. The shortest way to Canaan is eastwards along the Mediterranean coast, the Way of the Philistines, but since that was protected by Egyptian outposts, the Israelites avoided that (13:17). Instead they headed south-east towards the Bitter Lakes along the line of the modern Suez Canal. Geographers surmise that in the second millennium BC these lakes were connected with the Gulf of Suez, the western arm of the Red Sea, which could explain why the Israelites were trapped between the Red Sea and the Egyptian army. Alternatively, though the words *yam suf* can sometimes mean the Red Sea, it could be that here they have their more basic meaning 'sea of reeds', which might have been an apt description of the Bitter Lakes area.

For the initial stages of the route we follow Hoffmeier's suggestions. For the latter stages of the journey to Sinai, I prefer the suggestion of Harel 1968 that Sinai should be located at Jebel Sin Bishar in northern Sinai to the traditional view that locates it at Jebel Musa in the south. For further discussion see Wenham 1981, pp. 220–28.

Digging deeper:
THE PASSOVER

Try to build up a picture about the celebration of the Passover in Old Testament times, by comparing the instructions given in Exodus 12—13 with those in Exodus 34:18; Leviticus 23:4–8; Numbers 9:1–14; 28:16–25; Deuteronomy 16:1–8 and the descriptions of Passover in Joshua 5:10–12; 2 Kings 23:21–23; 2 Chronicles 35:1–19.

What similarities and differences do you notice? How do you explain them?

The Passover is mentioned several times in the New Testament (Luke 2:41–43; 1 Cor. 5:6–8), indeed the Last Supper was a Passover meal (Matt. 26:17–30; Mark 14:12–26; Luke 22:7–23).

Jews still observe the Passover today. As a result of the destruction of the temple in AD 70 they no longer offer the Passover lamb in sacrifice, but in other respects there is still much similarity to ancient custom. (Find a video or Internet site illustrating the Passover.) The Samaritans, who live in Nablus in Palestine, still sacrifice lambs at Passover.

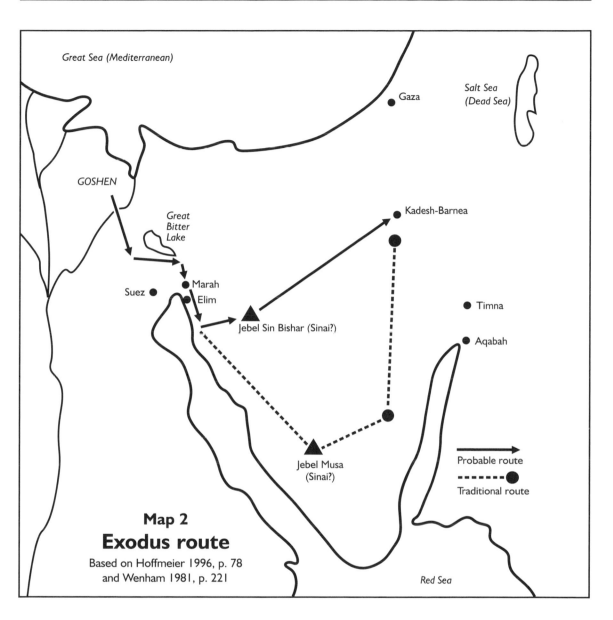

Great Sea (Mediterranean)

Salt Sea
(Dead Sea)

Gaza

GOSHEN

Great
Bitter
Lake

Kadesh-Barnea

Suez

Marah

Elim

Timna

Jebel Sin Bishar (Sinai?)

Aqabah

Jebel Musa
(Sinai?)

Probable route

Traditional route

Map 2
Exodus route
Based on Hoffmeier 1996, p. 78
and Wenham 1981, p. 221

Red Sea

But it is not so much where the Red Sea was but what happened there that really interests Exodus. The providential timing of the east wind, which allowed the Israelites to slip through the Red Sea, and its equally well-timed dropping away, which trapped the Egyptian chariotry in the rising waters was the final proof that the God of Israel was stronger than the superpower Egypt. It was the obstinacy of the Pharaoh in trying to prevent the Israelite escape that led to the elite of his army perishing in the sea. So Moses and the people join in singing the Song of the Sea (15:2–18) celebrating God's triumph over his enemies. It recalls the particular defeat of the Egyptians at the Red Sea:

> I will sing to the LORD, for he has
>   triumphed gloriously;
> the horse and his rider he has thrown
>   into the sea. (v. 1)

But the event has universal significance too: it does not just signal the LORD's supremacy over earthly powers, but over all supernatural powers as well. Moses asks rhetorically:

> Who is like you, O LORD, among the
>   gods? (v. 11)

His triumph at the Red Sea is a pledge that he will bring Israel into the promised land.

> You will bring them in and plant them
>   on your own mountain,
> the place, O LORD, which you have
>   made for your abode. (v. 17)

Finally the exodus experience proves that

> The LORD will reign for ever and ever.
> (v.18)

The style and vocabulary of this poem make it likely that it is one of the oldest in the Bible. So well does it express core Jewish beliefs that it is still recited by them every day in morning worship, as well of course on the seventh day of Passover to recall the occasion of its first recital.

15:22—18:27: Journey to Sinai

The glorious power of God witnessed at the Red Sea led to the people praising God in this great song and it evoked faith in him and in Moses. In the words of 14:31: 'Israel saw the great power that the LORD used against the Egyptians, so the people feared the LORD, and they believed in the LORD and his servant Moses.' But, as often in the Pentateuch, a great experience of God or act of faith is followed by doubt or disobedience (cf. Gen. 12; 20; Exod. 32; Lev. 10; Num. 13—14).

In this instance the crossing of the Red Sea is followed by three episodes of grumbling against Moses and by implication against the LORD, whom they blame for bringing them into this deadly wilderness, where they will probably die. After three days' journey they reached Marah, where the water was too bitter to drink (15:22–27). God answered Moses' prayer, and the water could be drunk. A month after leaving Egypt they arrived at the wilderness of Zin, where the people grumbled bitterly against Moses and Aaron because there was no bread or meat to eat. Meat soon arrived in the form of quails, low-flying birds of the pheasant family, which regularly migrate over Sinai (16:13). But this provision is not to be their regular fare; this takes the form of manna described in 16:14, as 'a fine, flake-like thing', and in 16:31, 'like coriander seed, white, [tasting] like wafers made with honey'. It has been suggested by Bodenheimer 1947 that manna was produced by the secretions of aphids living in the tamarisk trees of the region. Though this possibility cannot be ruled out, the text gives no indication that it was a natural phenomenon, unlike the quails, and the manna certainly seems to have been available in unnatural quantities.

Once again, just as in the account of the Passover, Exodus is not merely interested in recording the history of the event. It wants to draw lessons from the past for the present. Israel's ingratitude and disobedience are clearly being held up for censure, but more than that the episode illustrates the Sabbath principle and its importance. Before even they reach Mount Sinai, where the Ten Commandments were declared, the Israelites discovered why they should observe the Sabbath. God provided a double portion of manna on Fridays so that there was no need to collect it or cook it on the Sabbath (vv. 22–30).

The final episode in this trio of grumbling stories is clearly the most serious, often referred to in other parts of the OT (e.g. Deut. 6:16; Ps. 95:8). After the experience at Marah and the daily provision of manna, the vicious complaints to Moses about the lack of water at Rephidim seem a bit over the top: 'Why did you bring us up out of Egypt, to kill us and our children and our livestock with thirst?' (17:3). This was nothing less than a rejection of the whole divine programme to bring Israel into the land of Canaan. Nevertheless the rock was struck and water provided for all to drink.

Lack of water was not the only problem faced at Rephidim. A fierce and apparently unprovoked attack by the Amalekites (cf. Deut. 25:17–19) would have destroyed Israel before they reached Sinai. But as in

Egypt divine power mediated through Moses' staff saved Israel (17:8–14).

Finally in the run-up to the law-giving at Sinai, Jethro, Moses' father-in-law reappeared. Both the content of Exodus 18 and references to this episode in Numbers 10:11, 29–32 and Deuteronomy 1:9–17 imply that Jethro arrived and left after the law-giving, so why should this episode be inserted here? There is no obvious answer. Some suggest it is because the Kenites (= Midianites) are mentioned just before the Amalekites in 1 Samuel 15:6 in similar contrasting roles of friend and foe. Another suggestion is that the Midianites were descended from Keturah, Abraham's second wife (Gen. 25:2), and that both branches of Abraham's descendants had to be present at the law-giving. Maybe it is to show that even after the law had been given Moses would still be needed to ensure its fair administration.

THE LAW-GIVING

19:1—20:21: The Revelation at Sinai

The book of Exodus builds to its first climax at the Red Sea, but its second and even more dominant peak is the law-giving at Sinai. In fact the law-giving at Sinai dominates the narrative to Numbers 9, so that perhaps it would be better to speak of a mountain range, not a mere narrative peak. Nevertheless there is unmistakable drama about the first revelation at Sinai: its high prose style becomes almost poetic.

The Sinai revelation begins quite abruptly with the statement that the Israelites arrived at Mount Sinai (see map on p. 65) on the third new moon, that is six weeks, after leaving Egypt. Immediately Moses is summoned to the mountain, where the LORD sums up the essence of the covenant that he is about to make with Israel.

> You yourselves have seen what I did to the Egyptians, and how I bore you on eagles' wings and brought you to myself. Now therefore, if you will indeed obey my voice and keep my covenant, you shall be my treasured possession among all peoples, for all the earth is mine; and you shall be to me a kingdom of priests and a holy nation. (19:4–6)

Here several points are made. First, that the covenant is based on God's saving initiative. He has intervened like a great eagle and carried the people out of Egypt to make them his own. Second, they are expected to respond in obedience by keeping the covenant law, which is about to be revealed. Third, this obedience will be rewarded by ever greater intimacy with God: they will be his treasured possession, like the crown jewels of a king (Eccl. 2:8). Fourth, this intimate relationship will benefit all the peoples of the world, as Israel will function as a priest to all the nations. Priests both declare God's will to people and also pray for them and offer sacrifice on their behalf, and this is what Israel is expected to do for the surrounding peoples (cf. Gen. 12:3; Deut. 4:5–8).

After this introduction the people are summoned to prepare for their encounter with God. As is explained more fully in the book of Leviticus, God is supremely holy and people dare not meet him unless they are completely pure. So the Israelites are ordered to wash their clothes, abstain from sexual intercourse, and keep off the mountain. Mount Sinai is about to become a sacred place, where only those authorized by God may enter. Like the tabernacle (see figure 3, p. 75), whose construction is ordered in Exodus 25—30, Mount Sinai is divided into three zones. The summit corresponds to the innermost sanctum, the Holy of Holies, to which only Moses could go to meet the LORD. Then the rest of the mountain, corresponding to the holy place, could be accessed by a chosen few such as priests or elders (Exod. 24). The foot of the mountain corresponds to the tabernacle court, open to lay people, where the altar stood and sacrifice could be offered.

After allowing three days for the people to prepare themselves, God then appears in a terrifying storm on the top of Mount Sinai accompanied by fire and cloud, thunder and lightning and loud trumpet blasts. Some of the description makes Mount Sinai appear volcanic: 'the smoke of it went up like the smoke of a kiln, and the whole mountain trembled greatly' (19:18). But this imagery should not be taken so literally that we should suppose that Sinai was a real volcano: rather it is a way of expressing the inexpressible, the power and holiness of God which humans approach at their peril (19:21–24).

20:2–17: The Ten Commandments
The Ten Commandments are the core of the Sinai covenant and recognized as uniquely authoritative throughout the Old

and New Testaments. Other passages refer to them as the 'Ten Words' (Exod. 34:28; Deut. 4:13; 10:4). While all the laws are said to have been spoken by God to Moses, only the Ten Commandments are said to have been written by the finger of God (Exod. 31:18; 34:1, 28). This expresses the unique quality of their inspiration and their total authority. There are various views on how the commandments should be divided. Jews make verse 2 the first commandment, and verses 3–4 the second. Catholics make verses 3–6 the first commandment and split verse 17 into two commandments. An alternative Jewish tradition, followed by most English Bibles, makes verse 2 a prologue and verse 3 the first commandment. However, the different ways of dividing them make little difference to the understanding of the commandments.

Verse 2, 'I am the LORD your God, who brought you out of the land of Egypt, out of the house of slavery', like 19:4 reminds Israel of the basis of the covenant, namely Yahweh's saving grace demonstrated in the exodus from Egypt. Obedience to the commandments is viewed as a response of gratitude for salvation, not a means of earning it.

The commandments themselves fall into two sections. The first four deal with duties towards God: the others deal with responsibilities to one's neighbour. Interestingly the command to honour father and mother heads the manward commandments. This is not simply because the obligation to care for one's parents was seen as the most fundamental of human duties in traditional societies such as Israel, but because the authority and role of parents towards their children in many ways echoes the authority and role of God towards mankind. Just as God created the human race and continues to sustain it, so parents procreate and bring up their children. In both situations man is supposed to reciprocate, by honouring his heavenly Father on the one hand and his earthly parents on the other.

The first of the godward commands, 'You shall have no other gods before me' (v. 3), reminds Israel of her duty of exclusive allegiance to the one God. The acknowledgement of only one God distinguished Israel from all the other peoples of antiquity. Later the confession from Deuteronomy 6:4, 'Hear, O Israel: The LORD our God, the LORD is one', became the opening line of the Jewish creed, which is recited morning and evening.

Just as central to biblical thinking is the abhorrence of idolatry enshrined in the second commandment: 'You shall not make for yourself a carved image ... you shall not bow down to them or serve them' (vv. 4–5). Though the first clause could be, and has been, taken as a prohibition on all artwork or sculpture, that is not how the law should be read. What the command is forbidding is the manufacture of images with the intention of worshipping them. The tabernacle and temple contained a number of striking works of art, such as cherubim, which the text expressly sanctions (25:18–20). This shows that what matters is the use to which art is put, not art in itself. Characteristic of a covenant text this commandment appends a threat to those who flout it: the whole household from grandfather to his grandchildren (third generation) or great-grandchildren (fourth generation) could be affected. But there is the promise that God's steadfast love will extend to the thousandth generation of those who keep his commandments.

The third commandment prohibits the misuse of God's name in perjury, witchcraft, or even as a swear word (cf. Lev. 24:10–16).

The fourth commandment reminds Israel of the Sabbath, an institution unique to the Old Testament: no other ancient culture is known which had a weekly day of rest. Genesis 1 pictures God resting on the Sabbath, while Exodus 16 explains how it first came to be observed by the Israelites. Here special emphasis is placed on the whole household observing the Sabbath, even the slaves and domestic animals.

The sequence of the sixth to ninth commandments, murder, adultery, theft, lying, is interesting as it seems to reflect the relative gravity of the offences to judge from the various punishments imposed in the laws: the former offences are treated more harshly than the latter. The last commandment, 'you shall not covet', deals with an offence that is merely in the mind and therefore cannot be brought to court. This shows that the Ten Commandments

are much more than a law-code for ancient Israel: rather they are a distillation of the fundamental theological and moral principles of the Old Testament.

> **What do you think?**
> **THE TEN COMMANDMENTS IN TODAY'S SOCIETY**
>
> The New Testament reaffirms the continuing validity of the commandments for the early Church, e.g. Matthew 19:16–19; Mark 10:17–20; Romans 13:9–10.
>
> But how enforceable are they today in modern Western society? If you were Home Secretary or Attorney General, which commandments would you try and enforce, and which would you forget about? Of those that you would try to enforce, which would you be most strict about and penalize their violation most harshly? Compare your list and its order with that of Exodus, bearing in mind that the order in Exodus roughly reflects their importance in Bible times. What do the differences tell you about what modern society values and what the Bible values?

20:22—23:33: Laws and rules

This section contains great diversity of legal material, all set within the context of the law-giving at Sinai. Picking up the terminology of Exodus 24:7 commentators often call this section 'the book of the covenant'. Many of these rules and regulations have parallels within other ancient law codes, just as several of the Ten Commandments are paralleled elsewhere. Thus their inclusion here gives them the stamp of divine authority and brings them within the covenant framework.

The first part, 20:22–26, gives some rules about worship, evidently intended for the situation where there was no national central sanctuary. Certain basic principles – no idols, no hewn stone altars, no steps up to the altar – should characterize the design of these local shrines.

The second part, 21:1—22:17, is a selection of case laws, sometimes called casuistic law. It is a collection of judicial decisions or principles on interesting legal topics from slaves to seduction, from theft to assault, from goring oxen to arson. Many of these topics are dealt with in other collections of Near Eastern law emanating from the second millennium BC. These collections include the Laws of Eshnunna and Hammurabi (eighteenth century BC), the Middle Assyrian Laws (eleventh century BC) and the Hittite Laws (seventeenth century BC). It is not clear how far these collections represent actual decisions made in ancient courts or how far they are the musings of armchair lawyers illustrating traditional principles of Near Eastern law. What is clear is that none of these collections is a code, that is, a presentation of a complete system of law. Many basic issues are not discussed, and only unusual aspects of a problem are handled. For example, what is to be done in the case of premarital intercourse is discussed in 22:16–17, but not the normal procedures for marriage. To obtain a fuller picture of the principles being illustrated in the biblical law, it is necessary

to study them against the wider background of Near Eastern law in the manner exemplified by Westbrook (1988).

Another point to recognize in reading these case laws is that they do not express Old Testament ideals: they only deal with problems. If everyone loved his neighbour as himself, there would be no slavery, murder, theft or seduction. These laws define what must be done, if the Ten Commandments and the principle of neighbour love are ignored. And of course they ignore minor transgressions of these principles, such as anger, bitchy comments or lust. They deal with serious contraventions of the law and thereby set a floor for social behaviour. There is thus quite a gap between the ethical ideals of the Old Testament, that is how it was hoped people would behave, and the laws which define minimum standards of behaviour. Someone might covet his neighbour's ox, which was ethically wrong but not punishable by law. But if he stole that ox, the law came into play forcing him to make recompense (22:1). The modern reader must bear this in mind in reading these laws. They are designed to curb the worst excesses of Old Testament society: they do not define its ideals.

After the selection of case laws in 21:1—22:17, there is a collection of moral and religious injunctions in 22:18—23:19. Although on first reading there appears to be little rhyme or reason about the choice of topics and their arrangement, there is a considerable degree of organization and coherence within this section (see Sprinkle 1994). Unlike the case laws which are cast

Digging deeper:
TWO PROBLEMS IN THE LAW: SLAVERY AND THE *LEX TALIONIS*

Even if it is admitted that these laws are setting minimum standards of tolerable behaviour and are not defining what ideally ought to happen, modern readers are often shocked by the Pentateuch's acceptance of slavery and its affirmation of the *lex talionis*, that is the 'eye-for-an-eye and tooth-for-a-tooth' principle. Are these customs really compatible with justice and human dignity? We shall look at each briefly.

Slavery
Ancient Israelite society was very different from our own. Most people were self-employed smallholders. Extended families lived on the land they farmed. As long as the rains came and the harvests prospered, they enjoyed a great degree of independence. But too often the rains failed, and the families were reduced to destitution. Then one had to choose between emigration (Gen. 12:10; 45:6–10; Ruth 1:1) and indenture, that is selling one or more members of the family to be employed by a rich landowner, preferably a relative of the family. In return for working for him, the employee would receive board and lodging, and sometimes even a wife (cf. Jacob in Gen. 29). Typically then slavery was an institution whereby the wealthy provided employment to the destitute self-employed small farmers. It was seen as an act of charity to take people into slavery in such circumstances (cf. Gen. 47:13–25). Indeed the comfort and security of slavery with a good master might make a slave reluctant to claim his freedom (Exod. 21:5).

Nevertheless the Old Testament shows its unhappiness with slavery in two ways. First, it insists that slaves ought to have the right to freedom after they have worked for six years (Exod. 21:2). Second, it places the law on slave release right at the beginning of this section, whereas in other oriental legal collections laws about slaves are tucked in near the end. In that God redeemed Israel from Egyptian slavery, so human slave owners ought to make it possible for slaves to go free.

The *lex talionis*
The *lex talionis* occurs three times in the Pentateuch. First, as a principle to determine damages after a miscarriage caused by a fight (Exod. 21:23–25). Second, to determine damages after injuring a neighbour (Lev. 24:19–20). Third, to determine the appropriate punishment for someone giving false witness in court (Deut. 19:16–21).

The last example shows that the principle is that of exact retribution. Suppose someone falsely accuses someone else of a crime whose punishment is X. When the false witness is detected, he will suffer punishment X instead of the person he wrongly accused. 'The judges shall inquire diligently, and if the witness is a false witness, and has accused his brother falsely, then you shall do to him as he had meant to do to his brother' (Deut. 19:18–19). A similar logic applies to the situations envisaged in Leviticus 24 and Exodus 21.

Second, it should be noted that the principle was rarely applied literally. 'You shall pay life for life, eye for eye, tooth for tooth, hand for hand, wound for wound, stripe for stripe' sounds terribly brutal and literal. But the laws that follow, dealing with injuries to slaves and goring oxen, show the principle being applied quite differently. The slaves are compensated by being given their freedom and the owner of the goring ox has to pay damages for his ox's rampage (Exod. 21:26–32).

Third, the *lex talionis* is a way of limiting revenge. Lamech (Gen. 4:24) promised to wreak 77-fold revenge on anyone who attacked him: this principle limits revenge to exactly the damage done. In Old Testament times there were no police or public prosecution service, so all prosecution and punishment had to be carried out by the injured party and his family. Thus it would be quite possible for injured parties not to insist on their full rights under the *lex talionis*, but negotiate a lower settlement or even forgive the offender altogether. The *lex talionis* simply fixed the maximum that could be demanded.

Jesus encouraged his followers to forgo all their claims under the *lex talionis* (Matt. 5:38–42).

What principles do you think should determine (a) punishment in the courts and (b) personal attitudes? If they differ, how do you reconcile them?

in the third person, 'If a man does x', and state a penalty, 'he must do y', these are moral injunctions in the second person, 'you shall not do z', which do not specify a penalty for non-compliance. They are often called apodictic law to distinguish them from casuistic or case law. Many of the topics dealt with in this section are discussed more fully in the legal sections of Leviticus and Deuteronomy.

The epilogue of the book of the covenant, 23:20–33, ends as ancient legal documents usually do with threats and promises: a warning about disobedience in 23:21 and a promise of success in 23:22 if Israel is obedient. But the promise is here expanded greatly, with a vision of good harvests, good health and success in battle, so that Israel's boundaries will stretch from the Red Sea in the south to the Euphrates in the north, from the Mediterranean in the west to the wilderness in the east. This rosy vision of the future depends on Israel's total fidelity to the law (23:25), which at this stage in her history might still be hoped for. But later events will dull this optimism, and more emphasis will be placed on the warnings than on the promises (cf. Lev. 26; Deut. 28).

24:1–18: Making of the covenant
With chapter 24 the narrative resumes, after the long digression setting out the laws revealed on the mountain. In chapter 19 the appearance of God on the mountain top was so frightening that no one wanted to go up. Now Moses and Aaron, two sons of Aaron, and 70 elders are invited up the mountain, where they

are privileged to a vision of God's glory (24:9–11). This transformation in divine–human relationships was made possible by the sealing of the covenant described in 24:3–8.

In this rite Israel agrees to all the terms of the covenant: 'All that the LORD has spoken we will do' (24:7). An altar was erected symbolizing God's presence and 12 pillars were set up nearby symbolizing the 12 tribes of Israel. Sacrifices were offered, a typical element of covenant-making ceremonies, and the blood of the animals was caught in basins. Usually the blood was then splashed over the altar, but this time half of it was splashed over the altar and half over the people, or maybe over the pillars that represented them. This act linked God (the altar) and Israel (the pillars) in a sacred union, and thus made it possible for the priests and elders of Israel to ascend the mountain to meet the LORD.

Even so the elders could not go right to the summit, the holiest point, only Moses could. There he received the tablets inscribed with the Ten Commandments. This too was an indispensable part of covenant-making procedure. Unless legal arrangements such as treaties were sealed in written form, they were not valid in the ancient Near East. But such documents had to be stored in the sanctuary and that was one reason why the narrative now moves on to tell how the tabernacle must be constructed. The other reason for making the tabernacle was to make possible God's continuing presence among his people. At Sinai the mountain was the divine dwelling place. But Israel had been told to move to Canaan, and that meant leaving Sinai. Only with a portable shrine could they continue to enjoy God's presence among them and enter the promised land.

THE TABERNACLE

25:1—31:18: Directions for constructing the tabernacle

A good third of the book of Exodus is concerned with the tabernacle. Chapters 25—31 give detailed instructions about the design and manufacture of the tabernacle, while chapters 35—40 tell how these instructions were carried out. Modern readers tend to share the outlook of the Greek translators of Exodus, who, not seeing the point of the repetition, left out much of chapters 35—40. But the sheer space and detail devoted to the tabernacle show its importance for the writer, and we must therefore make some attempt to grasp both the elements of its design and its significance for ancient Israel if we are to appreciate why Exodus regards it as so important.

Basically the tabernacle was a large frame tent or small marquee surrounded by a screened courtyard in which stood a large altar and laver for washing.

Various features of the tabernacle are described in detail in chapters 25—31, and I shall not repeat them here. Rather we shall focus on the symbolic significance of the tabernacle as a whole: what it meant to the ancient Israelite as

Figure 3: **THE TABERNACLE**

N

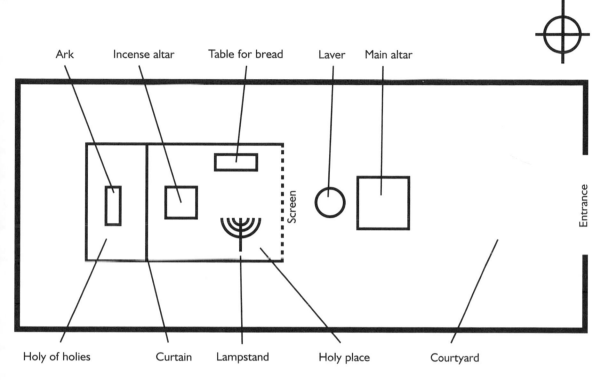

Ark · Incense altar · Table for bread · Laver · Main altar

Holy of holies · Curtain · Lampstand · Holy place · Courtyard

an edifice and what individual features in the design symbolized. Unpacking ancient religious symbolism is very difficult, so some of the suggestions that follow should be regarded as tentative. But without some understanding of the religious thinking behind the design these chapters will remain just a puzzling collection of numbers and measurements.

The fundamental idea embodied by the tabernacle was that it was God's earthly dwelling place. 'Let them make me a sanctuary, that I may dwell in their midst' (25:8) expresses this notion most clearly. This earthly sanctuary was modelled after a heavenly design. Several times Moses is told to make it 'after the pattern ... which is being shown you on the mountain' (25:40). It is not clear whether what Moses saw was just a blueprint for the earthly tabernacle, or a heavenly tabernacle in which God dwelt in heaven which had to be imitated on earth. However freely one interprets this imagery, it is clear that the design of the tabernacle, like other temples of antiquity, is of divine inspiration.

The tabernacle resembled a royal palace with its throne room, the holy of holies, right at the heart of the structure. It thus expressed the idea that the LORD was Israel's king dwelling among his people.

Its drapes of purple suggested royalty and its blue curtains suggested heaven. The sequence of metals, from bronze in the outer court, silver round the base of the tent, and pure gold covering the furniture inside the tent, indicated increasing nearness to the divine king.

The tabernacle's design also evoked the Garden of Eden, where God used to live harmoniously with man. The gold, the cherubim, the tree of life, the high-priestly jewels, and the entrance from the east are some of the features that the tabernacle and the Garden of Eden had in common. Most obvious was the presence of God in the tabernacle as he had been in Eden. The tabernacle thus pointed to a restoration of peace between man and God that was lost in the fall.

Chapters 25—31 are organized quite systematically: 25—27 detail the design of the tabernacle and its furniture, while 28—31 focus on the personnel of the tabernacle, the priests and constructors. The instructions in chapters 25—27 move from the holiest items, such as the ark of the covenant, to the least holy, the tabernacle courtyard.

25:10–22: The ark was the most sacred item in the tabernacle and was kept in the holy of holies completely out of sight. It was a gold-plated box, roughly 3 feet by 2 feet, which served as a container for the tablets of the Ten Commandments and as the throne of God. On the lid of the ark, the 'mercy seat', the most important rites of the Day of Atonement were carried out (Lev. 16:11–16). On the mercy seat stood two cherubim, traditional guardians of holy places (cf. Gen. 3:24).

> **Digging deeper:**
> **WHAT DID THE CHERUBIM LOOK LIKE?**
>
> In traditional Christian art cherubs are pictured as chubby babies with wings. Modern archaeological discovery has suggested they were much fiercer creatures. In Mesopotamia entrances to palaces and temples were guarded by winged bulls or lions with human faces. Assyrian texts mention *kuribu*, but what they looked like is uncertain. Ezekiel's description of the living creatures accompanying the divine presence (Ezek. 1:4–14) makes it probable that the biblical Cherubim were more like these Mesopotamian beasts than cherubs!

25:23–40: The table and the lampstand were the two most important pieces in the outer part of the tent, the holy place (see figure 3). The gold-plated table stood on the north side of the tent. On it were placed 12 flat loaves of bread symbolizing the 12 tribes. Opposite stood the seven-branched lampstand designed to look like a flowering tree, perhaps the tree of life. The continual light from the lamps symbolized the life-giving power of God shining out and blessing the bread on the table opposite, which represented the people of Israel.

26:1–37: The tent and its curtains Four layers of different materials, linen, goats' hair, and two kinds of leather covered the wooden framework of the tent. Inside, the tent was divided into two parts by the veil (26:31–35). The innermost section, the holy of holies was a perfect cube (15 feet, 4.5 metres) in each direction. The outer section was the same height and breadth but twice as long: it was called the holy place (see figure 3).

27:1–21: The courtyard of the tabernacle

As the holy of holies corresponded to the summit of Sinai in holiness, and the holy place to the zone midway up the mountain, the courtyard of the tabernacle (see figure 3) corresponded to the area around the base of Sinai. In both zones there was an altar for burnt offering, another symbol of God's presence among his people. As a holy, but not super-holy, area it could be entered by lay people if they prepared themselves properly (cf. 19:14–15). The courtyard itself was screened off by brightly coloured hangings, so that people could not enter this sacred zone inadvertently.

28:1—29:46: The priests

In a religion that made such a contrast between the holiness of God and the sinfulness of man, priestly mediation was crucial. Laity who deliberately or inadvertently trespassed into the holy were liable to instant death (cf. 19:12–24). Even priests could approach God only with extreme caution (28:35, 43). As mediators priests had a dual role: they represented God to Israel and they represented Israel before God. Their godly authority was expressed by their splendid robes, which evoked the majesty of God himself. The high priest represented Israel before God by offering sacrifices on the nation's behalf and by carrying the names of the 12 tribes engraved on the jewels he wore (28:9–10, 21). The priests were initiated into their office by donning their garments and offering many sacrifices in a lengthy ceremony that lasted a full week. Their offering of daily sacrifice ensured that God would continue to dwell with Israel, so the instructions conclude with the promise: 'I will dwell among the people of Israel and will be their God' (29:45).

30:1—31:17: Additional instructions

After dealing with the main issues, the section mentions a few extra points that were necessary for worship to proceed smoothly. It concludes with a reminder of the importance of observing the Sabbath 'as a covenant for ever. It is a sign forever between me and the people of Israel', and the handing over of the stone tablets as a sign of that covenant (31:16–18). But hardly has the eternity of the covenant been so emphatically affirmed when its very existence is put in peril by Israel's behaviour.

32:1—34:35: Making the golden calf

Abruptly and without warning we plunge into the greatest crisis in divine–human relationships since the flood. Then the whole human race was nearly wiped out for its sin, now the same fate threatens the people of Israel. In a parody of 25:1–9 where God tells the people how to make a tabernacle to symbolize his presence with them, the people make a golden calf to do just that (32:1–6). In so doing they flout the first two commandments, 'You shall have no other gods before me,' and 'You shall not make for yourself a carved image.'

The consequences are catastrophic. Moses smashes the tablets with the Ten Commandments, thereby cancelling the covenant between God and Israel, which has just been concluded. The LORD himself threatens to destroy Israel, and start again with Moses (32:10). In the event, a massacre and a plague destroy thousands of the people, which, though horrific, is not so terrible as their total annihilation, which had been threatened.

But it is not these punishments that save the situation, so much as Moses. His passionate intercession, with its appeal to the covenant with the patriarchs and to God's international reputation, persuades the LORD to hold back from his planned destruction (32:11–14). However, God says that he will not accompany them into the land of promise, lest their hard-heartedness provokes him again to destroy them (33:3). His presence was to be guaranteed and symbolized by the tabernacle accompanying them into the land. Since the design of the tabernacle expressed the notion of God walking among his people, God's threat not to go with them is in effect a cancellation of all the plans for the tabernacle set out in chapters 25—31, for without God within it the tabernacle would be just an empty shrine.

But Moses refuses to lead Israel into Canaan unless the LORD accompanies them (33:12–16). So God relents, and by way of reassurance allows Moses a partial vision of his glory, 'his back', and reiterates the terms of the covenant set out in Exodus 20—23 (33:17—34:26). However, this reiteration is not mere repetition: there are significant changes made to the earlier account. Most obviously the new terms highlight the danger of idolatry (34:12–17), but they also stress the mercy of God over against his anger (34:6–9).

In all these ways this section stresses the unique role of Moses: without his mediation Israel's mission to be the people of God would have been aborted. His advocacy of Israel despite their sin prevented the termination of the covenant. He was the one with whom the LORD spoke face to face in the tent of meeting outside the camp (33:7–11), and whose face shone so brightly after such encounters that he had to put a veil over it (34:29–35). It was he who brought down a second copy of the Ten Commandments as a sign of the renewal of the covenant. It was he who, by securing the LORD's willingness to accompany Israel into Canaan, reinstated the plan to construct the tabernacle.

35:1—40:38: Construction of the tabernacle

The final section of Exodus tells how Moses commissioned Bezalel and Oholiab to build the tabernacle, its furniture, and the priests' vestments according to the instructions Moses had received in the mountain. It tells of the enthusiasm of the ordinary people to make donations of gold, silver and precious materials for the tabernacle. It includes an inventory of the amounts collected.

The attention to detail is impressive, but many modern readers regard all the repetition of points already covered in chapters 25—31 as unnecessary. That is to miss the significance of this section. It comes after a crisis that threatened Israel's existence. The sin of the golden calf could have led to the nation's destruction, had it not been for Moses' intercession. Even then they might have had to enter the land unaccompanied by symbols of God's presence. The creation of the tabernacle showed that the divine programme had been reinstated. Israel's divine king was willing to dwell among them. The Garden of Eden had been brought back to earth. The LORD was going to walk among his people as he had in Eden. So the book closes with the cloud of God's glorious presence filling the tabernacle. 'The cloud of the LORD was on the tabernacle by day, and the fire was in it by night, in the sight of all the house of Israel throughout all their journeys' (40:38).

THE NEW TESTAMENT AND THE BOOK OF EXODUS

Within the OT the exodus from Egypt is often looked back to as the great saving event, especially in the Psalms and prophetic books (e.g. Pss 105; 106; 114; Isa. 11:11; Ezek. 20; Hos. 11:1). So it is not surprising that the NT can describe its key saving act, the death of Christ, as his exodus 'which he was about to accomplish at Jerusalem' (Luke 9:31). But it is not just Jesus who must participate in the exodus; Paul sees every Christian as passing through the Red Sea in the act of baptism

(1 Corinthians 10:2). For the epistle to the Hebrews the life of Moses demonstrates what is involved in living by faith in what is invisible (Heb. 11:23–28).

Linked with the exodus was the Passover and the same linkage is maintained in the New Testament. Not only did Jesus celebrate a Passover meal the day before he died at which he said, echoing Exodus 24:8, 'this is my blood of the covenant' (Matt. 26:28), but both John and Paul see Jesus as the true Passover lamb, whose blood takes away the sin of the world (John 1:29; 19:36; 1 Cor. 5:7). His death inaugurates the New Covenant just as the Passover ushered in the Old Covenant at Sinai.

Finally, tabernacle imagery is taken up in the New Testament. In the tabernacle God walked among his people, so the NT easily transfers this image to the incarnation, 'the Word became flesh and dwelt [tabernacled] among us, and we have seen his glory' (John 1:14), and to the body of the believer, who also is the dwelling place of the Spirit (1 Cor. 6:19). For the epistle to the Hebrews the rites in the tabernacle foreshadow in all sorts of ways the saving ministry of Christ (Heb. 9:1–28).

FURTHER READING

COMMENTARIES
U. Cassuto *A Commentary on the Book of Exodus*. Jerusalem: Magnes Press, 1967. Straightforward sensitive interpretation.
B. S. Childs *Exodus*. London: SCM Press, 1974. A classic.

N. M. Sarna *The JPS Torah Commentary: Exodus*. Philadelphia: Jewish Publication Society, 1991. Helpful modern commentary.

HISTORICAL BACKGROUND
F. S. Bodenheimer 'The Manna of Sinai' *BA* 10, 1947, pp. 1–10.

M. Harel *Masei Sinai*. Tel Aviv: Am Oved, 1968.

J. K. Hoffmeier *Israel in Egypt*. Oxford: Oxford University Press, 1996. Up-to-date scholarship.

G. Hort 'The Plagues of Egypt' *ZAW* 69, 1957, pp. 84–103; 70, 1958, pp. 48–59.

G. J. Wenham *Numbers: an Introduction and Commentary*. Leicester: IVP, 1981. Discusses route of exodus.

THE LAWS
G. C. Chirichigno *Debt-Slavery in Israel and the Ancient Near East*. Sheffield: JSOT Press, 1993.

B. M. Levinson (ed.) *Theory and Method in Biblical and Cuneiform Law*. Sheffield: Sheffield Academic Press, 1994. Essays debating different approaches to law. Valuable essay by Westbrook on Exodus 21—23.

D. Patrick *Old Testament Law*. Atlanta: John Knox Press, 1985. Introduction to traditional critical approach.

M. T. Roth, *Law Collections from Mesopotamia and Asia Minor*. Atlanta: Scholars Press, 1997.

J. M. Sprinkle *'The Book of the Covenant': a Literary Approach*. Sheffield: Sheffield Academic Press, 1994. Valuable discussion of arrangement of the laws.

G. J. Wenham 'The Gap between Law and Ethics in the Bible' *JJS* 48, 1997, pp. 17–29.

R. Westbrook *Studies in Biblical and Cuneiform Law*. Paris: Galbalda, 1988. A brilliant discussion.

THE TABERNACLE AND WORSHIP
M. Haran *Temples and Temple Worship in Ancient Israel*. Oxford: Clarendon Press, 1978. A thorough analysis.

C. L. Meyers *The Tabernacle Menorah*. Missoula: Scholars Press, 1976. A study of the archaeological background and symbolism of the Menorah (golden candlestick).

G. J. Wenham 'Sanctuary Symbolism in the Garden of Eden Story', in R. S. Hess and D. T. Tsumura *I Studied Inscriptions from before the Flood*. Winona Lake: Eisenbrauns, 1994, pp. 399–404.

THE GOLDEN CALF
R. W. L. Moberly *At the Mountain of God: Story and Theology in Exodus 32—34*. Sheffield: JSOT Press, 1983. Rich theological insights.

Chapter 5

LEVITICUS

Leviticus, like the names of the other books of the Pentateuch, is borrowed from the Greek translation of the Bible. It is called Leviticus because it deals with many matters of particular interest to priests, who were members of the tribe of Levi or Levites. However, it is a mistake to regard it as a handbook for priests, for many of the issues it deals with concern lay people.

Its alternative name, 'the third book of Moses', is also very apt, for it is a continuation of the biography of Moses that begins in Exodus. Leviticus is in fact closely linked to Exodus by the storyline. In chapters 25—31 of Exodus Moses was instructed about constructing the tabernacle and its furniture, about the design of the priests' vestments, and about their ordination. Chapters 35—40 tell how the tabernacle and its furniture were made and also the priestly vestments, but nothing is said about the ordination of the priests. This is dealt with in Leviticus 8—10, where Moses occupies a key role. The other obvious narrative section is in chapter 24, which discusses how a blasphemer was punished after Moses had discovered what was God's will. These stories are the most obvious indicators that Leviticus is essentially a narrative work, but the introduction to nearly every chapter, 'the LORD spoke to Moses' or something similar, makes the same point. Unfortunately the very frequency of this introduction tends to make the reader overlook it and forget that he is reading the life of Moses.

STRUCTURE

Leviticus is characterized by clear organization. Titles mark the beginning of new sections, and summary formulae mark section endings. By and large the chapter divisions, introduced into the Bible in the Middle Ages, pick up these earlier division markers correctly and give a good detailed breakdown of the material. Here we shall just give a general overview.

Part 1	1:1—7:38	Laws on sacrifice
	1:1—6:7	Instructions for the laity
	6:8—7:38	Instructions for the priests
Part 2	8:1—10:20	Institution of the priesthood

Part 3   11:1—16:34   Uncleanness and its treatment

Part 4   17:1—27:34   Prescriptions for practical holiness

THE PROBLEMS OF READING LEVITICUS

Although Leviticus was the first book that Jewish children studied in the synagogue, it is often the last to be tackled by modern Christian readers, if they ever try! This is a great pity because this book gives some of the clearest insights into biblical religion and theology. It is fundamental to the New Testament's understanding of the atonement, and therefore can scarcely be disregarded. So before we review the contents of the book, I shall try to identify the problems and how they may be overcome.

Modern readers face three major problems in making sense of Leviticus. First, they find it difficult to visualize the ceremonies described. Second, they tend to believe that rituals are obsolete and irrelevant, especially sacrifices and the sort of rites described in Leviticus. Third, they find these ceremonies and regulations very hard to interpret: how can we discover the key to their significance in ancient Israel? I shall look at these issues in turn.

VISUALIZATION

It is very difficult for modern readers to picture the sacrifices described in Leviticus, because they, unlike ancient Israelites, have never seen, let alone participated in a sacrifice. What we really need is a video showing all the different kinds of sacrifices, the burnt offering, the peace offering, the sin offering and so on! Just as the stories in the Old Testament are designed for reading aloud, not silently, so these ritual texts are meant for people who already have a good idea of how to sacrifice. They are just underlining important or controversial points, so that anyone offering a sacrifice would do it in a way acceptable to God.

So how can we proceed? The best way is to act them out, or alternatively, if one is more artistically inclined, produce a sort of comic strip showing each step in the action. Then it becomes much easier to grasp the steps in the process and see the direction of the ceremony. But it will also show up the gaps in the instructions, things that the first readers just took for granted. For example, Leviticus never says that the sacrificial animals had to have their legs tied before being killed. But this was the procedure in other parts of the ancient Near East and Genesis 22:9 suggests it was done in ancient Israel. Another thing the Old Testament nearly always leaves out are the words said or sung during the ceremonies. But one can hardly suppose that the worshipper did not explain to the priest why he was bringing a sacrifice or afterwards that the priest did not give some assurance that the sacrifice had been accepted. In Leviticus one has the rubrics setting out how a ceremony is to be performed, but none of the accompanying words. It is often surmised that the Psalms were used in temple services, presumably as the sacrifices were being carried out, but again there is no hint of this in Leviticus. Therefore, readers need to use much imagination to recreate the mood and atmosphere of the rites as well as attending carefully to the exact procedures set out in the text.

SIGNIFICANCE

The instinctive modern aversion to taking ritual seriously is reflected in many Old Testament theologies, which tend to ignore these books at the heart of the Pentateuch when they discuss biblical theology. Yet anthropologists insist that rituals are the key to understanding a society's central values. Monica Wilson (1934) has put this point most forcibly.

Rituals reveal values at their deepest level ... men [people] express in ritual what moves them most, and since the form of expression is conventionalized and obligatory, it is the values of the group that are revealed. I see in the study of rituals the key to an understanding of the essential constitution of human societies.

That rituals express deep emotion is at first sight surprising, but on reflection is clearly correct. Greeting someone with a handshake is warmer than a mere word or nod, but a kiss is more affectionate still and a hug even more so. In church too, ritual gestures are an index of emotional involvement, whether it be crossing oneself before receiving the sacrament or raising one's arms in a hymn.

But the ritual gestures used depend on the social environment: in other words they are determined by convention. Table manners vary from country to country. What is acceptable practice in England may not be in Germany and vice versa. Young people's conventions on behaviour often differ from those of the older generation. Religious gestures common in one denomination, e.g. kneeling or clapping, may not be used in another denomination. In this way 'the form of expression is conventionalized'.

But as Monica Wilson points out it is also 'obligatory'. You must wear the right clothes to certain functions, e.g. funerals, weddings, graduations, parties. You must write a thank-you letter. You must take your hat off in church. You must wear a hat in a synagogue. You must visit your family and eat roast turkey at Christmas. You may not want to do these things, but society tells you to and will disapprove if you don't. These customs thus tell us what society regards as important or appropriate, not necessarily what the individual feels. You may be secretly pleased Uncle Harry has died because he has remembered you in his will, but woe betide you, if you do not dress and behave correctly at his funeral!

Analysis of national customs gives us an insight into what a particular society holds dear. The 12 July Orange marches in Northern Ireland and the Guy Fawkes' celebrations in England celebrate the Protestant ethos of these societies, while Thanksgiving Day in the USA and Bastille Day in France commemorate the key aspirations of these nations. The declining attention given to such Christian holy days as Good Friday, Whitsun, Lent, and Sundays highlights the increasing secularization of many Western societies. Leviticus defines the most important rituals of ancient Israel from sacrifice to cleansing ceremonies, the religious calendar and its high holy days, birth rites and funeral practices. If these can be understood, we unlock 'the essential constitution of [Israelite] society'.

INTERPRETATION

Anthropologists have problems understanding the rites and customs of the peoples they study, even though they live among them and can question them about the significance of their ceremonies. Old Testament scholars have a much more difficult task penetrating the mind of Leviticus and its rituals because there are no living informants who can explain the rationale for different procedures. What makes it even more difficult is the absence of the words that accompanied the actions: Leviticus tells us what had to be done when a 'leper' was cleansed, but not what was said. If we knew more about what was said, we should have a much clearer picture of the significance of each gesture within a rite, as well as the overall purpose of the rite. Evidently these things were so well known in Israel that they were taken for granted by the pentateuchal writers and not explained. Thus the interpretation of the rites in Leviticus is fraught with difficulty.

Nevertheless by the application of insights from other societies and careful attention to the text, it is possible to understand the main issues at stake in different rites. In the last twenty years a broad consensus has developed among Old Testament scholars about the interpretation of the ritual system. Space does not permit us to justify the method or its conclusions in detail, or to point out where guesswork rather than rigorous proof lies behind some of the following discussion. For further discussion of these issues the books at the end of the chapter should be consulted.

1:1—7:38: LAWS ON SACRIFICE

As already noted, the book of Exodus gives instructions about the ordination of priests but this is not done until Leviticus 8—9. Their ordination involves the offering of a wide variety of sacrifices, whose procedures have not yet been explained. So the book of Leviticus begins by setting out how all the different sacrifices are to be performed. Not all of the instructions are pertinent to the ordination of Aaron and his sons, but for the sake of comprehensiveness they are all brought together in these opening chapters.

Leviticus 1:1—6:7 deal with sacrifice from the viewpoint of the offerer. This section specifies what the worshipper must do in each case to ensure his sacrifice is acceptable: what animals may be offered on what occasion, what the offerer must do and what the priest must do, and so on. Leviticus 6:8—7:38 deals with the same sacrifices but from the priests' perspective, in particular which parts of which sacrifice belong to the officiating priest.

The structure of this section is very clearly delineated with titles, such as 'the LORD spoke to Moses' to mark distinct laws and subtitles, such as 'if his offering ...' or 'this is the law of' to mark paragraphs within each law. Using these criteria the major divisions within this section are as follows:

1:1–17	The burnt offering
2:1–16	The grain offering
3:1–17	The peace offering
4:1—5:13	The sin offering
5:14—6:7	The guilt offering
6:8—7:38	Instructions for priests about sacrifice.

Digging deeper:
STRUCTURE OF THE LAWS

The careful arrangement of these laws allows literary analysis to be carried out easily. Using the subtitle 'if his offering is' see how chapters 1 and 3 are organized. Using the subtitle 'this is the law of' do the same on chapters 6 and 7. What are the subtitles used in chapters 2 and 4?

NB For this you will need a Bible such as the RSV or ESV that translates the Hebrew exactly. Many modern versions obscure the structure by translating rather freely.

1:1–17: The burnt offering

This is so called because it is the only sacrifice which is entirely burnt on the altar. All the other sacrifices are partially burnt on the altar and the rest of the meat shared by priests and sometimes the worshipper.

After an introduction to the group of laws in 1:1–2, the rules about the burnt offering are given in three paragraphs 3–9, 10–13, 14–17. Groups of three are quite common in Leviticus. (Look for examples in the following chapters.) These paragraphs define the types of animal acceptable for a burnt offering and the role of the offerer and the priest in the ceremony. Only domestic animals that are without blemish may be offered: thus wild or damaged beasts may not be offered. The worshipper ('he') must bring the animal, lay his hand on its head, skin it, chop it up, and kill it. The priest ('Aaron's sons') must collect the blood, splash it over the altar, and put the pieces of the animal on the altar fire. The division of labour between priest and offerer is important but obscured in some English translations (e.g. NIV, NRSV). Only the priest may handle the sacred liquid, the blood, and approach the altar.

The central act of the burnt offering was the killing and burning of the animal on the altar. This represents the giving of the animal to God. But why give it to God, is it just an act of generosity? The text suggests it is more than that. It 'makes atonement for' the worshipper, 'that he may be accepted before the LORD' (Lev. 1:4,3). By placing his hand on the animal's head, the worshipper is saying, 'This animal is/represents me.' In other words the offerer is giving himself to God in the sacrifice. He is acting out the command, 'You shall love the LORD your God with all your heart and with all your soul and with all your might' (Deut. 6:5).

Digging deeper:
MAKING SENSE OF SACRIFICE

Modern readers, if not disgusted by sacrifice, at least think it is a bizarre form of worship. How on earth can it be understood?

To understand the place of sacrifice in Bible times, one must recall the nature of that society. Most people would have scraped a living on small farms. Meat was a rare luxury, which was eaten only at festivals or when guests came. When three men visited Abraham he cooked fresh bread for them, killed and roasted a calf for them, and doubtless plied them with wine, for the Hebrew word for feast literally means 'drinking feast' (Gen. 18:1–8).

Meat, grain or bread, and wine were the components of every sacrifice (see Num. 15:1–10). Thus animal sacrifice was like serving an excellent meal to an important guest, namely God

himself. God's presence was symbolized by the altar and the fire on it. Burning the animal and bread in the fire and pouring the wine on the side of the altar was an act of generous hospitality to the heavenly guest. Other cultures (see the Atrahasis story of the flood in chapter 2, Genesis 1—11) actually believed the gods lived off the food provided by these sacrifices, but the Old Testament rejects this idea. As Psalm 50:12–13 puts it: 'If I were hungry, I would not tell you, for the world and its fullness are mine. Do I eat the flesh of bulls or drink the blood of goats?'

In a poor peasant culture, where animals were your long-term savings, sacrificing them to God was a mark of great generosity, devotion and penitence. That is why they are frequently said to be a 'pleasing aroma to the LORD', not because God was hungry! (Lev. 1:9, 13, 17 etc).

But the animal also 'makes atonement for him'. This could be paraphrased 'pays a ransom for him'. Biblical ransoms are not the exorbitant sums demanded by terrorists and blackmailers, but lesser penalties that the injured party may accept instead of full compensation (e.g. Exod. 21:30; Prov. 6:35). The implication is that the worshipper ought to give much more than an animal for his atonement, perhaps even his own life, but God graciously accepts the animal instead. Two key sacrifices in Genesis illustrate the effect and function of the burnt offering. In Genesis 22 God accepts the ram in place

of Isaac. This leads to the promises to Abraham being reaffirmed with an oath that 'all the nations of the earth [shall] be blessed' (Gen. 22:18). Even more revealing are Noah's burnt offerings after the flood, which lead God to promise never to destroy the human race in another flood. Although the reason for the flood, man's continual propensity to sin (Gen. 6:5) is still present (Gen. 8:21), the threat of total destruction is lifted 'when the LORD smelled the pleasing aroma'. In the wilderness Israel had already shown its propensity to sin (Exod. 16—17; 32), so that even if a particular sin requiring atonement cannot be discovered in every context where a burnt offering is prescribed, it could be seen as dealing with general human sinfulness as well as being an expression of devotion to God.

2:1–16: The cereal offering

This may sometimes have been allowed as a poor person's alternative to a burnt offering, but usually it was offered in addition to the animal sacrifices. Like the burnt offering, it makes 'a pleasing aroma to the LORD', but unlike the burnt offering only part of it was burnt on the altar: the rest of it went to the priest. Indeed it formed part of their core income. The cereal offering could be presented in the form of raw flour, cooked cakes or roast grain.

3:1–17: The peace offering

This is another animal sacrifice often offered in connection with vows or whenever people wished to celebrate an occasion with a meat meal. If someone was very ill, or desperately wanted their prayers answered, it was customary to make a vow. 'O LORD of hosts, if you … will give to your servant a son, then I will give him to the LORD all the days of his life' (1 Sam. 1:11). So Hannah prayed in the temple of Shiloh. On this occasion the family offered sacrifice; but an especially generous sacrifice was presented when her prayer was answered (1 Sam. 1:24). This would have been a peace offering.

This was the only sacrifice in which the worshipper ate some of the meat. Some of the animal was burnt, some was given to the priests, but the rest went to the worshipper and his family and friends (Lev. 3:3 4; 7:31–35). Though this sacrifice is also said to make 'a pleasing aroma to the LORD', its dominant purpose is celebration rather than expiation. It tended to be offered on joyful occasions.

4:1—5:13: The sin offering

This is the sacrifice discussed in most detail in Leviticus. Its use is prescribed for

SACRIFICES: AN OVERVIEW (Complete this table by reading Leviticus 1—7.)

Name of Sacrifice	Types of Animal	Hand-laying	Use of Blood	Priestly Portions	Lay Portions
Burnt	Cattle, sheep, goats, birds				
Peace		Yes			
Sin			Smeared on altars, sprinkled inside tent		
Guilt				Yes	No

(For a completed version see end of chapter.)

87

a variety of situations. This section is mainly concerned with making atonement for unintentional mistakes and for sins of omission, i.e. forgetting to do something. But elsewhere it is prescribed that the sin offering should be offered after childbirth, skin disease or in the ordination of the priests.

The procedure of the sin offering differs radically from that of the burnt and peace offerings which have been discussed up to now. The table on p. 87 has been left unfinished. Complete it by using Leviticus 1—7 to fill the empty boxes.

In all the other animal sacrifices the blood, the liquid of life, is symbolically returned to God, the source of life, by being slopped over the sides of the altar, but in the sin offering it is used quite differently: depending on the status of the sinner, some of it is smeared on the main altar of sacrifice, or on the incense altar in the holy place, and once a year on the Day of Atonement on the ark itself in the holy of holies. (For a diagram of the tabernacle, see p. 75.)

What was this smearing and sprinkling of the blood supposed to achieve? First, it cleansed the altar or ark of the pollution caused by sin. Sin is viewed in Leviticus as leaving invisible but real dirt in the tabernacle, so that God would be unwilling to dwell there. This is a most serious worry, for the whole point of the tabernacle is that it should be God's earthly palace where he may live among his people. But the blood acts as a spiritual cleanser making it possible

for continued fellowship between God and Israel.

But it does more than this: it secures the forgiveness of the sinner. Most paragraphs conclude with the comment, 'and he shall be forgiven' (4:26, 31, 35; 5:10, 13; cf. 4:20). It is not clear quite how the application of the blood to the altars achieves the forgiveness of sins. One possibility is that the altar itself is a mediator between God and man, just as priests are. Priests represent man to God and God to man. If the altar does the same, cleansing it from the effects of sin by smearing it with blood would at the same time effect cleansing of the person whom the altar represents.

5:14—6:7: The guilt offering

This is described more briefly than the other sacrifices, perhaps because it was offered more rarely or because it had no place in the ordination of the priests and has simply been included for completeness. Unlike the other sacrifices only one type of animal was permitted for the guilt offering, namely a ram, which seems to be viewed as reparation to God for some unintentional act of sacrilege, failing to fulfil a vow, or a false oath. Examples of situations requiring this sacrifice are people who have recovered from skin disease (Lev. 14:12) or a Nazirite whose vow of holiness has been broken by someone dying very near to him (Num. 6:9).

6:8—7:38: Instructions for the priests

At first sight these laws seem to be going over much the same ground as chapters

1—5, though the order of presentation is different. In the opening chapters the order is determined thematically: the sacrifices producing a 'pleasing aroma' (chs 1—3) precede the sacrifices for the forgiveness of sins (4:1—6:7). But in this section frequency seems to be the determining factor: the commonest sacrifices, e.g. the burnt and cereal offerings, precede the rarer sin and guilt offerings, while the optional peace offering brings up the rear.

But the focus of interest differs in this section from chapters 1—5 too. Whereas the opening chapters chiefly address the concerns of a lay-person offering a sacrifice, e.g. the choice of animal, the details of procedure, chapters 6—7 predominantly deal with the concerns of the priests. Most sections begin with a command to Aaron and his sons (6:9, 14, 20, 25) and their content is largely concerned with which parts of the sacrifices must go to the priests. Only in 7:23, 29 dealing with peace offerings are the regulations primarily addressed to the laity, as their share of these sacrifices is clarified.

8:1—10:20: INSTITUTION OF THE PRIESTHOOD

Initially this longish account of the institution of the priesthood looks out of place in a book of rules and regulations. But it is arguably the centrepiece of the book of Leviticus. If the Pentateuch is essentially a biography of Moses, the headings at the beginning of each chapter,

'And the LORD spoke to Moses', are not superfluous, but a regular reminder that the whole work is the story of Moses' life. These chapters about the ordination of Aaron and his sons draw attention to another of Moses' great achievements, the installation of human mediators between God and his people Israel. This section of Leviticus shows Moses carrying out with scrupulous attention to detail the instructions given in Exodus 28—29. The other instructions about making the tabernacle, its furniture and the priestly vestments, given in Exodus 25—31, had been carried out in Exodus 35—40. But the ordination of Aaron has not been mentioned. By leaving this undone, the narrative leaves the reader in suspense at the end of Exodus: will Aaron, designer of the golden calf, be allowed to proceed to ordination?

This section demonstrates that God's forgiveness extends even to him. Indeed the whole book of Leviticus seems to be constructed around the episode of Aaron's ordination. As already noted, the opening chapters spell out how the sacrifices involved in that ordination were to be carried out. At the same time they spell out one aspect of the priests' ongoing duties, namely the regular offering of sacrifice. Offering of sacrifice was central to their God-orientated activity, in which they represented the people of Israel before God. The other side of their duty was instructing the laity in holiness, to be holy as God is holy: this was the manward aspect of their role as mediators. They spoke on behalf of God to Israel telling them what behaviour was appropriate, if they were to be his people. To this end from chapter 10 onwards the book is taken up with instructions on purity and cleansing and all sorts of moral and religious duties that the Israelites were expected to carry out. In between these two parts the ordination itself is described, in which Moses takes the leading role.

The account of Aaron's ordination falls into three scenes.

8:1–36 Day 1 of Aaron's ordination
9:1–24 Day 8 of Aaron's ordination: Aaron's first sacrifices accepted
10:1–20 Aaron's sons' sacrifice rejected: death of Nadab and Abihu.

Chapter 8 describes Moses clothing Aaron in his splendid vestments, which befitted his status as supreme mediator between God and Israel (8:6–13). But as yet he does not fulfil that role, for he brings a sin offering, a burnt offering and a peace offering and carries out all the actions (hand-laying, killing, etc) that the lay worshipper normally did. It is Moses who carries out the priestly duties (handling the blood, burning the animal on the altar), for as yet Aaron and his sons are not qualified to act as priests (8:14–21). But some of the blood from the peace offering is treated in an extraordinary way: some of it is smeared on Aaron's ear, thumb and toe and the rest thrown over the altar. This is akin to the action in Exodus 24 when blood was thrown over the people and over the altar. In both cases the actions seem to symbolize linking God to his people, to Israel in general in the Exodus

ceremony and to Aaron in particular in Leviticus 8.

But a week later the situation is different. Now Moses slips into the background and Aaron is in charge. He offers a variety of sacrifices on behalf of himself and the people, but Moses does not have to do anything until the end when he accompanies the new high priest into the tabernacle for the first time. God's approval of the new high priest is demonstrated by the divine glory appearing and fire from before the LORD burning up the sacrifices on the altar. 'When all the people saw it, they shouted and fell on their faces' (9:24).

The first two scenes demonstrate Moses and Aaron carrying out God's instructions to the letter and climax with the public divine approval of them just described. The third scene is a horrible contrast. Its phraseology echoes the last words of chapter 9, but the outcome is totally different. 'The sons of Aaron ... offered unauthorized fire before the LORD, which he had not commanded them. And fire came out from before the LORD and consumed them' (10:1–2; cf. 9:24). Various details of this episode are obscure. (Were these priests drunk, cf. 10:9? Where did they get their illicit fire from?) But these uncertainties do not obscure the main points being made by the story, namely that Israel, and its priests in particular, have an absolute duty to follow God's commands exactly. 'Among those who are near me I will be sanctified' (10:3). It is their duty 'to teach the people of Israel all the statutes that the LORD has spoken to them by Moses' (10:11), and therefore they have a special obligation to keep his instructions strictly themselves.

11:1—16:34: UNCLEANNESS AND ITS TREATMENT

One of the duties of the priests according to 10:10 is 'to distinguish between the holy and the common, and between the unclean and the clean'. So the next five chapters are devoted to explaining the difference between cleanness and uncleanness, while chapter 16 prescribes how national uncleanness is to be dealt with on the Day of Atonement. These principles must be understood if Israel is to fulfil the repeated demand of Leviticus to 'be holy, for I am holy.'

But if the Israelites found these principles hard to grasp, modern readers find them unfathomable. What makes eagles, geckos, menstruation and mildew all to be classified as unclean, whereas locusts, goats and baldness are not? These are the sorts of issues raised by these chapters. Needless to say they have led to endless debate as commentators have tried to find some rhyme or reason in these categorizations. Here we shall not enter this debate, but simply set out some modern conclusions, which owe much to anthropology and careful reading of the texts.

11:1–47: Unclean foods
If 'fitness for worship' is the distinguishing feature of cleanness, we can see that is what distinguishes clean and unclean animals in Leviticus 11. Sacrificial animals had to be domesticated clean animals: wild

Digging deeper:
CLEAN AND UNCLEAN

Cleanness is not the same as cleanliness. It has little to do with hygiene, but much to do with religion. Something or someone unclean may not enter God's presence in worship: only the clean may do so. God is the super-holy and should anyone unclean come near God, he is liable to be destroyed. This explains the death of Nadab and Abihu in Leviticus 10 and the frequent warnings about the risk of death, if one approaches holy places unprepared (Exod. 19:21; 28:35; 30:20–21; Lev. 8:35; 10:7; 16:2, 13). Clean could be paraphrased as 'fit for worship'.

clean animals, e.g. deer, were not allowed, for as David put it, 'I will not offer burnt offerings to the LORD my God that cost me nothing' (2 Sam. 24:24).

Sheep, goats, cattle and birds were the main sacrificial animals of ancient Israel, so that creatures that resembled their habits, particularly their herbivorous eating habits, were judged to be clean and therefore fit for human consumption. Thus various birds, which seem to be birds of prey (Lev. 11:13–19), are pronounced unclean and therefore unfit for human consumption, let alone sacrifice. The definition of clean animals is drawn rather more tightly: like cattle and sheep they must both have cloven hooves and chew the cud. This rules out such creatures as camels, pigs and hares, which only partially fit the criteria (Lev. 11:2–8). Aquatic creatures must look like ordinary

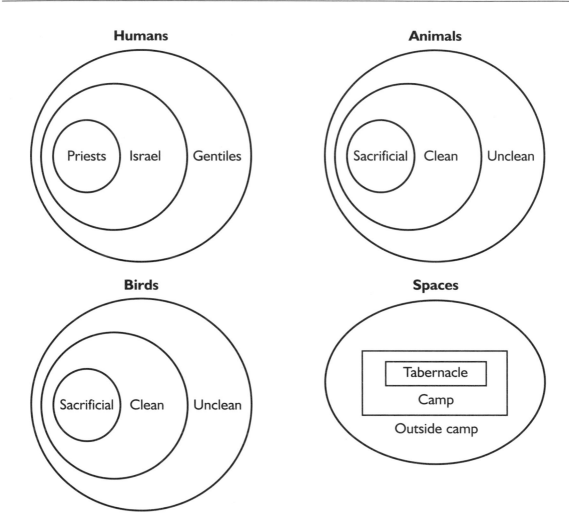

Figure 4: **CLEANNESS RULES**

We could express the information in Figure 4 in a table:

CLEANNESS RULES

Human	Animal	Bird	Fish
Priests	Sacrificial animals, cattle, sheep, etc	Sacrificial birds, doves, pigeons, etc	
Israel	Clean animals, cloven-hooved cud-chewers	Clean birds, all except birds of prey	Fish with fins and scales
Other nations	Unclean animals	Unclean birds	Water creatures without fins and scales

fish with fins and scales to count as clean: others were unclean. As there were no domesticated fishes from fish farms, no fish counted as sacrificial. It therefore is apparent that the animal, bird and fish world is structured like the human world.

These categories meant that ancient Israelites had certain restrictions on their diet and did not eat certain creatures. Not that that is unique to Judaism. Dogs, snakes, snails or frogs do not figure in the typical British diet, though other peoples eat them quite happily! But whereas our dislikes are merely conventional, the Old Testament restrictions have their own rationale. First, the rules reminded Israel that they were the chosen people. As God had restricted his choice among the nations of the world to the Israelites, so in turn the Israelites had to limit their choice of meat to the clean animals that in the symbolic world corresponded to themselves. Every meat meal was therefore a celebration that God had chosen them to be his people.

Second, these rules have another effect: they remind the Israelites of the vegetarian ideal of Genesis 1:29–30, an ideal that was relaxed in Genesis 9:3–4 on condition that blood was not eaten. These rules in Leviticus set limits on the animals that could be killed for food, and so foster respect for life. It may be noted that the unclean birds of prey and carnivorous animals disregard the principle of not eating blood and this may constitute another reason for their uncleanness.

It is the distinction between life and death that is at the heart of the biblical principle of cleanness and uncleanness. The worst kind of uncleanness is generated by death, hence the corpses of clean animals are particularly defiling (Lev. 11:24–40). God on the other hand is the source of abundant perfect life, and it is therefore wrong to bring into his presence anything that suggests death. It is these principles that underlie the regulations in Leviticus 12—15.

12:1–8: Uncleanness after childbirth
The lochia, a bloodlike discharge that follows childbirth, makes a woman as unclean as she is when menstruating. This means she should not attend the sanctuary (12:4). Apparently losing blood, she is not enjoying fullness of life, and she should therefore not come into the realm of perfect life. But after the discharge dries up, she can bring a small sacrifice to ensure both she and the sanctuary are cleansed.

13:1–59: Unclean skin diseases
The traditional translations supposed the skin disease described in this chapter was leprosy (Hansen's disease). But since it had not arrived in the Middle East in Old Testament times and does not spontaneously clear up as some of these conditions do, modern translations drop the term. But although the disease in question may just be eczema in some cases, it is treated very seriously. Peeling, raw skin is not perfect life, so it is understandable why it is regarded as unclean. Similarly a fungus rotting away a fabric or plaster in a house is suggestive of death and therefore counts as unclean. In all the situations described in chapter 13

priests may be called on to pronounce whether the condition is unclean or not, but they have no ability to cure the complaints. They act more like health inspectors than doctors.

14:1–57: Cleansing after skin disease

People suffering from skin disease were excluded from the community and treated almost as though they were non-Israelites. If they recovered from their complaint, they had to undergo an elaborate ceremony that symbolically cleansed them and reintegrated them into the community. This was not a healing service led by the priest. Rather, if he was satisfied that the skin disease had cleared up, then he conducted these rites, which like the ordination of the priests lasted a week. These included letting a bird fly off carrying the impurity away, offering several animal sacrifices and smearing the blood of one of them on the cleansed person. Only then was he restored to fullness of life in fellowship with all Israel.

15:1–33: The uncleanness of bodily discharges

Less serious than skin disease were discharges from the sexual organs of men and women. Gonorrhoea in men and bleeding from the vagina in women made them unclean. Again this is not a medical judgement, but a religious one: once more the underlying rationale seems to be that to lose a life-liquid, such as blood, meant that the person who was suffering was under the shadow of death and therefore unfit to approach the God of life. Only when these discharges cleared up and a small sacrifice had been offered could fellowship resume. Even normal

discharges of semen or menstrual blood led to uncleanness, but the effect of these discharges could be cleansed just by waiting and washing. Though modern readers may be surprised at these rules, they did, among other incidental effects, exclude the practice of ritual prostitution, a widespread custom in the ancient world. Their importance for Israel is underlined by verse 31, 'Thus you shall keep the people of Israel separate from their uncleanness, lest they die ... by defiling my tabernacle.'

16:1–34: The Day of Atonement

The Day of Atonement is the holiest day in Israel's calendar. It falls on the tenth day of the seventh month, which is about early October. Its main purpose was to cleanse the tabernacle from the pollution caused by sin and uncleanness. As already explained sin and uncleanness are conceived of as giving off a toxic vapour that pollutes holy objects such as altars and holy places in the tabernacle. If these things are not cleansed by sacrificial blood being smeared or sprinkled on them, it becomes impossible for God to dwell there (16:16, 19). Ultimately this would lead to the Israelites dying 'by defiling my tabernacle' (15:31), just as Nadab and Abihu did (16:1 cf. 10:1–3). The ceremonies of the Day of Atonement were designed to avoid this calamity being repeated.

There were three major elements to the Day of Atonement ceremonies. First, there were special sin offerings made by the high priest for himself and the people. The usual sin offerings are described in

Leviticus 4. They all involve smearing of blood on the main altar in the tabernacle courtyard or the incense altar in the holy place (see diagram on p. 75). But on the Day of Atonement the blood was taken right into the holy of holies, the innermost part of the tabernacle, where the ark was kept, and the blood was sprinkled in there (16:11–19). This cleansed it of pollution. However, this was a very dangerous operation. The tabernacle was God's earthly palace, and the holy of holies was the throne room. So it was extremely risky for a sinful high priest to enter there. He therefore had to don special clothes and enter wreathed in incense smoke, so that he did not die (16:2–4, 12–13).

The second major element of the Day of Atonement ceremonies was the so-called scapegoat ceremony. One goat was used as the people's sin-offering as described above: the other was sent away into the wilderness carrying the sins and impurities of the nation. This was done by the high priest laying his hands on the goat and confessing all the sins of the people, thereby symbolically transferring the nation's sins on to the goat. A man then drove the goat into the wilderness, so that they were removed for good (16:20–26).

The third element of the Day of Atonement was fasting by all the people. It was regarded as an ultra-strict Sabbath, when no work was done, but also a fast day when no food or water was drunk for 24 hours (16:29–31).

17:1—27:34: PRESCRIPTIONS FOR PRACTICAL HOLINESS

The last eleven chapters of Leviticus are frequently perceived as being rather different in character from the preceding chapters. These latter chapters address a much broader range of issues than Leviticus 1—16 do, with their focus on sacrifice and uncleanness: chapters 17—27, while not forgetting cultic issues, range over many moral and social issues. The frequent reminders to 'Be holy, for I the LORD your God am holy,' have led to them being dubbed the Holiness Code. However, the topics, while they may seem to be distinctly different to the modern reader from issues of sacrifice and uncleanness, were in the mind of ancient readers not so far removed. What we may view as essentially moral concerns, murder, adultery, incest, or as religious concerns, e.g. idolatry, were also issues of uncleanness. Indeed these sorts of offences constituted the very gravest causes of uncleanness. They do not simply pollute the offender and the sanctuary, they pollute the land, so that the land will

---

Digging deeper:
CLARIFYING THE ORDER OF CEREMONIES ON THE DAY OF ATONEMENT

For clarity I have simplified the outline of events on the Day of Atonement as described in Leviticus 16. Work through the chapter carefully and work out at what points the high priest changed his vestments, offered sacrifices and entered the holy of holies.

SPECTRUM OF CONDITIONS FROM HOLY TO UNCLEAN

God				
Life				Death
Holy				Unclean
Priests	Handicapped priests	Clean laity	Unclean, e.g. skin-diseased	Corpses
Sacrificial animals	Blemished sacrificial animals	Clean animals	Unclean animals	Dead animals

'vomit them out' (18:28; 20:22) or God himself will cut off the sinner (17:9, 14; 20:5), i.e. the offender will die suddenly and mysteriously. There is thus a spectrum of uncleanness from the mildest caused by natural conditions, through skin disease, to the most serious originating in sins like homicide and idolatry.

What is the connection between the uncleanness dealt with in Leviticus 11—15 and the uncleanness caused by the sins specified in Leviticus 17 onwards? Most fundamental is the association of uncleanness with death, with less than perfect life. At the other extreme God is identified with fullness of life. Thus handicapped priests may not officiate in the sanctuary, because only those enjoying completeness of health may enter the divine presence. Analogously, blemished animals may not be given to God in sacrifice (Lev. 21:17–23; 22:19–25). There is a polarity in these biblical texts between God/life at one extreme and death/sin at the other.

    God – sin
    life – death
    holiness – uncleanness

Thus murder is an assault on life, which is given by God, and therefore must be viewed as causing grave uncleanness. Similarly idolatry, which substitutes another god for the God of life, also causes serious uncleanness. Finally, sex, the God-given power to procreate life, when misused becomes a source of grave pollution. In this perspective there is not such a big jump in ideology between chapters 16 and 17 of Leviticus as sometimes perceived.

GRADES OF UNCLEANNESS

Tolerated	Punishable/Sinful
Discharges (Leviticus 12,15)	Forgotten cleansing (Numbers 5—6,19)
Skin diseases (Leviticus 13—14)	Idolatory, homicide, illicit sex (Leviticus 17—20; Numbers 35)

17:1–16: Irregular sacrifice and the consumption of blood

Here worship away from the tabernacle is banned lest it becomes a cover for worshipping other gods, such as goat demons (17:7). The ban on eating meat whose blood has not been drained away is repeated (cf. Gen. 9:3–4; and remarks on Lev. 11, pp. 91–93 above). Consuming blood shows flagrant disregard for life and so produces grave uncleanness.

18:1–30: Unlawful sexual relations

These cause such grave uncleanness that the land vomited out the Canaanites and will do the same to the Israelites if they behave similarly (18:24–28). Most attention is devoted to incest, sexual intercourse with people too closely related to each other (18:6–17), perhaps the most likely aberration in the tight-knit extended families of ancient Israel. But adultery, homosexual acts and bestiality are condemned too (18:20–23). All these actions are seen as contrary to life as designed by the creator, and therefore cause uncleanness.

19:18: Love your neighbour as yourself

This is the best-known verse in Leviticus and it well sums up the great variety of moral injunctions in chapter 19. But how do these topics relate to the idea of cleanness and holiness? Holiness is the essence of God's character which mankind is expected to emulate: 'Be holy for I am holy.' God is also perfect life, so the actions being commended here are those that are compatible with fullness of life, while those being criticized are those that conflict with these ideals. Mary Douglas (1966, pp. 53–54) has summed up the thinking behind this list well.

Developing the idea of holiness as order, not confusion, this list upholds rectitude and straight-dealing as holy, and contradiction and double-dealing as against holiness. Theft, lying, false witness, cheating in weights and measures, all kinds of dissembling such as speaking ill of the deaf (and presumably smiling to their face), hating your brother in your heart (while presumably speaking kindly to him), these are clearly contradictions between what seems and what is.

20:1–27: Punishments

Sins such as those listed in chapter 18 cause such serious uncleanness that Israel is liable to be expelled from the promised land. To avoid such a disaster, draconian human punishments are laid down to nip problems in the bud. If transgressors escape human detection and imagine they are safe, they are warned that they will not escape divine vengeance (20:5–6, 18–21).

21:1–24: Implications of holiness for priests

It is fundamental to the theology of Leviticus that holiness and uncleanness must not mix. For an unclean person to approach the holy God is to court death. Conversely holy people, such as priests, must shun uncleanness, particularly the uncleanness of corpses. This means that the ultra-holy high priest may not even attend the funeral of his parents (21:11). Ordinary priests face less severe restrictions, but again the principle that holy people should shun uncleanness is apparent (21:1–9).

22:1–33: Rules on eating when unclean

Only holy people, i.e. priests and their families, could eat holy food, i.e. the parts of sacrifices given to priests. But what happens if a priest becomes unclean, and who counts as members of a priest's household? These are the problems tackled in chapter 22. Once again the principle of keeping separate, clean and holy is vital. Thus priests must abstain from holy food as long as they suffer from uncleanness, whether it is caused by a discharge, skin disease or contact with death (22:1–9). Laity may not eat of priestly food, unless they have been fully incorporated into a priest's family, such as a slave or a widowed priest's daughter (22:10–16). Meat could only be eaten as a result of sacrifice, so the chapter closes with rules on acceptable and unacceptable animals (22:17–30).

23:1–44: The national festivals

Apart from great family events the main occasions for eating meat were at the national festivals, when all males were expected to go up to Jerusalem and offer the appropriate sacrifices. This could be the reason these regulations come at this point in the book, just after the discussion of what makes an acceptable animal for sacrifice. The focus is certainly on what the lay-person should do on these occasions. After yet another reminder of the weekly Sabbath, three festivals are mentioned and two holy days, the Feast of Trumpets and the Day of Atonement. Together with the Feast of Booths, that makes three celebrations in the seventh month, making the seventh month of the year holy, just as the seventh day of the week, the Sabbath, is holy.

24:1–9: Bread for the tabernacle

The golden lampstand and the table that stood opposite it are described in Exodus 25:23–40. On this table were placed 12 loaves of bread, symbolizing the 12 tribes of Israel basking in the light of the tree of life, which the lampstand represented. But why this detail about the bread should be placed here is obscure, unless it could be the mention of all the harvest-related festivals in chapter 23.

Nor is it clear why the episode of the blaspheming Egyptian should come here. But it is a reminder that Leviticus is essentially a narrative in which Moses is the chief actor, here not only receiving God's words but carrying them out (cf. Lev. 8—10). On the *lex talionis* (24:17–22) see Chapter 4 pp. 72–73 above.

FESTIVALS

Festival	Date	Modern Time of Year	Reference
Passover	14th–21st of first month	Easter	23:4–14
Weeks	1st of third month	Pentecost	23:15–21
Trumpets	1st of seventh month	Late September	23:24–25
Day of Atonement	10th of seventh month	September/October	23:27–32
Booths	15th–22nd of seventh month	October	23:34–43

25:1–55: Holy years

After dealing with holy days and holy weeks in chapter 23, a discussion of holy years logically follows. Exodus 23:10–11 prescribes that every seventh year the ground shall lie fallow and anything that grows be left for the poor and the wild animals to eat. Leviticus 25 develops these principles in a far-reaching way. After reaffirming the principle of a fallow year every seventh year, it institutes a jubilee or super-sabbatical year every 50 years. In the jubilee year the land enjoyed another fallow year, but those who had mortgaged their land or houses received their property back without payment. Those who had sold themselves into slavery because they were in debt were released. These arrangements were designed to prevent any family being forced into permanent destitution and the accumulation of land and property in the hands of a few rich people. In this way the nation as a whole celebrated the fact that they had once all been slaves in Egypt but the LORD had released them (25:55).

What do you think?
THE JUBILEE TODAY

Destitution through crop failure and consequent indebtedness is still a big problem in third-world countries. Slum dwellers are often destitute peasants forced off their ancestral land. How could the principle of the jubilee be applied in their situation?

26:1–46: Blessings and curses

Ancient legal texts such as treaties and law codes usually ended with a series of blessings and curses, that is promises of prosperity if the laws or treaty were observed and warnings of punishment if they were disregarded. Leviticus 26 and Deuteronomy 28 are clearly in this mould. From reading the blessings we can see what Israel most longed for in the future: good crops, victory when attacked, and the presence of God (26:3–13). The curses show what they most feared: disease, drought, famine, defeat and exile (26:14–39). Indeed their exile will give the land the sabbatical rest that the disobedience of the people denied it (26:43). In this way chapter 26 links back to chapter 25 with its advocacy of the sabbatical and jubilee years.

27:1–34: Vows

Throughout history people in distress have made promises to do something for God if he answered their prayers. In Israel these vows took the form of promising oneself, or one's children, to God's service, or pledging an animal in sacrifice (Gen. 28:20–22; Judg. 11:30–31; 1 Sam. 1:11). This chapter gives guidance about which sorts of vow can be changed, and at what cost.

THE NEW TESTAMENT AND LEVITICUS

Leviticus tells of the institution of the priesthood and the role of the high priest, who on the Day of Atonement entered through the veil to sprinkle blood on the mercy seat in the very presence of God. The Epistle to the Hebrews views Jesus as acting as the perfect high priest, entering heaven not with the blood of bulls and goats but with his own blood. And whereas the Israelite high priest had to keep on offering sacrifices and was allowed to enter the holy of holies only once a year, Jesus offered just one sacrifice and is seated at God's right hand continually making intercession for his people (4:14—10:25). The gospels also record that when Jesus died the veil of the temple separating the holy of holies from the outer shrine was torn in two from top to bottom: this too seems to imply that the death of Christ makes for easier access to God (Matt. 27:51; Mark 15:38; Luke 23:45).

The other great concern of Leviticus is the differentiation of clean and unclean, which we suggested relates to the contrast between life and death. This contrast pervades Scripture, including the New Testament e.g. John 5:24: 'Truly, truly, I say to you, whoever hears my word and believes him who sent me has eternal life. He does not come into judgement, but has passed from death to life.' It is because Jesus brings life and healing that he overrides many of the uncleanness regulations of Leviticus by touching the dead or those suffering from skin disease or discharges (e.g. Matt. 8:2–4; 9:18–31). More radical still, because the gospel invites peoples of all nations to enter God's kingdom, the food laws, which symbolized the unique status of the Jews as the only people of God, are abrogated (Matt. 15:1–28; Acts 10:1–29).

FURTHER READING

COMMENTARIES

L. L. Grabbe *Leviticus*. Sheffield: Sheffield Academic Press, 1993.

J. Milgrom *Leviticus*. Garden City: Doubleday, 1991–2001. Three long volumes by the leading expert on the book.

G. J. Wenham *The Book of Leviticus*. Grand Rapids: Eerdmans, 1979.

STUDIES OF THE RITUAL SYSTEM

M. Douglas *Purity and Danger*. London: Routledge and Kegan Paul, 1966. Contains the very influential chapter 'The Abominations of Leviticus'.

M. Douglas *Implicit Meanings*. London: Routledge and Kegan Paul, 1975.

M. Douglas *Leviticus as Literature*. Oxford: Oxford University Press, 1999.

E. Feldman *Biblical and Post-Biblical Defilement and Mourning: Law as Theology*. New York: Yeshiva University Press, 1977. Shows the importance of death in biblical thought.

W. Houston *Purity and Danger: Clean and Unclean Animals in Biblical Law*. Sheffield: JSOT Press, 1993.

P. P. Jenson *Graded Holiness: A Key to the Priestly Conception of the World*. Sheffield: JSOT Press, 1992.

J. Klawans *Impurity and Sin in Ancient Judaism*. Oxford: Oxford University Press, 2000.

V. W. Turner *The Ritual Process*. London: Routledge and Kegan Paul, 1969.

M. Wilson *American Anthropologist* 56, 1934, p. 242 quoted by Turner 1969, p. 6.

D. P. Wright 'Unclean and Clean (OT)' *ABD 6*, New York: Doubleday, 1992. pp. 729–41.

STUDIES OF SACRIFICE

N. Kiuchi *The Purification Offering in the Priestly Literature*. Sheffield: JSOT Press, 1987. Tightly argued study.

J. H. Kurtz *Sacrificial Worship of the Old Testament*. tr. by J. Martin, Edinburgh: T & T Clark, 1863. Old-fashioned but comprehensive and sensible.

SACRIFICES: AN OVERVIEW (Completed, see p. 87)

Name of Sacrifice	Types of Animal	Hand-laying	Use of Blood	Priestly Portions	Lay Portions
Burnt	Cattle, sheep, goats, birds	Yes	Poured on altar sides	No	No
Peace	Cattle, sheep, goats	Yes	Poured on altar sides	Yes	Yes
Sin	Cattle, sheep, goats, birds	Yes	Smeared on altars, sprinkled inside tent	Yes, usually	No
Guilt	Rams	Probably	Poured on altar sides	Yes	No

Chapter 6

NUMBERS

Humour and magic, messianic prophecy and laws about worship are not what a reader would expect to find in a book called Numbers, a title which like those of the other books of the Pentateuch originated with the Septuagint, the Greek translation of the Old Testament. Its Hebrew title 'In the Wilderness' is not much more illuminating, though it does aptly describe Israel's situation throughout the narrative. Once again the old sub-title 'the Fourth Book of Moses' is most fitting, as it covers the last 40 years of his life journeying from Sinai to Mount Nebo, where he will give his farewell sermons to the nation, which are recorded in Deuteronomy. There he will die, overlooking the promised land but denied entry to it.

Numbers is most similar to Exodus, in that both books mix plenty of narrative with legal material, and both clearly form part of a biography of Moses. Both books also tell of a major crisis, which threatens the future survival of the nation: in Exodus this is the golden calf episode, in Numbers it is the unbelief of the spies. In both cases it is the intercession of Moses that leads God to relent of his threat to destroy Israel. Both books end optimistically: Exodus with the erection of the tabernacle and its filling with the divine glory as a pledge of God's ongoing presence with Israel, Numbers with the prophecies of Balaam predicting Israel's security in the land and with the laws about festivals and land inheritance confirming where the nation's future lies. There is only one cloud in the sky as the book ends: Moses' imminent death outside Canaan, from which he is excluded because of his unbelief at Meribah.

STRUCTURE

Unlike Genesis and Leviticus, whose structure is clearly marked by recurring formulae, Numbers runs on as a continuous narrative, so that it is not clear exactly how it should be divided. Traditionally commentators have split it into three parts based on the geographical setting of each part of the narrative.

Part 1   1:1—10:10: Near Sinai
Part 2   10:11—22:1: Near Kadesh
Part 3   22:2—36:13: In the Plains of Moab

STRUCTURE OF NUMBERS

Law-giving	Sinai	(Exodus 19:1)—Numbers 10:10
Journey	Sinai to Kadesh	Numbers 10:11—12:16
Law-giving	Kadesh	Numbers 13:1—19:22
Journey	Kadesh to Plains of Moab	Numbers 20:1—22:1
Law-giving	Plains of Moab	Numbers 22:2—36:13

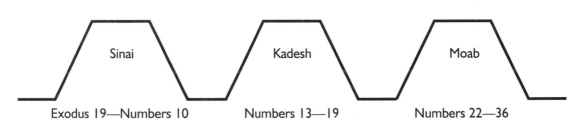

Sinai	Kadesh	Moab
Exodus 19—Numbers 10	Numbers 13—19	Numbers 22—36

Figure 5: **ARRANGEMENT OF MATERIAL IN EXODUS IN RELATION TO NUMBERS**

A variation on this schema is to see Numbers as structured like the preceding two books with sections of law-giving linked by accounts of journeys in between – see the 'Structure of Numbers' table. Graphically this table may be illustrated as shown in Figure 5.

Recently Olson (1996) has suggested that the book of Numbers falls into two halves: chapters 1—25 tells of the generation of Israelites who died in the wilderness, while chapters 26—36 of those who entered the land. He draws the parallels between the two halves shown in the 'Two halves of Numbers' table.

What do you think?
THE STRUCTURE OF NUMBERS

What do you think about the structure of Numbers? Which of the suggestions about structure given here fits the contents of the book best? Consider how much of the material fits into the proposed schemes naturally and how much must be left out because it does not fit.

TWO HALVES OF NUMBERS

Censuses	Chapters 1—4	Chapter 26
Laws about women	5:11–31	27:1–11
Laws on vows	6:1–21	Chapter 30
Laws about offerings	Chapter 15	Chapters 28—29
List of spies/land-distributors	13:4–16	34:17–29

THE CONTENTS OF NUMBERS

1:1—10:10	**Israel prepares to enter the promised land**	
1:1—4:49	Censuses	
5:1—6:27	Cleansing the camp	
7:1–89	Offerings for the altar	
8:1–26	Dedication of the Levites	
9:1–23	The second Passover	
10:1–10	The silver trumpets	
10:11—12:16	**Journey from Sinai to Kadesh**	
10:11–36	Departure in battle order	
11:1—12:16	Three complaints	
13:1—19:22	**Forty years near Kadesh**	
13:1—14:45	The rebellion of the spies	
15:1–41	Laws on offerings	
16:1—18:32	Prerogatives of the priests	
19:1–22	Laws on cleansing	
20:1—22:1	**Journey from Kadesh to the Plains of Moab**	
22:1—36:13	**In the Plains of Moab**	
22:1—24:25	Balaam and Balak	
25:1–18	National apostasy	
26:1–65	Census	
27:1—30:16	Laws about land, offerings and vows	
31:1—32:42	Defeat of Midian and settlement in Transjordan	
33:1–49	List of camp sites	
33:50—36:13	Laws about land	

1:1–46: The first census

The two censuses in chapters 1 and 26 prompted the Greek translators to call this book Numbers. Although superficially similar, they in fact serve different purposes. Here the focus is on the imminent campaign to conquer Canaan, so the census serves to list all men aged 20 or over 'able to go to war'. After the victories in Transjordan described in chapter 21 the narrative takes for granted that Canaan will be conquered, so that the purpose of the second census is to see how much land ought to be allotted to each tribe.

1:47—4:49: The duties of the Levites

The Levites were the religious tribe in ancient Israel and one clan of the Levites were the priests, who offered sacrifice. The other Levites had a dual function: on the one hand they acted as religious police preventing unauthorized laity entering the tent of meeting, on the other they were responsible for dismantling, carrying, and re-erecting the tabernacle whenever it moved. This was a highly responsible and dangerous task. As we saw

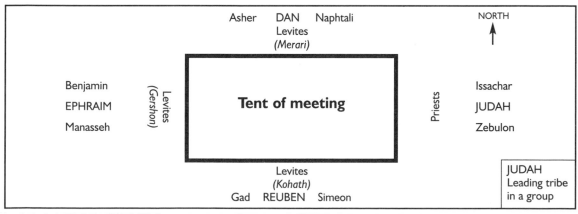

Figure 6: **ISRAEL IN CAMP**

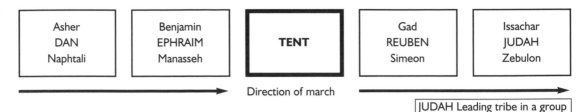

Figure 7: **ISRAEL ON THE MARCH**

in Leviticus, accidental contact between the holy divine world and the unclean human world must be avoided at all costs. Should it occur, God's anger would be visited on the transgressors and they might die. The Levites are charged with preventing this happening by camping between the tent of meeting and the tribes, see Figure 6.

The priests guard the eastern end of the tent of meeting, where its entrance is. On

---

FURTHER REFLECTION ON THE CENSUS RESULTS

According to the first census there were 603,550 warriors in Israel over 20 years old (Num. 1:46). The total in the second census is similar (26:51).

Assuming an equal number of females, and perhaps as many under 20 as over 20 years old, the total Israelite population implied by the census must have been about two million.

This everyone agrees is an unlikely number. The present population of Bedouin in the Sinai Peninsula is about 5,000, and it is estimated that before modern methods of agriculture the land of Canaan could have supported at most one million people. Yet Exodus 23:29–30 observes that there are too few Israelites to occupy the land.

Various explanations of these large figures have been put forward including:

a) They represent the figures of a later period, perhaps the time of David.

b) The numbers now read as thousands, originally meant clan or family, so the original total should come to between 5,500 and 72,000 depending on how the figures were misinterpreted.

c) The numbers are symbolic. Links with Babylonian mathematics or astronomy have been proposed to explain how the figures were generated. However, the symbolic meaning of the numbers is not clear on this interpretation.

It is very difficult to know which, if any, of these interpretations is right: the evidence is inconclusive. But whatever the historical truth behind these numbers, in their present context they surely point to the fulfilment of the promise to Abraham that his offspring would be as numerous as the dust of the earth and the stars of heaven (Gen. 13:16; 15:5). This partial fulfilment of the patriarchal promise should have given the Israelites confidence that the land promise would also be fulfilled.

the march the Levites were entrusted with carrying the different components of the tabernacle, with six tribes marching ahead of them and six marching after them. See Figure 7.

5:1—6:27: Cleansing the camp

One of the chief duties of the Levites was to prevent unauthorized people intruding into the holy area surrounding the tabernacle (1:51; 3:10). As we saw in studying Leviticus holiness and uncleanness must never mix (see pp. 91–94). If that happened the whole enterprise of the holy LORD travelling in the midst of his people Israel to the promised land would be put in jeopardy. So the next two chapters of Numbers are concerned not just with preventing intrusion, but with eliminating sources of pollution among the people.

First, clear cases of uncleanness must be removed. Leviticus 12—15 spells out what conditions make people unclean. Anyone suffering in this way was made to live outside the main camp, presumably in separate tents (5:1–4), until he or she recovered. Other risks to national purity could be caused by unresolved disputes over property (5:5–10). Adultery, like murder and idolatry, caused the most severe form of uncleanness, so even the suspicion of adultery had to be cleared up. Numbers 5:11–31 provides a rite designed to put an end to any such suspicion.

Death, particularly human death, is again a source of severe uncleanness, so another possible area of risk is dealt with in chapter 6. Nazirites were the holiest lay people in ancient Israel, the Old Testament equivalent of monks and nuns. To become a Nazirite you took a vow to abstain from all forms of alcohol or grape products and never cut your hair (Samson is the best known Nazirite in the Bible, more distinguished for breaking his vows than keeping them! see Judg. 13—16). Numbers 6 deals with the situation that would occur if such a holy person did become polluted through accidental contact with death and what must be done to remedy the situation (6:6–12).

Chapters 5—6 are thus concerned with dealing with actual, suspected or potential cases of uncleanness in Israel. They demonstrate with what seriousness it was taken: failure to preserve the purity of the nation could lead to God abandoning them and their never reaching the promised land. Such strictness could lead to the conclusion that God was not well disposed to Israel. So the chapter concludes with the famous priestly blessing, which sets out his comprehensive love for Israel:

> The LORD bless you and keep you;
> The LORD make his face to shine upon you and be gracious to you;
> The LORD lift up his countenance upon you and give you peace (Num. 6:24–26).

In the Hebrew each line is longer than the preceding: three words in the first, five in the second, and seven in the third. It consists of 15 words in total, three being God's name the LORD, and 12 others, perhaps one for each of the 12 tribes. It concludes with a promise of peace.

Beyond the imminent struggle for the land God's ultimate purpose for Israel is peace, security and prosperity.

Digging deeper:
ANCIENT VERSIONS OF THE PRIESTLY BLESSING

The priestly blessing has been found engraved on two silver amulets found in Jerusalem. They date from about 600 BC, which makes them the oldest texts from the OT yet discovered and indicates the popularity of this blessing. The first line may also be quoted in an inscription from Kuntillet Ajrud (in the northern Sinai) dated about 800 BC.

Its popularity is also indicated by echoes of it in the Psalms, especially in the Psalms of ascents (120—134) and Psalm 67. See what echoes of the blessing you can find in these Psalms. Start with Psalms 67 and 121, looking out for important words like bless, keep, face, peace, the LORD, etc.

7:1—8:26: Dedication of tabernacle furnishings and personnel

The story now includes a flashback to events a month earlier, when the tabernacle was first erected. This records how the secular tribes gave the Levites wagons to transport the tabernacle in, and how each tribe presented utensils and animals for use in worship. Each tribe gives exactly the same. This stresses the equal standing of each tribe and their joint responsibility to support worship in the tabernacle.

Then the rites for the dedication of the Levites are described (8:5–26). These are much less complicated than the procedures for the ordination of the priests (see Lev. 8—9). Throughout this section Moses' role as mediator of God's requirements and executor of his will continues to be stressed. The people do exactly what God asks them through the agency of Moses.

9:1—10:10: Ready to go

This stress on the exact compliance with God's instructions continues in chapters 9 and 10. The anniversary of the exodus from Egypt is celebrated in the Passover: this festival *par excellence* had last been celebrated just before they left Egypt. Now and in the future its celebration will commemorate the past. Its mention here implicitly reminds the reader of the intended destination of the Israelites: not Sinai, not the desert, but the land of Canaan. But although it is of the utmost importance to celebrate Passover, for sudden death may befall those who fail to observe it (9:13), uncleanness caused by death is an insuperable obstacle to worship. So those who are unclean must delay their celebration by a month (9:1–14).

These measures ensure God's continued goodwill towards his people, indicated by the pillar of fire hovering over the tabernacle by day and night (9:15–23). With the manufacture of the silver trumpets to summon Israel to break camp and move on, everything is in place to journey from Sinai to Canaan (10:1–10).

10:11–36: A hopeful start

The journey from Sinai to Kadesh begins brilliantly. Just a year after leaving Egypt the Israelites are on their way to the promised land, marching exactly as prescribed in chapters 2—4. Their complete obedience is rewarded by the cloud of the LORD accompanying them on the route (10:33–36). Everything bodes well.

11:1—12:16: Three complaints

But abruptly this optimism is shattered. Three stories tell of different groups complaining about Moses' leadership and the difficulties of the journey. The first and shortest complaint is typical of all three and includes four elements: first, the people's complaint (11:1); second, God's anger and judgement (11:1); third, Moses' intercession (11:2); fourth, naming the place (11:3).

Digging deeper:
PARALLELS IN COMPLAINT STORIES

Read the next two complaint stories in 11:4—12:16 and see how the four elements found in 11:1–3 appear in them.

Complaints by the Israelites form a regular feature of the journeys in the Pentateuch. In this section of Numbers there are clear parallels with the journey from the Red Sea to Sinai: the same topics and characters reappear.

Clearly readers are expected both to remember the earlier incidents in Exodus as they read Numbers and to compare them. It is quite obvious in several of these incidents that things have deteriorated from Exodus to Numbers. In Exodus

PARALLELS BETWEEN EXODUS AND NUMBERS

Miriam's song of praise	Exodus 15:20–21	Miriam and Aaron rebel	Numbers 12
Three-day journey to Sinai	Exodus 15:22	Three-day journey from Sinai	Numbers 10:33
Complaint about water	Exodus 15:22–26	Complaint unspecified	Numbers 11:1–3
Manna and quail	Exodus 16	Manna and quail	Numbers 11:4–15, 31–35
Water from rock	Exodus 17:1–7	Water from rock	Numbers 20:1–13
Advice from Moses' father-in-law	Exodus 18:1	Advice from Moses' father-in-law	Numbers 10:29
Leaders appointed to assist Moses	Exodus 18	Leaders appointed to assist Moses	Numbers 11:16–30
Israel defeats Amalek	Exodus 17:8–16	Israel defeated by Amalek	Numbers 14:39–45

15:20–21 Miriam is praising God, but in Numbers 12 she is leading a protest against Moses. In Exodus 17 Amalek attacks Israel and Israel defeats them, but in Numbers 14 it is the other way round. More intriguing are the different treatments of the complaints about food and water in Exodus and Numbers. In Exodus, though the people are ticked off for complaining, they are not punished for their behaviour: the LORD sends the manna and the quails in Exodus 16 and there are no dire after-effects, but in Numbers 11:33 we read 'While the meat was yet between their teeth ... the anger of the LORD was kindled against the people, and the LORD struck down the people with a very great plague.' Similarly there are no long-term consequences in Exodus 17 after Moses brings water from the rock, but in Numbers 20 he is condemned to exclusion from the land.

> **What do you think?**
> **WHY WERE LATER COMPLAINTS TREATED MORE HARSHLY?**
>
> Why should the complaints in Numbers have been treated more severely than those in Exodus? Were the complaints any worse in Numbers? What had happened between Exodus 19 and Numbers 10? Could this have affected God's attitude?

Miriam and Aaron's complaint deserves special consideration, if the Pentateuch is a biography of Moses. Though we might be tempted to dismiss it as just a case of family bitchiness, that is not the perspective of the author. He regards it as a full-blooded challenge to Moses' role as intermediary between God and Israel. He is not just a prophet, but one with whom God speaks 'mouth to mouth'. He even 'beholds the form of God' (12:8). This sets him apart from every other prophet. These points have already been made before (Exod. 33:7–23), but their reaffirmation here and at the end of the Pentateuch underlines Moses' unique status (Deut. 34:10–12).

Miriam's skin disease (cf. Lev. 13) and Aaron's prayer for her and for himself are almost incidental to the story, but they serve as a reminder that even those closest to Moses are susceptible to sin and therefore liable to judgement. It will not be long before Moses too stumbles and forfeits his right to enter Canaan.

13:1—14:45: The spies

Arriving at Kadesh-Barnea (see maps 2 and 3, pp. 65 and 119) the Israelites had reached the southern border of Canaan as defined in Numbers 34:4. They will very shortly enter the promised land. At God's command a man from each tribe is sent out to spy out the land. They return with a glowing account of its wealth and fertility, but claim it will be impossible to conquer. This of course is a direct contradiction of the age-old promise to Abraham that his descendants would inherit the land, and a denial of the whole purpose of the exodus from Egypt. Indeed they say 'Let us choose a leader and go back to Egypt' (14:4). This precipitates the greatest crisis in the national history since the golden calf episode of Exodus 32.

It prompts God to threaten to annihilate Israel and start again with Moses (14:12 cf. Exod. 32:10). Once again it is Moses' intercession on behalf of Israel that leads God to relent and to pardon Israel (14:20). But as elsewhere in the Pentateuch forgiveness does not mean exemption from punishment, but its reduction. The ten faithless spies die in a plague, and the people who had expressed the wish to die in the wilderness (14:2) do eventually die there (14:32; 26:64–65). Only their children, who they said would die in the conquest of Canaan, will enter it (14:3, 31), but not until they have wandered for 40 years in the wilderness.

Ever afterwards these experiences were looked back upon and retold to warn later generations not to make the mistake their fathers did (e.g. Deut. 1:19–40; Ps. 95:10–11; 106:24–27).

Digging deeper:
THE SPIES AND THE GOLDEN CALF

Make a comparison of the golden calf story (Exodus 32—34) with the spy story (Numbers 13—14). What features do they have in common and how do they differ?

Why?

15:1–41: Laws that give hope
After being sentenced to 40 years in the wilderness and being defeated by the Amalekites, Israel could have concluded that they were doomed. But these laws specifying what sacrifices must be offered,

'when you come into the land you are to inhabit' (15:2, 18), are a reassurance about the nation's future. It lies in Canaan, and there they will be able to offer all manner of lavish sacrifices, bulls, rams, lambs, flour, oil and wine. It will in other words prove to be the land flowing with milk and honey.

Sacrifice will be necessary there to atone for unintentional sin. But deliberate sin, as illustrated by the episodes of the spies and the Sabbath breaker (15:32–36), will be punished. As a constant reminder of their duty to keep the law, all Israelites must wear tassels on their clothes so that they do not follow after their own heart and eyes (15:39).

Figure 8: **SCALLOPED LOINCLOTH**

111

Digging deeper:
ARCHAEOLOGY AND THE TASSELS

Paintings and sculptures from the ancient Near East portray nobles with tassels on their clothes. The OT adopts the idea and encourages everyone to have tassels.

The blue or violet strand within the tassel is the colour of heaven and is also used in priestly vestments: it reminded the Israelites that they were called to be a kingdom of priests and a holy nation (Exod. 19:6). Jesus wore tassels (Matt. 9:20), and some Jews still do.

16:1—18:32: More leadership challenges

The reassurance that Israel will eventually reach Canaan is soon eclipsed by further challenges to the leadership of Moses and the priests. First, there is a two-pronged assault led by the Levite Korah on the high priesthood of Aaron, and by Dathan and Abiram on the leadership of of Moses. This collapses when the ground opens under their feet and swallows them up (16:1–35).

This prompts a mass protest the next day by all the leading men of the community against Moses and Aaron. This leads to another outbreak of the plague in divine judgement on them, which is only stopped by Aaron rushing in and offering incense. This proof of the value and efficacy of the priesthood is followed the next day by the test of their staffs being placed overnight near the ark (17:7). Evidently each tribal chief had such a staff. Miraculously in one night Aaron's sprouts, flowers and produces almonds. This makes all the

people realize the necessity of priests if they are to survive. They cry out, 'Behold we perish ... we are all undone. Everyone who comes near ... to the tabernacle of the LORD, shall die' (17:12–13).

This demonstration that only priests should approach God leads into chapter 18, which summarizes the duties and income of the priests and Levites. The Levites' role as guardians of the tabernacle preventing unauthorized persons from entry is reaffirmed (18:1–7). Then the income of the priests from sacrifices and new-born animals is set out (18:8–20). The Levites receive tithes in acknowledgement of their service in guarding the tabernacle and thereby protecting the people from God's wrath. More precisely they are given a tithe of all agricultural produce, from which they in turn give a tithe to the priests (18:21–32).

19:1–22: The red cow rite

Death, as we noted in discussing Leviticus, causes the worst form of uncleanness. Those who come near to God must be free of all pollution. But in the last few chapters people from every walk of life have died, and the whole community has been polluted. It is possible to deal with such pollution by offering a sin offering (see Lev. 4), but that is expensive and complicated. Here an instant sin offering is provided instead. By burning a red cow, cedar-wood, hyssop, and scarlet yarn, all of which have atoning properties, special ash is created. When mixed with water, another cleansing agent, the ash can be sprinkled on people to purify them from corpse pollution.

20:1—22:1: The final journey

Within the Pentateuch the journey from Egypt to Canaan falls into three stages: Egypt to Sinai (Exod. 12:37—19:1), Sinai to Kadesh (Num. 10:11—12:16), and Kadesh to the Plains of Moab (Num. 20:1—22:1). It is the final stage of the journey not just for the Israelites, but in another sense for Miriam and Aaron as well, who die during this part of the journey. Miriam's death is briefly recorded in 20:1.

The next episode (20:2–13) resembles in a number of ways the episode much earlier at Meribah (Exod. 17:1–7), when Moses struck the rock to bring water out of it for the people. Then, apart from a few sharp words, everything ended sweetly. This time it ends with Aaron and Moses being sentenced to die outside the land of promise (20:12). Why? What is the difference that leads to such a harsh outcome for Israel's leaders?

The answer is not obvious and many suggestions have been made. The retort of Moses and Aaron, 'Hear now, you rebels: shall we bring water for you out of this rock?' (20:10) could be interpreted as arrogance on Moses and Aaron's part: are they suggesting they have power that belongs only to God? Thus it may be that there is something in their words that led to their condemnation. Later on (20:24), God says Aaron rebelled at Meribah. Rebellion suggests disobedience, and indeed a careful reading of the story shows that Aaron and Moses did not obey God exactly. He told them to take the staff and speak to the rock, whereas Moses

struck the rock twice. Though this may seem a minor deviation, the leaders of Israel were meant to be scrupulous in exact obedience to the law and God's instructions. Leviticus 10:1–2 tells of two sons of Aaron dying for offering unauthorized fire. Now father and uncle make a similar mistake. Clearly the Pentateuch is anxious to encourage exact compliance with its laws.

Aaron's death is recorded in 20:22–29. Then follows the first of several victories over the Canaanites, who lived in the south of the promised land, and over the Amorites, who lived east of the Jordan (21:1–3, 21–35). These victories heralded

Digging deeper:
THE BRONZE SNAKE IN THE TIMNAH TEMPLE

A few miles north of Eilat lies Timnah where there were copper mines in Bible times. In an abandoned Egyptian temple at Timnah Israeli archaeologists found that Midianites had erected a tent shrine in the twelfth century BC. One of the items in this shrine was a copper snake, 5 inches (12 cm) long. Its purpose is obscure and it cannot be the Israelite bronze serpent. Nevertheless the archaeologists were intrigued by the coincidence that they had found a tent shrine with a copper serpent in the area, where according to the book of Numbers, the Israelites had wandered with similar objects perhaps about a century earlier. Had perhaps the Midianites seen the Israelite shrine and bronze serpent?

the promised campaign to conquer Canaan itself and panicked the king of Moab to look for supernatural protection from the Israelites. This forms the topic of the next three chapters (22—24), the story of Balak and Balaam.

But there is one last occasion of grumbling about food described in 21:4–9, a topic which also occurs in the other journey passages (Exod. 16; Num. 12). This time they are not punished by plague but by an attack of deadly snakes. Once again it is Moses' prayer that saves the people. In reply to his prayer God tells him to make a bronze serpent, and put it on a pole, so that anyone bitten by a snake could look at it and be healed.

22:2—36:13: Israel in the Plains of Moab
The alternation of journeys and places of encampment in Exodus to Numbers ends here. The first journey took Israel from Egypt to Sinai: the encampment there is described in Exodus 19 to Numbers 10. The second journey took the people from Sinai to Kadesh: the Kadesh story fills Numbers 13—19. The third and final journey brings the people to the Plains of Moab for their last encampment before crossing the Jordan into Canaan proper. Each encampment seems to include similar sorts of events: law giving, promises about the future, apostasy and judgement. All of them look for the fulfilment of the promises made to the patriarchs, but in these closing chapters of Numbers hope burns particularly brightly.

Nowhere in the book are the promises endorsed so emphatically as in the

prophecies of Balaam (chs 23—24). But they are preceded by one of the funniest tales in the Bible, which almost looks as if it is designed to send up Balaam, not add credibility to his message!

Balaam, the most famous diviner in the Middle East of his day, lived at Pethor in Syria, 400 miles (600 km) north of Moab. So when Balak, the king of Moab, saw the Israelites swamping the Plains of Moab just to the east of the Dead Sea, he sent for Balaam hoping that he would destroy Israel by cursing them. Balaam showed some initial reluctance to come, saying that he could go only if God gave him permission, but hinting that he would really like a higher fee! But God holds him to his word, permitting him to go only if he says exactly what God tells him. This insistence that Balaam utters only the words that God gives him underlines the inspiration and authority of Balaam's visions of Israel's future. The same point is made by the comic story of Balaam's donkey ride. Here we have the best diviner of his time unable to see an angel, but his donkey can! If God can make himself known to a donkey and make it

Digging deeper:
BALAAM AND HIS DONKEY

The table opposite is based on an analysis of recurring phrases, words, and ideas. Examine the story yourself and see how many key words or repeated phrases you can find, which support or contradict the outline given in the table.

speak, how much more is he able to make a money-grubbing pagan prophet declare the future!

The section is tightly structured to fall into two sections each containing an introduction and three scenes.

SCENES IN THE BALAAM STORY

22:2–6	Introduction
22:7–14	Balaam's first encounter with God
22:15–20	Balaam's second encounter with God
22:21–35	Balaam's third encounter with God 22–23: Donkey and angel 1 24–25: Donkey and angel 2 26–35: Donkey and angel 3
22:36–40	Introduction
22:41—23:12	Balaam's first blessing of Israel
23:13–26	Balaam's second blessing of Israel
23:27—24:25	Balaam's third blessing of Israel 3–9: Blessing part 1 15–19: Blessing part 2 20–24: Blessing part 3

All the focus in this section is on Balaam's blessings, for as the narrative keeps underlining, they represent exactly what God told him to say. Furthermore they are essentially an expansion of the promises made to Abraham in Genesis. (Look back at Genesis 12:1–3 to remind yourself of their exact wording.)

The promise to Abraham involved four elements. 1) A promise of numerous descendants: this is the key idea in Balaam's first oracle (see 23:10). 2) A promise of divine blessing and protection: this is reflected in Balaam's second oracle (see 23:21–23). 3) A promise of land: this

Digging deeper:
BALAAM OUTSIDE THE BIBLE

In 1967 parts of a text mentioning Balaam were found at Deir Alla, a place in Transjordan a little north of where the Israelites camped in the Plains of Moab. The text dates from about 800 BC, that is some 500 years after the exodus. It is hard to interpret, so it does not shed any real light on the biblical story. However, in both the Bible and this text, Balaam appears to be a seer with whom the gods can communicate. He can avert divine wrath by his mediation. In both sets of text he refers to God as El (God) and as Shadday (Almighty).

Here is a tentative translation of part of this text in which Balaam tells his dream foretelling a drought on the land.

> This is the account of Balaam, son of Beor, who was a seer of the gods.
> The gods came to him in the night, and he saw a vision according to the oracle of El. Then they spoke to Balaam son of Beor: 'This he will do ... in the future ...' And Balaam rose on the next day ... and he wept bitterly. And his people came up to him and said to him, 'Balaam, son of Beor, why do you fast and weep?' And he said to them: 'Sit down and I shall relate to you what the *shaddayin* are going to do.' (from Milgrom 1990, p. 474)

is the central topic of the first part of the third oracle (see 24:5–7). 4) A promise of blessing to the nations: this is the implication of the Israelite king promised in 24:16–17. He will bring peace to the warring nations, who threaten both Israel and each other (24:18–24).

25:1–18: National apostasy

While God's words are being proclaimed by Balaam on the mountain tops overlooking the Plains of Moab, down on the Plains the Israelites are whoring after other gods. The whole situation is reminiscent of the Golden Calf episode: when Moses was up Mount Sinai receiving the tablets of the law, down at the foot of the mountain the people were making and worshipping the golden calf. This is not the only similarity though.

FURTHER PARALLELS BETWEEN EXODUS AND NUMBERS

People sacrifice to other gods	Exodus 32:6	Numbers 25:2
Killing of apostates demanded	Exodus 32:27	Numbers 25:5
Levites' (Phinehas's) status enhanced	Exodus 32:28–29	Numbers 25:6–13
Plague on the people	Exodus 32:35	Numbers 25:9

These parallels suggest the people have learnt very little from their previous mistakes. But perhaps there is a glimmer of hope, in that Aaron was ringleader in the Golden Calf episode but his grandson Phinehas is exemplary in his loyalty in the Plains of Moab.

26:1–65: The second census

This offers another ray of hope. Despite the death of so many, indeed of nearly the entire generation that came out of Egypt, the total this time (601,730) is almost the same as in the first census (603,550). The catastrophic fall in the Simeonite numbers (59,300 (1:23) to 22,200 (26:14)) may reflect their leading involvement in the apostasy at Peor (25:14). Another encouraging change of focus is in the purpose of the census: it is designed to ascertain the size of the tribes so that each tribe may be given an area appropriate to its size (26:53–56). Entry to the land is now taken for granted.

27:1—29:40: Land and festivals

The same positive message emerges from the laws on land inheritance, festivals and vows in chapters 27—30. The daughters of Zelophehad raise the issue of female inheritance precisely because they anticipate the imminent conquest and distribution of the land (ch. 27). Similarly the calendar of festivals and the enormous number of sacrifices that they involve presuppose that the Israelites will soon be in the land enjoying an abundance of agricultural produce (chs 28—29). These chapters set out what the priests must offer on behalf of the nation, and to these regular sacrifices must be added all the offerings brought by lay people. In a single year the priests should offer 113 bulls, 32 rams, 1086 lambs, a ton of flour and a thousand bottles of wine and oil! These laws, like those in Numbers 15, are an implicit promise of entry into and great prosperity in the land.

These calendars serve not just as index of Israel's anticipated wealth but also of the relative importance of the different festivals.

ANIMAL SACRIFICES

Occasion		Bulls	Rams	Lambs	Goats
Daily (28:3–8)				2	
Sabbath (28:9–10)				4	
1st of Month (28:11–15)		2	1	9	1
Passover/Unleavened Bread (28:16–25)		2	1	9	1
Pentecost/Feast of Weeks (28:26–31)		2	1	9	1
1st Day of 7th Month (29:1–6)		3	2	16	1
Day of Atonement (29:7–11)		1	1	9	2
Tabernacles (29:12–38)	Day 1	13	2	16	1
	Day 2	12	2	16	1
	Day 3	11	2	16	1
	Day 4	10	2	16	1
	Day 5	9	2	16	1
	Day 6	8	2	16	1
	Day 7	7	2	16	1
	Day 8	1	1	9	1

30:1–16: Rules on vows

As already noted, the sacrifices listed above were offered by the priests. But lay-men were expected to attend the three great national festivals of Passover, Pentecost and Tabernacles. They would often be accompanied by other members of the

> **Digging deeper:**
> **FESTIVALS AND THEIR IMPORTANCE**
>
> Look at the table of animal sacrifices and consider what it shows about the importance of different festivals and different seasons in the year. How does that relate to other passages dealing with these festivals? (Look at Exod. 12—13; Exod. 23:14–18; Lev. 16; Lev. 23; Deut. 16.)

family and might offer their own sacrifices at the temple. They might well do this because they had made a vow, perhaps pledging a sacrifice if they recovered from illness or had a baby (e.g. 1 Sam. 1). If this happened it was essential that the vow be carried out. If a man made a vow, he could never go back on it. The same rule applied to a woman, unless her father or husband objected as soon as he heard about the vow. The Old Testament elsewhere underlines the importance of fulfilling vows (Deut. 23:21–23; Eccl. 5:4–6). Israel's entry to the promised land depended on God fulfilling his vow to Abraham, so Israel must be similarly punctilious about fulfilling her vows.

31:1—32:42: Defeat of Midian and settlement of Transjordan

The national apostasy at Peor involved two parties: Israel and Midianite Moabites. The sentence passed on Israel was that all the Israelite males and their leaders should be executed, and some 24,000 died in a plague (25:9). Chapter 31 records how the Midianites now suffer similarly, though this judgement is carried out by Israel herself at God's command mediated by Moses (31:1–2). Here is the first example of the holy war, a topic of great importance in Deuteronomy.

But the description of the battle is brief compared to the account of its aftermath. What really interests Numbers is the necessity of cleansing the warriors and the booty they have amassed. Although the war was mandated by God, the death of the enemy polluted the Israelite fighters, who had to undergo a week's cleansing ceremony before they re-entered the camp (31:19–24). The fighters bring some of the booty to make atonement for themselves (31:50). It is as if the text is saying, 'War, however just the cause, is incompatible with God's creative life-giving character. It may be necessary, but it is still evil.'

The request of the tribes of Reuben and Gad (ch. 32) to settle in Transjordan in the territories that had belonged to the Amorites (see map 3, p. 119, and ch. 21) is initially seen by Moses as another potential disaster. The area they requested lies outside the borders of the promised land set out in chapter 34, so their request reminded him of the episode with the spies, when the whole nation had bunked out of the conquest of Canaan (32:6–15 cf. chs 13—14). However, the Reubenites and Gadites assure Moses that they will send their fighting men to help with the campaign in Canaan. This satisfies him, and he allocates the land to them.

In chapters 31—32 we are given a foretaste of the future conquest of Canaan. In the battle against the Midianites, not a single Israelite was lost. The tribes of

Reuben and Gad have been allocated land to settle in. If Israel can enjoy such success outside the land of promise, how much more certain is the conquest of Canaan itself. This is the message of these closing chapters of Numbers.

This confidence is underlined by the list in chapter 33 of encampments between Egypt and the Plains of Moab. It is a condensed review of the great moments in Israel's experience of God in the preceding 40 years, including the exodus, the provision of water and food, the law-giving, and the victory at Hormah. If God has brought Israel this far, he surely will take them into the land. But let them be careful not to make the mistake they made at their last camp site in the Plains of Moab and adopt their pagan worship. If Israel does compromise on this, they will find themselves losing the land (33:56).

34:1–15: The borders of Canaan

After so much talk about the promised land of Canaan, what are its actual borders? Numbers 34 gives us the most precise definition anywhere in the Old Testament. The southern part comprises everything between the Jordan River and the Mediterranean, but the northern area is a little harder to define, as we do not know where all the places on the border are. The map opposite shows the probable limits. This definition seems to correspond to the Egyptian understanding of the boundaries of Canaan in texts from the fifteenth to thirteenth centuries BC. But Israel did not manage to conquer this whole area: it remained an aspiration not a reality.

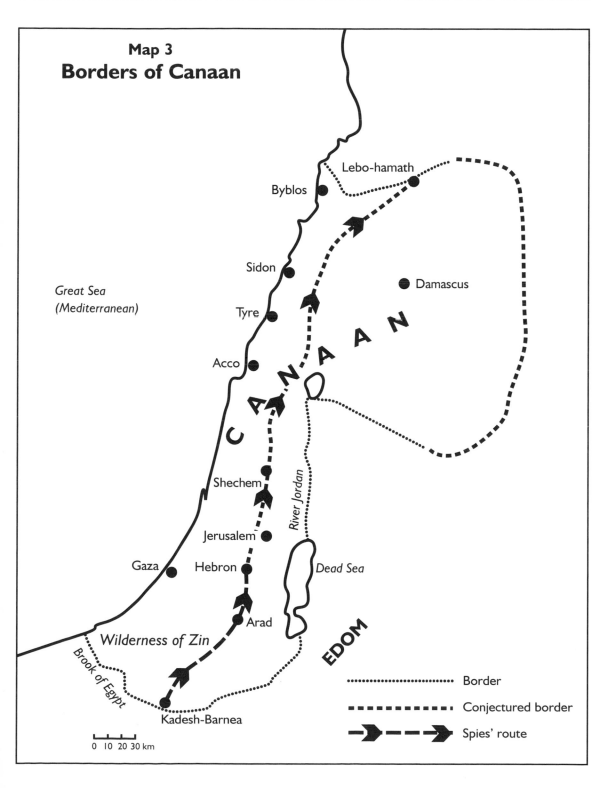

Map 3
Borders of Canaan

Lebo-hamath

Byblos

Great Sea
(Mediterranean)

Sidon

Damascus

Tyre

Acco

C A N A A N

Shechem

River Jordan

Jerusalem

Gaza   Hebron   Dead Sea

Arad

Wilderness of Zin   EDOM

Brook of Egypt

Kadesh-Barnea

0 10 20 30 km

•••••••••••••• Border

▪▪▪▪▪▪▪▪▪▪▪▪▪ Conjectured border

➤➤➤➤➤➤ Spies' route

34:16—36:13: A future in the land

The assumption that Israel's future lies in the land is already evident in the preceding chapters, but now it seems to be taken for granted. First, distributors of the land are appointed (34:16–29). Chapter 35 is concerned with establishing cities for the Levites and cities of refuge, to which homicidal killers may flee and be tried there. Although much of the passage is devoted to defining the difference between murder, which is punished by the death penalty, and manslaughter, which is punished by detention in a city of refuge until the high priest's death, the reason for including the law here is that the land must be kept pure. Death, especially violent human death, pollutes the land and makes it impossible for God to dwell there. This is why homicide must be taken so seriously. An even worse disaster for the nation than a human death would be for God to forsake it (35:33–34).

What do you think?
THE BIBLICAL DEFINITION OF MURDER

Different legal codes define the essence of murder differently. Look at the examples of different types of killing discussed in 35:15–23 and see what these laws regard as the vital difference between murder and manslaughter. Is it intention to kill that matters or pre-meditation? Premeditation involves planning and/or long-term hatred. Intention might not: in a sudden fight the participants might in their rage intend to kill each other. Scholars disagree whether intention or premeditation is the key issue. What do you think?

In chapter 36 the daughters of Zelophehad appear again. In chapter 27 they had won a concession, which allowed a man's daughters to inherit his land, if he had no sons. Why do they pop up again here? It is because the grant of land to the half-tribe of Manasseh to which they belonged (32:40) potentially created further problems. And the same problems could occur in the land of Canaan itself. If women inherited land and then married someone from a different tribe, their land would be transferred to that tribe. In this way the tribal territories could become muddled up and lose their integrity. To prevent this happening, it is laid down that land-owning women must marry someone from their own tribe. In this way the land of Canaan will belong to the tribes for ever (36:9).

The way that this apparently trivial problem is resolved expresses the conviction of the Pentateuch that the land of Canaan will be Israel's for ever (e.g. Gen. 13:15; 17:8). In this way it emphasizes the conviction that undergirds the closing chapters of Numbers that entry to Canaan is both certain and imminent. However, it also reminds us that Moses is barred from entry, yet he is still active and making important rulings. Last time, immediately after the daughters of Zelophehad appeared, Moses was told to climb the mountain to die (27:1–23). This time nothing is said, though it has been reiterated that he will soon die (31:2). The book thus ends in suspense. Israel will enter the land, but not under Moses' leadership. Yet he is still there. Another book is needed to resolve the issue.

NUMBERS AND THE NEW TESTAMENT

The New Testament draws on Numbers in two main ways: first to urge its readers not to make the same mistakes as the wilderness generation, and second to show that Jesus is a second and superior Moses.

The longest passage of the first type is 1 Corinthians 10:3–11, where, echoing Numbers, Paul urges the Corinthians to avoid idolatry and sexual immorality. Hebrews 3:16 says 'Who were those who heard and yet rebelled? Was it not all those who left Egypt led by Moses?' It goes on to cite other incidents in the wilderness wanderings. Jude 11 mentions Balaam's error and Korah's rebellion as reoccurring in the New Testament Church.

On the other hand the New Testament also uses these stories to show that Christ is even greater than Moses (Heb. 3:2–6). Jesus is the one who feeds his people not just with manna but with the bread from heaven (John 6:48–51). He pictures himself as the brazen serpent which gave life to the dying Israelites: 'As Moses lifted up the serpent in the wilderness, so must the Son of Man be lifted up, that whoever believes in him may have eternal life' (John 3:14–15).

The parallels between the experiences of Israel in the wilderness and those of the later Church have continued to inspire Christians of later generations. That most popular of hymns, 'Guide me, O thou great Jehovah, pilgrim through this barren land', sums up the story line of Numbers in three stanzas. It is a prayer that, fed by the bread of heaven, drinking from the crystal fountain, and guided by the fiery cloudy pillar, the Christian will eventually land on Canaan's side. In this way the life of every believer is identified with the experience of Israel.

It may also be used of the Church's corporate experience. As Olson puts it:

> Every succeeding generation of God's people could continue to return to the story of the wilderness in the book of Numbers and claim it as a tradition of continuing relevance for a people who had not yet entered fully into the land of promise. God's people will always find themselves at some stage of the wilderness journey, straining forward in hope but never fully at home in the promised land. (Olson 1996, p. 186)

Digging deeper:
THE NEW TESTAMENT'S APPEAL TO NUMBERS

Read all the New Testament passages cited above and find out which parts of Numbers they are referring to. What faults in the early Church are being equated with the mistakes of the Israelites?

FURTHER READING

COMMENTARIES

E. W. Davies *Numbers*. Grand Rapids: Eerdmans, 1995.

J. Milgrom *The JPS Torah Commentary: Numbers*. Philadelphia: Jewish Publication Society, 1990.

D. T. Olson *Numbers*. Louisville: John Knox Press, 1996.

G. J. Wenham *Numbers*. Sheffield: Sheffield Academic Press, 1997.

OTHER STUDIES

M. Douglas *In the Wilderness: The Doctrine of Defilement in the Book of Numbers*. Sheffield: Sheffield Academic Press, 1993.

J. Hackett *The Balaam Text from Deir Alla*. Chico: Scholars Press, 1984.

J. L. T. Kok *The Sin of Moses and the Staff of God*. Assen: Van Gorcum, 1997.

S. Niditch *War in the Hebrew Bible*. Oxford: Oxford University Press, 1993.

C. J. Humphreys 'The Number of People in the Exodus from Egypt' *VT* 48, 1998, pp. 196–213.

B. Rothenburg *Timna: Valley of the Biblical Copper Mines*. London: Thames and Hudson, 1972.

Chapter 7

DEUTERONOMY

Deuteronomy is arguably the most influential book of the Old Testament. It brings the Pentateuch to a climactic conclusion. It is at the same time the first of the prophetic books, with the greatest of Israel's prophets, Moses, giving his last impassioned sermons to Israel before he dies. Echoes of Deuteronomy's phraseology and ideology have been detected throughout the Old Testament, and it is one of the books most quoted in the New Testament.

Its title, the 'Second Law', is borrowed from the Greek translation, and in some ways it is quite an apt description, for it does repeat many of the laws, including the Ten Commandments, that are found in the earlier books of the Pentateuch. However, the presentation of the laws is quite different from the earlier books. In them the laws are presented as the words of God to Moses: in Deuteronomy Moses gives the laws himself and encourages the people to keep them with all the persuasiveness he can muster. It is preaching about the law rather than direct law-giving.

Though prophets are rarely described as preachers of the law, that was central to their mission even if explicit references to the law are rare (see Isa. 1:10; 2:3; 24:5; Jer. 7:9; Hos. 4:1–3; Amos 2:4; 3:2 etc). Here in Deuteronomy we are presented with Moses the archetypal prophet (18:15–22) expounding the law to the people, explaining its demands on the people in the present and setting out the implications of their obedience and disobedience for the future. Sometimes he looks far into the future, envisaging their future king (17:14–20), the tribal settlements (33:6–29), the exile, and even the return from exile (28:64–68; 30:1–3).

But mostly Moses focuses on their immediate situation as they wait in the Plains of Moab to cross the Jordan and conquer the land under their new leader Joshua. With great passion and urgency he incites them to total loyalty to the LORD: they must not deviate in any way. Past experience shows that they are easily seduced by idolatry: they must not make that mistake again. They failed to trust God's power in the past to give them victory or supply them with food. The campaign in Canaan must be characterized by fearlessness because they know God is fighting for them. Above all they must obey all the demands in the law, because that proves their fidelity to the covenant at Sinai. And keeping the law guarantees God's favour, success in battle and prosperity in the land.

Deuteronomy is thus full of the rhetoric of the preacher. It is pressing. It is repetitive. When it is talking about the law, its purpose is not to explain its niceties but to persuade the listener to keep it. When it recounts stories from the past, it is not for their antiquarian interest but to convince its contemporary listeners how to avoid such mistakes in the future. Thus 'prophetic sermon' would I think be the best way to characterize the genre of most of the material in Deuteronomy.

More precisely, though, it is a farewell sermon, akin to the deathbed blessings of Isaac and Jacob before Moses' time (Gen. 27:27–29, 39–40; 49:2–27) and after Moses' day to the farewells of Joshua and David (Josh. 23:2—24:27; 1 Kgs 2:2–9). These farewells typically review what God has done in the dying hero's lifetime, make predictions about the future, and urge their successors to be loyal to God. In its length and depth Moses' farewell dwarfs all others in the Bible. It is the master example of this genre.

But having observed that most of Deuteronomy consists of Moses' farewell sermons and songs, that is not exactly the best description of the book of Deuteronomy. For this farewell material is embedded in narrative, in an account of Moses' death. Numbers left the reader in suspense, wondering when Moses would ascend Mount Nebo to die. Deuteronomy opens with the people of Israel still in the Plains of Moab, then Moses' farewell begins and it is not long before he mentions that he must die outside the promised land (1:37). The imminence of his death hangs over the whole book, giving the speeches of Moses a peculiar urgency and poignancy: he is never going to enjoy the wonderful land he is describing to his hearers. And eventually at the end of the day's speeches the LORD speaks to Moses: 'Go up this mountain of the Abarim, Mount Nebo ... and die' (32:49–50). And after pronouncing blessings on the tribes he does. 'So Moses the servant of the LORD died there in the land of Moab' (34:5).

The book closes with a fulsome epitaph on Moses. 'There has not arisen a prophet since in Israel like Moses, whom the LORD knew face to face, none like him for all the signs and the wonders that the LORD sent him to do in the land of Egypt, to Pharaoh and to all his servants and to all his land' (34:10–11). The content of Deuteronomy thus makes it quite clear that it is the last part of a biography of Moses. In previous chapters I argued that the other books of the Pentateuch should be seen as the earlier parts of this biography. Whatever the merits of the description 'biography of Moses' for Genesis to Numbers, it seems inescapable in the case of Deuteronomy.

STRUCTURE

1:1–5	**Heading**
1:6—4:43	**First sermon**
1:6—3:29	Reflections on journey from Horeb to Moab
4:1–40	Israel's duty of obedience
4:41–43	Cities of refuge appointed
4:44–49	**Heading**
5:1—28:69	**Second sermon**
5:1–33	The giving of the Ten Commandments
6:1—11:32	The challenge of loving God with the whole heart
12:1—26:19	Exposition of the Law
27:1–26	Ratifying the covenant on entry to the Land
28:1–68	Blessings and curses
29:1—30:20 Third sermon	
31:1—34:12 Epilogue: Moses' last days	
31:1–30	Appointment of Joshua as successor
32:1–43	The Song of Moses
32:48–52	God's final command to Moses
33:1–29	The blessing of Moses
34:1–12	The death of Moses

To simplify the description of the book of Deuteronomy we could describe it as three sermons of Moses embedded in an account of the last days before his death. But he envisages his exposition of the law being renewed in regular covenant ceremonies every seventh year at the Feast of Tabernacles, that is, in early October. 'At the end of every seven years ... at the feast of booths ... you shall read this law before all Israel in their hearing' (31:10–11). The core of the book is thus envisaged as a covenant document that defines the relationship between God and Israel. It binds them to be God's loyal subjects promising them prosperity if they are obedient and punishment if they go their own way.

It is therefore not surprising that the core of Deuteronomy follows the pattern of Near Eastern legal documents, such as treaties, law codes and boundary stones. All these documents in the second millennium BC have a similar pattern. It is most apt to see the Deuteronomic covenant as a cross between a treaty and a

DEUTERONOMY'S STRUCTURE AS A CROSS BETWEEN A LAW CODE AND A TREATY

Law Code e.g. Hammurabi's 1750 BC	Deuteronomy	Treaty e.g. Hittite Treaties c. 1500–1200 BC
Historical prologue	Deuteronomy 1—3	Historical prologue
Laws	Deuteronomy 4—26	Treaty stipulations
Document clause	Deuteronomy 27:3; 31:9–13	Document clause
		Gods witnessing treaty
Blessings	Deuteronomy 28:1–14	(Curses)
Curses	Deuteronomy 28:15–68	(Blessings)

125

law code. It is treaty-like in that its principal concern is to establish Israel as the LORD's loyal vassal. Its chief concern is that Israel will love the LORD with all her heart, soul and might and have nothing to do with the gods of Canaan or their worshippers. Deuteronomy is also law-code-like, in that it takes up earlier laws, explains them, and applies them to Israel's new situation.

Interestingly the structure of the book of Deuteronomy is also a cross between a law code and a treaty (see the table on p. 125).

The historical prologue reviews the recent history between the parties concerned. In the treaties the suzerain boasts of his kindness towards his vassal e.g. in allowing the vassal to remain king despite his rebellion. In a similar vein Deuteronomy reminds Israel of God's goodness to them in bringing them from Sinai to the promised land despite their frequent acts of disobedience.

The parallel between the laws of Hammurabi and those of Deuteronomy is obvious, but the latter do have the flavour of stipulations. In a treaty the essence of the stipulations is vassal loyalty: the treaty spells out just what the vassal ought to do for the suzerain by giving him regular tribute or extraditing fugitive criminals or supporting his successor. The same outlook characterizes Deuteronomy's appeal to Israel: they must support the LORD unswervingly.

The document clause mentions that the treaty must be written down and stored in a sanctuary and then publicly read at regular intervals to remind the vassal of his obligations. Very similar motives are evident in Deuteronomy 27 and 31.

A god list does not appear in Deuteronomy for obvious reasons: Israel acknowledged only one God (5:7; 6:4).

Both treaties and law codes end with a section of blessings and curses, in which the gods are urged to reward the obedient vassal with long life, prosperity, good crops and so on, and to punish the disobedient with all sorts of woes. In the law codes blessings precede the curses, but in the treaties the curses come first and are much weightier than the blessings. Deuteronomy follows the law-code order by putting the blessings first, but resembles the treaties in the length of its curses.

Digging deeper:
THE TEN COMMANDMENTS AND ANCIENT TREATIES

The use of treaty/law-code ideas and structure did not begin with Deuteronomy: it can be found in the Ten Commandments. Elements of historical prologue, blessing, curse and of course law or stipulation are found in Exodus 20:2–17 and its parallel Deuteronomy 5:6–21. Reread the commandments and identify these elements. Compare the version of the commandments in Deuteronomy with that in Exodus: how would you characterize the differences?

1:1—3:29: From Sinai to the Plains of Moab

Deuteronomy begins with a review of Israel's history from their departure from Sinai, called Horeb in Deuteronomy, to their arrival in the Plains of Moab. These events will often be referred to in the subsequent exhortation, but here this retelling of the 40 years of wilderness wanderings sets the tone for the whole book.

The short summary of the book of Numbers in Deuteronomy 1:1–5 gives the context for Moses' first sermon, which begins in 1:6. Verses 6–8 serve as his text, a quotation of God's words at Sinai: 'You have stayed long enough at this mountain. Turn and take your journey ... See I have set the land before you. Go in and take possession of the land that the LORD swore to your fathers.'

God had said that 40 years earlier, but they still had not entered the land and Moses had been told he never would. What had gone wrong? What could the hearers do now to ensure the fulfilment of that promise? These are the issues that Moses addresses first. He reminds them of his appointment of leaders to share his burden of managing the nation, which was itself proof of the fulfilment of part of the promises to the patriarchs, that their descendants would be as numerous as the stars of heaven (Gen. 15:5). God had not failed them.

Indeed God had brought them from Horeb to Kadesh-Barnea to the very borders of the promised land. It was there that Israel failed. Moses then reminds them of the spies episode (see Num. 13—14), retelling it in summary fashion and laying the blame more directly on the Israelites than Numbers does. That is why none of the older generation, save Joshua and Caleb, would enter the land. Even Moses himself was excluded. Numbers of course connects this with another rebellion at Meribah (Num. 20:2–13), but Moses mentions it here as further confirmation of the reason for the long delay in entry to the land. His imminent death hangs over the book of Deuteronomy: not until Moses dies can the people enter the land.

Digging deeper:
SPIN AND THE SPIES

Compare the account of the spies in Numbers 13—14 with that in Deuteronomy 1:19–46. What parts of the Numbers version does Deuteronomy retain, and what does it leave out? What does Deuteronomy add or change in the Numbers version? How does this alter the spin put on this episode?

Deuteronomy 1:41–45 recalls that the Israelites changed their mind and contrary to God's instructions tried to invade the land. This was of course a failure (cf. Num. 14:39–45), and confirmation of the folly of disobeying God's word. He had sentenced them to 40 years wandering in the wilderness and that would be carried out.

Eventually the sentence was served and chapter 2 sees the Israelites on the move again, skirting the territories of Edom,

Moab and Ammon. They were not to be attacked because they were Israel's brothers. (Genesis makes Edom and Israel twin brothers and Moab and Ammon cousins of Israel, see Gen. 25:25–26; 19:37–38.) Just as important is the observation that God had given them their lands (2:5, 9, 19). God's gift of land to Israel's relatives is proof of his power to give land, and thus a reassurance to Israel that in due course they will also be given their land.

Further reassurance is provided by the successful campaigns against Sihon and Og in northern Transjordan. This story has already been told before (Num. 21:21–35), but here it is mentioned again as confirmation that Israel would be able to conquer Canaan. If Israel could conquer giants such as Og with his nine-cubit (4 metre) bed, they could surely conquer the Nephilim of Canaan who had so scared the spies (Num. 13:28, 33). The victories over Sihon and Og and the subsequent resettlement of the land by the tribes of Reuben, Gad and Manasseh, were a model for the other tribes to follow in Canaan, as Moses said to Joshua: 'Your eyes have seen all that the LORD your God has done to these two kings. So will the LORD do to all the kingdoms into which you are crossing' (Deut. 3:21).

Is there then perhaps a chance that after all Moses will be able to enter the land? But despite his successful prayers on behalf of Israel on other occasions, his prayer is rejected this time, because 'the LORD was angry with me because of you and would not listen to me.' He confirms his sentence, 'You shall not go over this Jordan. But charge Joshua, and encourage and strengthen him, for he shall go over at the head of this people, and he shall put them in possession of the land that you shall see' (Deut. 3:26–28).

In this way Deuteronomy portrays Moses' death as a necessary prerequisite for the fulfilment of the promise of the land. He dies so that the people may enter the land. Indeed it is because of the people's sin that he must die. Though his coming death is barely referred to again until the closing chapters of the book, we should remember that every reference to the entry to Canaan carries as its corollary the non-entry of Moses. Not until his death will the gates of the land be unlocked for Israel.

4:1–40: Israel's unique experience of God

Chapter 4 expresses the heart of the book's theology with passionate eloquence, namely that obedience to the law is the key to Israel's survival and success. The first and last verses of the section make this plain: 'And now, O Israel, listen to the statutes and the rules that I am teaching you, and do them, that you may live, and go in and take possession of the land, that the LORD, the God of your fathers, is giving you' (4:1 cf. 4:40).

The introductory 'And now' introduces a logical consequence of the historical review in the opening chapters. This showed that when Israel obeyed God's directions they succeeded in defeating their foes and settling their land, but that when the Israelites disregarded divine instructions they failed. Now they are challenged not to make the same mistake again: but this time the test is not obedience to specific military instructions but to the 'statutes and rules', that is the laws contained in the book of Deuteronomy, especially the prohibitions against the worship of other gods and idolatry.

Complete obedience is required, not rough-and-ready compliance. 'You shall not add to the word that I command you, nor take from it.' Recent experiences at Baal Peor showed the disastrous consequences of disobedience. Instead of learning from other nations Israel is urged to be an example to them. They are invited to show the world what it means to have God dwelling among them and to live by his laws (4:5–8). This is no straightforward matter as their experience at Sinai showed.

On the one hand it demonstrated why Israel should not make idols: at Sinai they heard God speak but did not see him, therefore it would be quite inappropriate for them to make idols to worship (4:15–24). And if they do, they will lose possession of the land, not live in it as they have been promised (4:25–30).

On the other hand the Sinai experience showed that God could draw near to man without destroying him, something unique in human history. 'Did any people ever hear the voice of God ... and still live?' (4:33). He of course did even more than that: he brought Israel out of Egypt 'by great deeds of terror, all of which the LORD your God did for you in Egypt before your eyes' (4:34). That same power enabled Israel to defeat the kings of Transjordan, and will enable them to enter the promised land and live in it, if only they 'keep his statutes and his commandments' (4:40).

4:44—5:30: Introduction to the second sermon

After briefly setting the scene again in 4:44–49 (cf. 1:1–5), the second sermon

STRUCTURE OF THE SECOND SERMON

A	Hear O Israel the statutes and the rules	5:1
B	The LORD our God made a covenant with us in Horeb	5:2
C	Ceremony on Mounts Ebal and Gerizim	11:29–30
A'	You shall be careful to do all the statutes and rules	11:32
A"	These are the statutes and rules that you shall be careful to do	12:1
D	The statutes and rules	12:2—26:15
A'''	These statutes and rules. You shall therefore be careful to do them	26:16
C'	Ceremony on Mounts Ebal and Gerizim	27:1–26
B'	The covenant that he had made with them at Horeb	29:1

begins where the first ended. It is essentially an exposition of the 'statutes and rules' (5:1), which have already been mentioned in 4:1, 5, 40. Moses again refers to the experience at Sinai where God spoke face to face with the people as a frightening occasion (cf. 4:10). In this way chapter 5 links back to what precedes it.

It also anticipates what follows. The second sermon in chapters 5—28 is encased by a series of concentric titles or conclusions which tie the sermon together.

But Deuteronomy 5 is much more than a bridge between chapters 1—4 and 6—28: it has its own important points to make. The first is that the covenant at Sinai is binding on the new generation standing in the Plains of Moab. In fact, although nearly everyone of the generation who came out of Egypt has died, Deuteronomy pictures its hearers as being present at Sinai. 'Not with our fathers did the LORD make this covenant, but with us, who are all of us here alive today. The LORD spoke to you face to face at the mountain' (5:3–4).

The second point being made is that Moses is the recognized mediator of the laws. He retells the story of the Ten Commandments to make the point that the people asked him to approach God and pass on his words to them because they were afraid of doing so themselves (5:24–27). Not only this, but God approved of their decision commenting, 'O that they had such a mind as this always, to fear me and to keep all my commandments' (5:29). In this way the

Digging deeper:
THE LOVE OF GOD IN DEUTERONOMY

The love of God is one of the most striking features of the teaching of Deuteronomy. In 6:5 Israel is being commanded to love God, but this is essentially a response to God's love for Israel. God showed his love for Israel by choosing the patriarchs (4:37), changing Balaam's curse into blessing (23:5) and will continue to show his love in the future by blessing and multiplying them (7:13).

Israel must respond to God's love for her by loving him in return (e.g. 7:7–9; cf. 10:18–19). She should show her love for God by being totally loyal to him, i.e. loving him with all her heart, soul and might. This sense of love = loyalty seems to be borrowed from the language of treaties, in which the sovereign often exhorts his vassal to love him. In Deuteronomy love for God is coupled with walking in God's ways, holding fast to him, and especially keeping his commandments (6:5; 10:12; 11:1, 13; 19:9). Deuteronomy recognizes the difficulty of achieving this whole-hearted love of God, but promises that one day 'The LORD your God will circumcise your heart ... so that you will love the LORD your God with all your heart and with all your soul that you may live' (30:6).

What do you think? Can feelings be command-ed? e.g. love, fear (3:2; 6:13), coveting (5:21), joy (16:14, 15), humility (17:20), etc.

How are feelings and actions connected? Compare Jesus' teaching in John 14:15.

book again emphasizes the absolute importance of keeping the law. The Israelites must not deviate from its demands in the slightest if they wish to live and enjoy long life in the land.

6:1—11:32: The challenge to love God with all the heart

Commandments, statutes and rules have a negative ring in modern ears, but, as far as Deuteronomy is concerned, keeping them demonstrates one's love for God. The central command addressed to Israel is this: 'Hear, O Israel: the LORD our God, the LORD is one. You shall love the LORD your God with all your heart and with all your soul and with all your might' (6:4–5).

This demand for total and abiding love for the one and only God is what runs through the whole book of Deuteronomy, but it is put with peculiar intensity and power in this section. Parents must be constantly teaching their children to love God (6:7–9, 20–24). When Israel enters the land, they must beware not to be seduced into loving the gods of the Canaanites instead. All traces of Canaanite religion must be obliterated, lest Israel is tempted to forsake its loyalty to the LORD (7:1–26).

Love for God is the proper response to God's love for Israel. He brought them out of Egypt, led and fed them in the wilderness, and is bringing them to a land like the Garden of Eden. Their imminent victories in Canaan and settlement of the land must not lead them to forget that this is all God's doing (8:1–18). It would be even worse if they turn their back on God

and follow the gods of Canaan. In that case Israel will share the fate of the Canaanites, namely expulsion from their land (8:19–20).

Unfortunately ingratitude and even apostasy are likely: just remember what Israel did at Sinai. While Moses was up the mountain receiving the Ten Commandments, Israel was making a golden calf (9:1–21). And this was not just a one-off mistake; the people rebelled again at Taberah, Massah, Kibroth-Hattaavah, not to mention Kadesh-Barnea (9:22–24; cf. Num. 12—14). It was only Moses' intercession that saved Israel from destruction (9:25—10:11).

If Israel is to enter the land and be successful, she must have a total change of heart. 'And now, Israel, what does the LORD your God require of you, but to fear the LORD your God, to walk in all his ways, to love him, to serve the LORD your God with all your heart and with all your soul, and to keep the commandments and the statutes of the LORD … Circumcise therefore the foreskin of your heart, and be no longer stubborn' (10:12–16). Notice how the appeal to history in 10:1–11 leads to practical application in 10:12, just as chapters 1—3 preface the application in chapter 4. In both cases the transition is marked by the key phrase 'And now' (4:1; 10:12, for other examples see 26:10; 31:19).

Other experience teaches the same lesson (11:1–7). If only they will keep the commandment, the future in the land is assured for it is 'a land the LORD your God cares for' (11:12). God's words must direct every thought and action: 'you shall bind them as a sign on your hand, and they shall be as frontlets between your eyes' (11:18). Though later Jews took these instructions very literally (see 'Digging deeper' below), even taken metaphorically these words encourage the Israelites to let God's commands guide their every thought and deed. And if they do, they will be successful in dispossessing the Canaanites and living securely in their land (11:22–25).

The choice though is theirs. Does Israel want God on their side or against them? The blessing or the curse? When they enter the land and reach Mounts Gerizim and Ebal, they will have to choose to follow the LORD or the gods of Canaan. This is an allusion to the ceremony to be carried out as described in chapter 27. Having pleaded with Israel in general terms to keep the laws, Moses is now ready to expound some of them in detail in chapters 12—26.

Digging deeper:
USE OF DEUTERONOMY IN JEWISH WORSHIP

These chapters of Deuteronomy contain two of the most quoted passages in Jewish worship. Deuteronomy 6:4–9 and 11:13–21 and Numbers 15:37–41 make up the Shema, the prayer most used by Jews. The Deuteronomy passages are also incorporated in the Tefillin and the Mezuzah.

Deuteronomy 6:7 encourages these words to be recited 'when you lie down, and when you rise', so from New Testament times (cf. Mark 12:29–30), if not earlier, the Shema has been part of morning and evening prayers. It serves as a Jewish creed, though in some respects it is more like the Lord's Prayer, in that the reciter accepts the rule of God over his life. As an assertion of God's unity it has reminded the Jews of their distinctive beliefs, as against ancient polytheism, Zoroastrian dualism, Christian Trinitarianism and modern atheism.

As well as reciting the whole Shema as part of daily prayers, Jews are expected to say the first paragraph just before they go to sleep and on their deathbed.

Tefillin, called phylacteries in the New Testament (Matt. 23:5), are little leather boxes containing these passages from Deuteronomy (see figure 9). These boxes have straps attached by which they may be fastened to the forehead and upper arm. Jewish men do this as part of morning prayers, symbolically binding themselves to keep the law both in what they do and in what they think. The custom is clearly based on a literal interpretation of 6:8; 11:18.

The same verses have prompted the making and use of Mezuzot. Every doorway of a Jewish house except the bathroom should have a Mezuzah attached to it. This is a thin box or tube containing a parchment inscribed with Deuteronomy 6:4–9 and 11:13–21.

Figure 9: **PHYLACTERY**

12:1—26:19: Exposition of the law
After the long and impassioned appeal in chapters 5—11 to keep the statutes and laws, their exposition at last begins in chapter 12. But right at the beginning and again at the end Israel is reminded why they should keep the laws: to enjoy life in the land (12:1; 26:16–19).

It is not easy to see the logic in the arrangement of the laws that follow, but a study of other Near Eastern collections of law has shed light on their arrangement. It is also apparent that this exposition of laws roughly follows the order of the Ten Commandments. These rules in Deuteronomy could be described as applications of the principles expressed most crisply in the Ten Commandments. For example, keeping the Sabbath entails celebrating other Holy Days and Holy Years, the topic of chapters 15—16. 'You shall not murder' is a cue for all the rules about homicide and war found in chapters 19—21. Kaufman (1978–9) has proposed that Deuteronomy 12—26 relates to the Commandments as follows:

DEUTERONOMY'S APPLICATION OF THE TEN COMMANDMENTS

Commandment	Deuteronomy's Application
1–2 'No other gods'	12:1–32 No worship at Canaanite shrines
3 'No taking of God's name'	13:1—14:27 No apostasy or compromise with Canaanite worship
4 'Observe the Sabbath'	15:1—16:17 Holy years and holy days
5 'Honour father and mother'	16:18—18:22 Respecting authorities
6 'No murder'	19:1—22:8 Respect for human life
7 'No adultery'	22:9— 23:18 Adultery and illicit mixtures
8 'No theft'	23:19—24:7 Property violations
9 'No false witness'	24:8—25: 4 Fair treatment of others
10 'No coveting'	25:5–16 Coveting wives and property

12:1–32: No worship at Canaanite shrines

Running through all the laws of Deuteronomy is the fear of religious disloyalty, whose worst expression is joining in Canaanite worship. Retellings of the Beth-Peor incident and the golden calf story have reminded the Israelites of their past failures. Now on the verge of Canaan they are liable to be tempted again, so their first priority must be to destroy Canaanite shrines. Their altars must be knocked down and their idols chopped up. Instead the Israelites must worship at 'the place which the LORD ... will choose' (12:1–5).

Only at the chosen place may sacrifices, tithes, vows and other offerings be brought, 'not at any place that you see' (12:13). Traditionally meat-eating was a corollary of sacrifice: the laity were allowed to share in the peace offerings. But in the new situation where the sanctuary might be a long way from someone's home, it would be permissible to kill an animal for food without offering a sacrifice as long as no blood was consumed (12:15–28). This change from earlier practice would reduce the temptation to use Canaanite shrines as a means of enjoying meat meals.

13:1–18: Apostasy

This still could be a threat. Prophets might encourage the worship of other gods. Other people could be tempted by their relatives or fellow citizens. Wherever the threat came from, it could not be tolerated and those who originated it must be wiped out. This will 'purge the evil from your midst' (13:5). Frequently in these chapters

Digging deeper:
THE CHOSEN PLACE OF WORSHIP IN DEUTERONOMY

Deuteronomy is particularly concerned that when Israel enters the land the people may adopt Canaanite worship practices, especially if they go to their shrines. To prevent this it orders that all such local shrines be destroyed, and that in future all sacrifices, offerings and festivals be celebrated at a national shrine, which it calls 'the place that the LORD will choose to make his name dwell there' (12:11). This phrase or an abbreviation of it keeps recurring in Deuteronomy. It is there that the national court sits (17:8), and where the whole nation gathers every seven years to hear the law read (31:11).

Deuteronomy does not expect this place to come into use until the LORD 'gives you rest from all your enemies around, so that you live in safety' (12:10), i.e. until the conquest is fully complete. It also never says where 'the place' is. The books of Kings identify Jerusalem as the chosen city (e.g. 1 Kgs 8:44), but never describe Jerusalem as the chosen place. However, many commentators suppose that Deuteronomy is making a covert reference to Jerusalem with this phrase. For further discussion see Chapter 9, Composition.

there is talk of 'purging evil' (17:7, 12; 19:13, 19; 21:9, 21; 22:21–22; 24:7). Most of these references refer to idolatry, homicide and adultery, the three sins that according to Leviticus pollute the land and make it impossible for Israel to dwell there (Lev. 18:28; 20:22–23).

Deuteronomy evidently shares this anxiety and this explains its drastic treatment of them. Canaan is to be the holy land where the LORD dwells but he tolerates no impurity.

14:1–29: Food and tithes

After the digression about apostasy, the issue of food and the bringing of tithes to the sanctuary is resumed. As we saw in Leviticus, the distinction between clean and unclean food was intended to remind the Israelites that they were a chosen people different from the nations. That is why they must not eat any abomination (14:1–21). Tithes must be brought to the sanctuary, but if it proves to be a long way from home, Israelites may sell the tithe and bring the money to the chosen temple.

The third-year tithe is to be given to the poor, one of Deuteronomy's humanitarian features. And that triggers off a mention of other poor-relief measures, as described in chapter 15.

15:1–18: Debt and slave release in the seventh year

Some of these provisions overlap with provisions in Exodus 21:1–6 and Leviticus 25, but Deuteronomy is notable for the generosity it urges the master to exercise when his slave's time of service is up. Doubtless the master thought he had been generous in the first place employing the destitute man as his slave (for the attitude to slavery see Chapter 4, Exodus), but Deuteronomy proposes that he be given a golden handshake when he leaves. 'You shall furnish him liberally out of your

flock, out of your threshing floor, and out of your winepress.' The master's generosity must match God's generosity: 'As the LORD your God has blessed you, you shall give to him' (15:14).

> **Digging deeper:**
> **DEUTERONOMY'S HUMANITARIANISM**
>
> One of Deuteronomy's striking features is its concern with the poor and disadvantaged members of society, e.g. slaves, immigrants (sojourners), orphans, widows and landless Levites. Look up the passages where they are mentioned. How does it want them to be helped? What reasons does it give for this help? See 5:14–15; 10:18–19; 12:18–19; 14:21, 29; 15:13–15; 16:11–12, 14; 23:7, 15–16; 24:7, 14–15, 17–22; 26:11–13.

15:19—16:17: Firstlings and festivals

Firstlings, that is first-born animals, also had to be given to God: that is brought to the sanctuary and sacrificed there (15:19—16:17). The easiest time to do this would be at one of the national Festivals of Passover, Pentecost or Booths (16:1–17). Whereas the Passover regulations in Exodus envisage only a home ceremony, Deuteronomy points out that in the land all these festivals must be celebrated at the national shrine. Every Israelite male had to participate in these pilgrimage feasts, but Deuteronomy obviously expects the women to join in too (16:11, 14, 16). It also hopes that the poor, the slaves, the orphans, the widows and the Levites will be included in these celebrations (16:11–12, 14).

16:18—18:22: Legal and other authorities

Entry to the land will require the appointment of judges and officers to maintain law and order. Their first priority is to deal with Canaanite worship practices that may be reintroduced, such as Asherah poles or sacred pillars (16:21–22). Should local people actually go and worship other gods, they must be immediately executed by stoning. Difficult murder cases must be tried in the national court manned by the priests and the judge in the capital city (17:1–13).

Should the time come for the appointment of a king, he should be different from the typical oriental monarch. He should not be distinguished by showy cavalry, multiple wives or great wealth, rather he is to be an exemplary student of the law. 'He shall read in it all the days of his life, that he may learn to fear the LORD his God by keeping all the words of this law' (17:19).

The king sounds more like a priest or a prophet than a secular ruler. All of them are responsible for making sure the nation does not adopt the magic practices of the Canaanites (18:9–14). In other words all the authorities in Israel must be on their guard against allowing foreign worship to pollute national life. This section concludes with a reminder of the authority with which Moses can make these demands. He alone mediated between God and Israel at Sinai; that is why Israel must listen to him now and to his successors in the future (18:15–22).

19:1—22:8: Protecting human life

We have noted that the exposition of the laws in chapters 12—26 follows the order of the Ten Commandments. The longest of these sections is devoted to explaining and applying the sixth commandment, 'You shall not murder.' Homicide is one of the most polluting of sins. It is said to defile the land, so that if it is not treated properly, it would make it impossible for Israel to remain in the land. The first law on the cities of refuge repeats many of the provisions of Numbers 35, but here the interest is slightly different. It is not so much on distinguishing murder from manslaughter, as on preventing accidental 'manslayers' being executed before being tried. In Israel there were no police or other professionals to maintain law and order. If someone was killed, it was the duty of his brother or nearest male relative to catch and execute the killer. Deuteronomy's concern is that manslayers who accidentally kill someone should have a chance to escape execution, and it therefore sets up extra cities of refuge for such people to flee to. It wants to minimize the loss of innocent blood in the land.

Moving a landmark reduces a family's land and its ability to survive (19:14). Falsely accusing someone of a capital offence is another way of eliminating him (19:15–21). So these crimes too are dealt with under the rubric 'You shall not murder.'

It is perhaps surprising to find laws on war under this heading, for of all human activities war tends to involve the greatest loss of life. But once again Deuteronomy's

Digging deeper:
WAR IN DEUTERONOMY

The imminent prospect of a fierce war against the Canaanites dominates the book of Deuteronomy. This conflicts with the book's concern to preserve human life, which is evident in 19:1—22:8. How does the book see the problem?

First, it holds that the land has been promised to the Israelites (1:8, 35; 6:10, 18, 23 and many times). Second, it affirms that the Canaanites have forfeited their right to live in the land through their sin (e.g. 9:5). Third, it is sure that the Israelites will be tempted to follow Canaanite religious practices, for they have such a track record of apostasy (4:3–4; 9:7–24). Indeed the central demand of Deuteronomy is total fidelity to the law and shunning of all other gods. It is a recurrent theme in the laws (e.g. 13:1–18; 17:2–7; 20:18) and in the final sermon and song (chs 29—30; 32). It is this fear of Israel's potential apostasy that prompts the apparent demand to exterminate the Canaanites.

However, this could be more rhetoric than literal demand. For example, after commanding that the Canaanites be devoted to total destruction, Deuteronomy 7:2–5 continues 'You shall make no covenant with them and show no mercy to them. You shall not intermarry with them, giving your daughters to their sons or taking their daughters for your sons, for they would turn away your sons from following me, to serve other gods.' These commands against making treaties and intermarriage would be superfluous if all the Canaanites had been wiped out. So how does the command continue? 'But thus you shall deal with them: you shall break down their altars and dash in pieces their pillars and chop down their Asherim and burn their carved images with fire' (7:5). It is evident that destruction of Canaanite religion is much more important than destroying the people.

Chapter 20:10–18 is the passage that seems most clearly to offer no quarter to the Canaanites, see verse 17. But this does suppose that the offer of peace in verse 10 does not apply to them. It is possible to understand the laws differently as follows:

Case 1 – Foreign Cities
    Offer of peace (v. 10)
    If accepted – Forced labour (v. 11)
    If refused – Males killed: others spared (vv. 13–14)

Case 2 – Canaanite cities
    (Offer of peace
    If accepted – Forced labour)
    If refused – All killed (vv. 16–17)

On this understanding, supported by Maimonides, the most famous medieval Jew, and Lohfink 1986, the leading modern authority on Deuteronomy, Canaanites could escape total destruction provided they surrendered. The law could certainly be read this way syntactically. But most commentators believe the law does not envisage the Canaanites being offered a chance to surrender.

Read the passages yourself (chs 7 and 20). Which view do you prefer?

Now consider 13:12–18. Does the treatment of an Israelite city shed light on the motives behind the rules in chapters 7 and 20?

concern is to limit loss of life in this bloody activity. It begins by listing all the men in Israel exempt from call-up: men with new houses, vineyards or wives. Even the faint-hearted are allowed to discharge themselves. Here the book is clearly showing how it values civilian pursuits over military glory (20:1–9).

Its fundamental rule about the exercise of war is that besieged cities must be offered surrender terms. Only if they refuse such terms may all combatant males be put to death when the city falls. This is the rule for cities outside the land (20:10–15). In the case of cities within the promised land all their inhabitants must be executed, so that they do not lead Israel into the worship of foreign gods (20:16–18). The rest of the section contains further laws dealing with the pollution caused by death (e.g. 21:1–9), and others intended to preserve life (e.g. 22:8) including plant and animal life (20:19–20; 22:1–4).

22:9—23:18: Relations between the sexes

The misuse of sex is seen as highly polluting, and this section may be viewed as an extended exposition of the seventh commandment, 'You shall not commit adultery.' Some applications of this principle are discussed in 22:13–30. These laws on unethical sex are preceded by laws forbidding mixed cropping, ploughing and textiles, which do not seem to have much relationship to irregular sexual liaisons (22:9–11). However, as we saw in discussing the food laws in Leviticus 11 (see Chapter 5, Leviticus), these rules reminded Israel of their status as the chosen people and served to segregate them from Gentiles. It is probable that these laws on mixtures had a similar function and thereby discouraged intermarriage with Canaanites and others.

One law on transvestism (22:5) is apparently in the wrong section as it is clearly intended to promote proper relations between the sexes. We would expect it to be included somewhere between 22:9 and 23:18. However, it is placed towards the end of the section on preserving life as a trailer for the section on sexual relations that begins in 22:9. This device for linking up sections of law codes can be seen in other oriental collections such as the laws of Hammurabi. Another example of a trailer is found in 23:15–16 allowing an escaped slave to keep his freedom. This law has nothing to do with the misuse of sex but it does anticipate the property laws in 23:19—24:7.

23:19—24:7: The property laws

These apply the eighth commandment, 'You shall not steal', to a range of ancient problems. Taking interest, for example, is banned because it makes the plight of the debtor even worse (23:19–20). Property pledged to God in a vow must be given (23:21–23). It is not immediately obvious how the law in 24:1–4, forbidding a husband from remarrying his former wife, fits into a section on property rights. However, Westbrook (1986) has plausibly argued that the issue involves a scam whereby the husband acquires his wife's dowry by making a false accusation against her. Understood in this way it also acts as a trailer for the section on false witness that begins in 24:8.

24:8—25:4: No false witness

This is the theme of the next section, which begins with a reminder of the unwarranted accusations Miriam made against Moses (Num. 12). But false accusation is not the only way people can be destroyed as human beings: the rich can exercise their power over the poor to demean them even further. Some undesirable practices of this sort are condemned in 24:10—25:4.

25:5–16: You shall not covet

This roughly covers the contents of the last section. The prohibition on coveting wives may lie behind the rules on Levirate marriage and brawls (25:5–12). Coveting property can lead to theft, and so too the possession of false weights and measures may lead to cheating the customer (25:13–16).

One of the best antidotes to coveting is giving. So the exposition of the laws concludes with a reminder of the Israelites' duty of giving to God and the poor. The first fruits of all crops had to be offered to God in the sanctuary, and 26:1–11 prescribes what must be said on this occasion. The worshipper's prayer recalls God's rescue of Israel from Egyptian slavery and his gift to them of the land (26:5–10). It is God's generosity that makes this annual gift of the first fruits possible.

Every third year a tithe of all agricultural products had to be given to the needy in Israel, such as the Levites, widows and orphans. Again a prayer is prescribed, in which the worshipper declares that he has been scrupulous in his giving and not retained anything he should not have done (26:13–15).

A final exhortation to keep the law and a reminder of Israel's unique status as the chosen people rounds off this part of the sermon (26:16–19).

27:1–26: Ratifying the covenant in the land

The ceremonies to be carried out on Mount Ebal are unusual. Though there are oriental parallels to writing and reading treaty or law texts in sanctuaries, there is nothing like it in the Old Testament. Mounts Ebal and Gerizim overlook the modern town of Nablus, which is near the site of ancient Shechem (see map 3, p. 119). It was here that Abraham was first told where the promised land was, where he built his first altar, where Jacob bought a plot of land, and where Joseph was buried (Gen. 12:7; 33:19; Josh. 24:32). Thus it was a place already full of historic significance before Moses' day. There is therefore something appropriate about it being the first place for the people to visit after they have entered the promised land. Going there they identified with the promises and with the patriarchs to whom they were made.

On Mount Ebal they were to write the law, and renew their pledge to keep it. In particular they pledged themselves to keep even the humanly unenforceable parts of the law by invoking curses on anyone who transgressed. The sins singled out were those people might do in secret and hope to remain undetected e.g. secret idolatry, moving landmarks, misleading the blind, sexual sins, or secret murder. But they conclude with a broad general curse on 'anyone who does not confirm the words of this law by doing them' (27:15–26). Once again the book rams home the obligation to keep the whole law.

28:1–68: Blessings and curses

Ancient treaties and law codes usually ended with a section of blessings and curses. The appearance of this feature here is an indication that Deuteronomy is not just a sermon but was used in covenant renewal ceremonies, such as the one on Mount Ebal prescribed in the previous chapter.

However, in the context of Moses' second and longest sermon it constitutes his final appeal to the nation to keep the law. A glorious prospect of peace and prosperity awaits Israel, if they 'faithfully obey the voice of the LORD your God, being careful to do all his commandments' (28:1). On the other hand all manner of personal and national disasters will befall the nation, if they do not keep the law. All the promises of prosperity and happiness in the land will be nullified. Drought, famine, plague, defeat by their enemies, and exile from the promised land will be their fate. Having been released from slavery in Egypt, they will be forced to return there as slaves and suffer the plagues of Egypt themselves (28:60, 68).

These blessings and curses are of course conditional. Israel can choose which she enjoys by choosing to obey the law or to reject it. Nevertheless, the much greater space given to the curses suggests a certain pessimism on Moses' part: he thinks it more likely that they will disobey the law than keep it. Indeed from verse 45 onwards the curses begin to sound more like prophecy than conditional curses as Israel's defeat and exile is described in horrifying detail. Of course prophecies of doom are conditional, in that the prophet pronouncing them hopes that his hearers will repent and avert the calamity. Nevertheless, casting the message in this form does prepare the way for the next section.

29:1—30:20: Moses' third sermon

In the last of his three sermons Moses reinforces the points he has already made: these chapters are full of allusions to earlier passages in the book. He reminds them of the way that God has led them from Egypt to Moab (29:1–9). Now they are standing ready to renew the covenant first made at Sinai (29:10–15). They must all give wholehearted assent: individuals must not secretly opt out, or the land will become as desolate as Sodom and Gomorrah (29:16–29).

Indeed Moses fears that all the dire warnings he made in chapter 28 will come true and Israel will find herself exiled in foreign lands (30:1). But should this happen, they should not lose hope, for, if they repent, God will bring them home (30:2–3). Indeed he promises to give them a new heart, 'so that you will love the LORD with all your heart and with all your soul, that you may live' (30:6).

But now is the moment to decide. 'See, I have set before you today life and good, death and evil' (30:15). Will they choose life, 'by loving the LORD your God ... by keeping his commandments and his statutes and his rules'? Or will they choose to perish by worshipping other gods? (30:16–18). His last word to them is: 'Choose life, that you and your offspring may live' (30:19).

31:1–29: The appointment of Moses' successors: Joshua and the law

Moses had urged Israel to choose life, but he sadly must die, because of his failure to obey God exactly. His fate is an object lesson to Israel on the necessity of keeping the law. So at last he hands over the reins to Joshua to lead the people into the long-promised land. He assures Joshua that the LORD will be with him and that he will therefore succeed (31:7–8).

However, unlike Moses, Joshua is no prophet: the LORD will rarely speak to him face to face. God's word to the new generation consists of the last sermons of Moses and they must be enshrined in this book of Deuteronomy. In future it will have to be read to the entire nation once every seven years at the Feast of Booths (October). Moses therefore writes his words down, and, as befits a sacred text, it is stored by the ark to remind the people of their obligations (31:9–13, 24–27).

32:1–47: The Song of Moses

A law-book stored beside the ark may be forgotten: what the people need is something short enough to be committed to memory that will make the same point

as his sermons. This is what the song offers. It describes God's justice and Israel's unfaithfulness (32:4–6). Then it recalls God's choice of Israel and all he has done for them (32:7–14). It relates Israel's disloyalty (32:15–18), and the decision to punish their betrayal (32:19–25). However, the LORD will limit their enemy's oppression and ultimately deliver his people (32:26–43). A final word to the people urges them to take to heart the words of this song and the teaching of the law that they may 'live long in the land that you are going over the Jordan to possess' (32:47).

Now once again God tells Moses to ascend Mount Nebo to die (32:49–52). The wording is almost the same as Numbers 27:12 and 20:11–13. In explaining his exclusion from the land, Moses, in Deuteronomy, glosses over the mistake he made at Meribah, apparently blaming the Israelites for his failure to obey God precisely (e.g. Deut. 1:37; 3:26). But here God reminds him and the reader why he never entered the land, 'because you broke faith with me.' History as well as exhortation challenges the reader to obey God totally.

33:1–29: The blessing of Moses

Moses is denied entry to Canaan, but here in his final words of blessing to his people he foresees their future destiny in the land. Each tribal territory is pictured in glowing terms, protected by God and sated with his blessings. Such deathbed blessings were conventional in Israel (cf. Gen. 27) and there is a close parallel to this blessing in the blessing of Jacob in

141

Genesis 49. There, Jacob, father of the tribes, foresees their future prosperity in the land. Here, Moses, father of the nation, does the same.

However, there are interesting differences in their presentation. Moses prefaces his blessing of the tribes by recalling God's coming to Sinai and the law-giving there (33:2–5). Once again the law's importance is emphasized by this unusual introduction. And this is reinforced in the tribal blessings. Whereas Jacob picks out the most important political tribes, Judah and Joseph, for extended treatment, Moses devotes most attention to Levi, 'who observed your word and kept your covenant. They shall teach Jacob your rules and Israel your law' (33:9–10). Thus even in his final blessing Moses keeps the key theme of Deuteronomy to the fore: enjoyment of the land and observance of the law go hand in hand.

34:1–12: The death of Moses

Forty chapters after he was first told to climb Mount Nebo and die, Moses does so. It is a sad moment. Readers who have identified with Moses' desire to enter the land share his disappointment that he never reached it. His first and last glimpse of it is described in verses 1–3. As he wistfully surveys the whole land from north to south, the LORD speaks to him for the last time: 'This is the land of which I swore to Abraham, to Isaac, and to Jacob, "I will give it to your offspring". I have let you see it with your eyes, but you shall not go over there' (34:4).

With this expanded quotation of the promise to Abraham in Genesis 12:7 we are reminded of the beginning of the biography of Moses, which I have suggested begins with Genesis. Now we reach the end, with him dying at the grand old age of 120. But it is not his age, so much as his prophetic gifts, that his biographer wants us to remember him for. 'There has not arisen a prophet since in Israel, whom the LORD knew face to face' (34:10). No one in the Old Testament stands higher than Moses.

DEUTERONOMY AND THE NEW TESTAMENT

Deuteronomy is one of the most quoted books in the New Testament. Many of the passages where it is quoted show the actors' familiarity with the book. Jesus quotes 8:3 'man does not live by bread alone', when tested by the devil in Matthew 4:4. He quotes the Shema (6:4–5) 'Hear O Israel, the LORD our God, the LORD is one. You shall love the LORD your God with all your heart and with all your soul' (Mark 12:29–30), when asked by a scribe which is the greatest commandment in the law. St Paul cites Deuteronomy 32:35 in the Greek version 'Vengeance is mine, I will repay' in Romans 12:19 to discourage vendettas, and 25:4 'You shall not muzzle an ox when it is treading out the grain' to encourage payment of Christian workers (1 Cor. 9:9). Many other quotations of this type could be found.

However, several of the New Testament writers do more: they imply that Jesus is the prophet greater than Moses. Matthew presents Jesus not simply as the mediator of the law on the mountain but as the law-giver (Matt. 5:1; 7:28–29). He feeds the multitudes in the wilderness (Matt. 14:13–21; 15:32–39). He is the one to whom all authority in heaven and on earth has been given (Matt. 28:18)

FURTHER READING

COMMENTARIES

P. C. Craigie *The Book of Deuteronomy*. Grand Rapids: Eerdmans, 1976.

J. G. McConville *Deuteronomy*. Leicester: Apollos, 2002.

J. H. Tigay *The JPS Commentary: Deuteronomy*. Philadelphia: Jewish Publication Society, 1996.

OTHER STUDIES

D. L. Christensen *A Song of Power and the Power of Song*. Winona Lake: Eisenbrauns, 1993. A collection of important essays about Deuteronomy.

S. A. Kaufman 'The Structure of the Deuteronomic Law', *Maarav* 1/2, 1978–79 pp. 105–58.

N. Lohfink *'haram, herem'* Theological *Dictionary of the Old Testament* 5, 1986, pp. 180–99.

J. G. Millar *Now Choose Life: Theology and Ethics in Deuteronomy*. Leicester: Apollos, 1998.

D. T. Olson *Deuteronomy and the Death of Moses*. Minneapolis: Fortress Press, 1994.

M. Weinfeld *Deuteronomy and the Deuteronomic School*. Oxford: Clarendon Press, 1972.

R. Westbrook 'The Prohibition on Restoration of Marriage in Deuteronomy 24:1–4' in *Studies in the Bible* ed. by Sara Japhet, Scripta Hierosolymitana 31. Jerusalem: Magnes Press, 1986, pp. 387–405.

Chapter 8

THEME OF THE PENTATEUCH

Earlier we tried to define the genre of the Pentateuch, that is, to specify what kind of literature it is. I suggested that it is best described as *Torah*, instruction about how to live, in the form of a biography of Moses. The traditional titles of Genesis to Deuteronomy as books of Moses may be taken this way. We can see Genesis as explaining the background to Moses' life, while the following books trace his life from the cradle to the grave.

But can one be more precise? Can one specify the theme or themes of the Pentateuch? Indeed, what do we mean by a theme in connection with a book, or in this case a series of books? Different scholars have different understandings of theme, and in this chapter I shall outline some of the most influential views in recent years.

MARTIN NOTH ON THE THEMES OF THE PENTATEUCH

Martin Noth (1902–68) was the outstanding German Old Testament historian of the mid-twentieth century,

whose critical theories dominated biblical scholarship till quite recently. He believed that to understand the theology of the Bible one must trace its growth from short, simple original stories into the long developed books that now make up the Pentateuch. For example, the story of the conquest of Canaan was once passed on by word of mouth either by storytellers in the home or in acts of worship that brought the tribes together. In its earliest form this story was quite brief and terse and known only by a few Israelites. But as it was told to generation after generation it grew in length and also spread among the whole Israelite league of tribes to become a national saga. In the course of time it was also linked up and connected to other stories told by other tribes and was eventually put in writing. This process of accretion and expansion of the stories continued down the centuries until at last the present Pentateuch was formed.

The next chapter will explore this development in more detail. Here it is sufficient to note that Noth believed that by identifying the core original stories of the Pentateuch, which he called themes, one can grasp the message of the Pentateuch as a whole. Noth believed the Pentateuch was built around five core themes: 'Guidance out of Egypt', 'Guidance into the Arable Land', 'Promise to the Patriarchs', 'Guidance in the Wilderness', and 'Revelation at Sinai'. I shall therefore explain what, Noth argued, each of these themes involved, how they grew over the course of time, and were then connected together.

According to Noth the oldest and most fundamental of these themes is the theme 'Guidance out of Egypt' or, as it is usually known, the story of the exodus. In the laws, the prophets and the psalms Yahweh is often called 'the LORD who brought Israel out of Egypt'. He holds that this is the kernel of the whole Pentateuch: the whole story of Genesis to Deuteronomy started with this confession. Though Noth thinks that only a few of the tribes came out of Egypt, the assertion that the LORD brought Israel out of Egypt was the first to be accepted by all the tribes as an affirmation of their identity. He posits that when the nation gathered for worship 'men skilled in speech would have recited the substance of this faith over and over again' (Noth 1972, p. 51). They would have told of the slavery in Egypt, their flight and the destruction of the Egyptians in the Red Sea.

The second theme identified by Noth is 'Guidance into the Land', i.e. the story of the conquest and settlement of Canaan. Like the exodus theme Israelites used the 'Guidance into the Land' theme when they came to make offerings at their holy places (see Deut. 26:1–11). Originally it was unrelated to the exodus theme and different tribes told different stories of how God brought them into the land. But eventually the story told by the central tribes of Ephraim, Manasseh and Benjamin displaced all rival versions and then the theme was linked to the exodus theme in a pan-Israelite account of the exodus from Egypt and conquest of the land.

The third theme, 'Promise to the Patriarchs', originally had nothing to do with the themes dealing with the exodus and conquest. Stories about God promising the patriarchs land were told at various worship centres throughout the land. When the Israelites settled in the land, they learned these stories and they were combined with the story of the exodus and conquest to create essentially the present outline of the Pentateuch. It was a story that began with God promising the land and ended with Israel receiving the fulfilment of the promises by settling in the land. Noth suggests that originally the stories about God making promises to Abraham and Isaac had nothing to do with the stories of promises made to Jacob: they were different versions of the 'Promise to the Patriarchs' theme told in different places. Later storytellers, wanting to preserve the different versions of the theme, linked them together by making Abraham the grandfather and Isaac the father of Jacob.

Like the patriarchal promise theme, the fourth theme, 'Guidance in the Wilderness', originally had nothing to do

146

with the other themes. It was added later to fill the gap between the exodus story and the conquest account. It was, according to Noth, based on the experience of the southern tribes who lived close to the Sinai wilderness and knew what sort of things happened there. With the inclusion of this theme the Pentateuchal story now had the shape found in summaries of Israel's early history such as Joshua 24, Psalms 135 and 136.

Missing from these summaries of the Pentateuchal story is any reference to the law-giving at Sinai. According to Noth, originally this also had nothing to do with the rest of the Pentateuchal story. It was a story related at the national shrine when the LORD's covenant with Israel was celebrated and renewed. But eventually this theme 'Revelation at Sinai' was combined with the other four themes to produce an outline of our present Pentateuch.

It must be stressed that this 'five-theme' Pentateuch was just an outline. In the course of retelling it was greatly expanded. The story of the plagues was added to the account of the exodus, the Balaam stories to the 'Guidance into the Land' theme, and the stories about Jacob at Shechem to the patriarchal promise theme, to name just a few of the expansions of the Pentateuchal story. Moses originally had nothing to do with the story of the Pentateuch, but perhaps he was first mentioned in the 'Guidance in the Wilderness' theme. He was then introduced into all the other themes

except the patriarchal promise theme, so that in the course of time he became more and more important, eventually becoming 'the overwhelmingly prominent human figure of the Pentateuchal narrative' (Noth 1972, p. 174).

What do you think?
REFLECTING ON NOTH'S THEMES

Skim through the Pentateuch, asking yourself how far Noth's five themes adequately capture the message of the books.

Noth offers no hard evidence for his theory about how the Pentateuch grew. How plausible does it seem to be to you?

GERHARD VON RAD AND THE PENTATEUCH

Von Rad (1901–71) was a contemporary of Martin Noth and they often appealed to each other's work in developing their own ideas. But whereas Noth was first and foremost a historian, von Rad was primarily a theologian. Indeed, his Old Testament theology is still the richest and most stimulating resource for anyone working in this area. His key publications on the Pentateuch are his form-critical *The Problem of the Hexateuch* (1966), *Old Testament Theology I* (1962) and commentaries on Genesis and Deuteronomy.

The title of his first major work immediately differentiates his approach from Noth's. Whereas Noth was happy to speak about the Pentateuch, though he actually regarded Deuteronomy as the start of a new work, von Rad spoke of the Hexateuch, by which he meant Genesis to Joshua. He sees the book of Joshua as intimately connected with Deuteronomy and forming the conclusion of the Pentateuchal story. But in broad approach to defining the theme of the Pentateuch both Noth and von Rad had much in common. They both believed that by tracing the development of the Pentateuch from its earliest beginnings through its subsequent expansions one can grasp the essential message of these books.

Von Rad held that the earliest form of the Pentateuchal story is encapsulated in Deuteronomy 26:5–9 which he dubbed the little historical creed.

> A wandering Aramean was my father.
> And he went down into Egypt and
> sojourned there, few in number,
> and there he became a nation, great,
> mighty and populous. And the
> Egyptians treated us harshly and
> humiliated us and laid on us hard
> labour. Then we cried to the LORD, the
> God of our fathers, and the LORD heard
> our voice and saw our affliction, our toil
> and our oppression. And the LORD
> brought us out of Egypt with great
> deeds of terror, with signs and wonders.
> And he brought us into this place and
> gave us this land, a land flowing with
> milk and honey.

This short creed sums up the major episodes in the Pentateuchal story: the call of the patriarchs, the slavery in Egypt, the exodus, and the conquest of the land. This confession of Israel's core beliefs used to be recited at the sanctuary of Gilgal at the annual Feast of Weeks (Pentecost) when the tribes gathered to celebrate their unity. For von Rad it is very significant that the oldest form of the confession of Israel's faith as expressed in Deuteronomy 26 is in essence so similar to the final shape of the Pentateuch. There is clear continuity between its earliest observable form and the final statement found in Genesis to Deuteronomy.

But according to von Rad the greatest influence on the Pentateuch comes from the so-called Yahwist (for further explanation see next chapter), an author in the time of David (tenth century BC), who put the Pentateuchal story into its first written shape. He elaborated the basic creed by adding many details of the patriarchs' lives, the plagues, and wilderness wanderings. But the Yahwist was also responsible for adding the primeval history (Genesis 1—11) as a preface to the patriarchal stories and introducing some mention of the lawgiving at Sinai.

This early Yahwistic Pentateuch was focused on two covenants, the covenant with the patriarchs and the covenant at Sinai. The patriarchal covenant centred on the promise of the land of Canaan to Abraham and his successors. Von Rad supposes that originally the patriarchs expected the immediate realization of this promise, i.e. that having arrived in the land they expected to stay there. But in the present Pentateuch there is a delay in the fulfilment of the promise, indeed throughout the five books there is a looking forward to the unrealized hope of settlement, something which was not achieved until the time of Joshua. Originally, von Rad surmises, the promise was just made to a few of Israel's ancestors, but in the present Pentateuch it is made to all Israel.

The covenant with the patriarchs was essentially a promise, the promise of land, which required little response except acceptance and faith on the patriarchs' part. Von Rad believes that in the Yahwistic account the Sinai covenant is also essentially 'a unilateral protective relationship' (von Rad 1962, p. 131), that is God is basically guaranteeing Israel's future. But he notes that already other old additions to the account of the Sinai covenant are expecting an obedient and active response by Israel to God's commands, so that the law is becoming visible within a context of grace.

At a later stage in the writing of the Pentateuch another huge corpus of material, called the Priestly source (see next chapter for further discussion) was incorporated into the Yahwistic Pentateuch. This made a considerable difference to the balance and perspective of the material. Most of the Priestly material is found between Exodus 25 and Numbers 36 and is predominantly laws about worship and similar issues. These make the demand for obedience to the LORD, which is already present in the earlier version of the Sinai covenant, completely explicit.

But von Rad also suggests that the Priestly additions led to a nuancing of the covenant with the patriarchs. The covenant with Abraham now contains three promises. First, that Abraham will become a people. Second, that he will have a new relationship with God, 'I will be your God'. Third, that he will possess the land. Already the Yahwistic covenant with Abraham implied that he would become a great nation, but von Rad did not think nationhood was part of the covenant. The really fresh element in the Priestly version of the Abrahamic covenant was the promise of a special relationship.

As a result of the combination of the Yahwistic and Priestly materials the final form of the Pentateuch emerged. The opening chapters describe the creation and fall of the human race, followed by a fresh start with Noah. Then comes the covenant with Abraham with its threefold promise of numerous descendants, a special relationship, and the land. The rest of the Pentateuch describes the progressive fulfilment of these three promises. The first promise was fulfilled by the Israelites becoming a great and numerous people in Egypt. The second promise was implemented at Sinai, when Israel's special relationship with God was defined and regulated by the establishment of means of worship and the giving of the law. The rest of the Pentateuch and the book of Joshua relate the fulfilment of the third promise, the gift of the land of Canaan. In this way von Rad sees the promises to Abraham and their fulfilment as constituting the unifying theme of the Pentateuch.

DAVID CLINES ON THE THEME OF THE PENTATEUCH

David Clines, an Australian by birth, has for over 30 years taught at the University of Sheffield. One of his early and most influential works is entitled *The Theme of the Pentateuch* (1978). It was a harbinger of a fresh approach to Old Testament study. For two centuries biblical scholars had been preoccupied with historical questions, such as 'Did Joshua capture Jericho?', 'What was biblical leprosy?' or 'How was the book of Genesis written?'. Indeed, it was often asserted that the key to understanding texts was to understand the circumstances of their composition. The important questions were: who wrote them, when and why? The works of Noth and von Rad are excellent examples of this approach: they try to establish the message of the Pentateuch by describing the process of its composition from short oral stories or creeds to the present lengthy books of Genesis to Deuteronomy.

But David Clines and many other modern scholars have argued that this is the wrong approach to literature. First of all, it is wrong because it concentrates on the detail at the expense of the whole picture: minor issues are discussed at length whereas the overall message is ignored. Second, this approach is misguided because it is so speculative. We really do not know how biblical books came to be written, especially in their early stages, so to base our interpretation of them on guesses about how and when they came into existence is a very dubious procedure. Instead, interpretation should begin with the final form of the text, the only form of the text we can be sure of. It may be possible, having established the meaning of the final text, to make suggestions about earlier forms of the text and what they may have meant. But these inferences will be much less certain than interpretations of the final form. Clines' book is therefore a discussion of the theme of the Pentateuch in its final form: for him, unlike Noth and von Rad, it is irrelevant how the Pentateuch grew into its present form. While he does not rule out conventional critical theories on the composition of the Pentateuch, they are of little value to his study of theme.

But first of all one must define what is meant by theme. Clines uses 'theme' in a different way from Noth, for whom theme was just a short element of the plot, e.g. the exodus, or revelation at Sinai. For Clines there can only be one theme in a literary work, not five as Noth held. Theme is not the same as a statement of content, such as 'The Pentateuch tells the story of mankind and especially Israel to the death of Moses' (Clines 1978, p. 17). Nor is the theme the same as the plot of a story. In a plot causality is important, i.e. why one event triggered the next event and so on. Clines defines theme as 'plot with the emphasis on conceptualized meaning' (p. 18), such as 'how power corrupts' or 'the divergence between Yahweh's and man's plans'. Put more crudely it is the author's agenda in writing his work, the main point in what he wants to convey to his reader through telling his tale. If the theme of a literary work is correctly identified, it will show how the diverse materials within that work cohere together, and prevent large-scale misunderstanding of that work. Though some literary texts proclaim their theme at the beginning, more usually it has to be inferred by careful and repeated reading.

Having clarified what he means by the theme of a book Clines then proceeds to approach a definition of the theme. He observes that Deuteronomy seems to end in mid-air with Moses dead but Israel still outside the promised land. Genesis also ends with a lack of plot resolution: Joseph dies in Egypt leaving instructions that he should eventually be buried in Canaan. Clines argues that Exodus, Leviticus and Numbers also end with a forward look towards Canaan. Canaan, he says, has been the goal of the Pentateuchal narrative ever since it was promised to Abraham in Genesis 12, but though Israel gets ever closer to the land as the story progresses they never finally reach it.

This leads him to define the theme of the Pentateuch as:

> the partial fulfilment – which implies also the partial non-fulfilment – of the promise to or blessing of the patriarchs. The promise or blessing is both the divine initiative in a world where human initiatives always lead to disaster and a re-affirmation of the primal divine intentions for man. (Clines 1978, p. 29)

Like von Rad Clines holds that the patriarchal promises have three elements, descendants, a divine–human relationship, and the land. The descendants element dominates Genesis 12—50 as the patriarchs gradually father children. The establishment of a special divine–human relationship is the concern of Exodus and Leviticus, while Numbers and Deuteronomy look forward to the conquest of the land. He argues that each element of the promise implicitly involves the other two elements. A promise of land is pointless unless one has descendants to live in it. And those descendants need to be reassured of God's benevolent protection in the land. If God told Abraham to 'go to the land that I will show you', that implies he will guide and protect him on the way.

Explicit promises of posterity, relationship and land are most frequent in Genesis and early Exodus, but allusions to these promises pervade the Pentateuch, especially the book of Deuteronomy where they are too many to list in full.

But the theme relates not just to the promises embedded in the story, but to the story itself. As one reads the Pentateuch the gradual fulfilment of the promises is illustrated. For example, Genesis illustrates how the promise of innumerable descendants is partially fulfilled. Sarah, after many years of waiting, has one son. Isaac's wife, Rebekah, after 20 years of marriage eventually has twins. Rachel, Jacob's favourite wife, has two sons, and his other wives another ten between them, so that when they migrate to Egypt, they number 70 all told (Gen. 46:27). According to Clines less attention is paid in Genesis to the relationship and land promises, but they too begin to be partially fulfilled (e.g. Gen. 17:7). All these promises are more fully fulfilled in Exodus to Deuteronomy, but even by the end of that book Israel is still waiting to enter the land. This is why he describes the theme as dealing with the partial fulfilment of the promises, rather than, as von Rad does, with the fulfilment of the promises.

Digging deeper:
STORY AND FULFILMENT OF PROMISES

Pick at random a chapter or two from Genesis or early Exodus, and ask yourself how it relates to the fulfilment of the promises made to Abraham in Genesis 12:1–3.

The first time promises are made to the patriarchs is in Genesis 12, so it is not immediately apparent how the opening chapters of the book relate to the theme of fulfilment of the promises. Indeed, many discussions of the theme of Genesis 1—11 seem to proceed without much consideration of what follows. Clines therefore reviews several suggestions about the theme of chapters 1—11.

One idea is that the theme of these chapters is Sin – Speech – Mitigation – Punishment. For example, Adam and Eve's sin is followed by a speech condemning them (Gen. 3:14–19), mitigation of the sentence (God provides them with clothes) (3:21), and finally punishment (3:22–24). Similar patterns have been discerned in the Cain and Abel story, and the flood story. Though Clines sees some validity in this approach he notes it fails to account for chapter 1 and the long genealogical sections in chapters 5, 10 and 11.

Another suggestion is that the theme of Genesis 1—11 is Spread of Sin – Spread of Grace. There is an avalanche of sin from Adam's mistake in chapter 3, to Cain's murder of his brother in chapter 4, to the outbreak of universal violence in chapter 6, which prompts the flood. But each new stage of human depravity is marked by divine grace: God does not punish Adam and Eve with death as he threatened, he puts a mark on Cain to protect him, and he saves Noah and his family from the flood. Clines finds this a better suggestion than the first because it does seem able to handle the opening chapter and the genealogies.

But there is yet a third way to read Genesis 1—11 as Creation – Decreation – Recreation. Genesis 1—2 describe creation, chapters 3—7 decreation. Sin leads to a progressive disruption of the relationships established at creation between man and the animals, and then disrupts relationships between humans. But it all culminates with the flood in which the world returns to its original state, uninhabited and covered in water (Gen. 1:2). The retreat of the flood waters allows a new creation to appear. Land is separated from water. Plants grow again. The animals emerge from the ark to repopulate the world, and Noah, like Adam before, is told to be fruitful and multiply.

152

Clines thinks there are valid insights in both the second and third proposals, but he cannot decide whether Genesis 1—11 is essentially pessimistic – whatever God creates man tends to spoil by sin – or essentially optimistic – however drastic man's sin God always starts afresh. But by connecting the opening chapters with Genesis 12ff. the problem is resolved. The two eras of increasing sin, Eden to the flood, the flood to Babel, are succeeded by an era marked by the promise to the patriarchs. God's grace will ultimately triumph over human sin. Indeed, as Clines puts it, these promises to the patriarchs are 'a re-affirmation of the primal divine intentions for man' (Clines 1978, p. 29). Originally God told Adam to be fruitful and multiply: now he promises Abraham that he will be the father of many nations. At the first God gave Adam a garden to cultivate: now he promises Abraham a land. In Eden Adam and Eve walked with God in the cool of the day: now Abraham is assured: 'I will bless you and make your name great.' In this way Genesis 1—11 is no longer an irrelevant preface to the rest of the Pentateuch, but integral to it. It sets the promises to the patriarchs in a cosmic context.

REASSESSMENT

Clines' discussion of the theme of the Pentateuch is not only the fullest, but also the most satisfactory so far. In many ways it recasts some of von Rad's insights. Von Rad saw the Pentateuch plus Joshua as constituting a single work, so he spoke of a Hexateuch rather than a Pentateuch. And because Joshua tells of the conquest and allocation of the land of Canaan among the 12 tribes, von Rad could speak of the fulfilment of the promises to the patriarchs constituting the theme. But because Clines restricts his discussion to the Pentateuch, he redefines the theme as the partial fulfilment of the patriarchal promises. In other words the Pentateuch is open-ended: it looks for a greater fulfilment eventually. Clines makes an important contribution by relating the promises to the patriarchs to creation: God promises to the patriarchs what was given to the human race at creation but lost through the fall: land, descendants and a close relationship with God.

But though Clines is an advance on earlier discussions, it should not be seen as the last word. In three respects his ideas need adjusting. First, the definition of the patriarchal promises as threefold, land, descendants, and relationship, needs modifying. This leaves out the climax of the promises, the fourth promise of blessing to the nations. Second, it needs to be considered how far the promises are fulfilled within the Pentateuch. Is it the case that they are only partially fulfilled? Obviously this is the case in the land promise, but in the case of the other promises it is not so obvious. Balaam asks, 'Who can count the dust of Jacob, or number the fourth part of Israel?' (Num. 23:10). He may be exaggerating, but as far as the promises of descendants and relationship are concerned, they do appear to be substantially fulfilled even before Moses' death. Third, in defining the theme of the Pentateuch, no mention is made of Moses, although he is the dominating personality from Exodus to Deuteronomy. If it is right to define the Pentateuch as *Torah*, or law, in the form of a biography of Moses, some account needs to be taken of him in formulating the theme of the Pentateuch.

It is widely agreed that Genesis 12:1–3 is programmatic, that is it sets out the direction of the succeeding narrative.

> Now the LORD said to Abram, 'Go from your country and your kindred and your father's house to the land that I will show you. And I will make of you a great nation, and I will bless you and make your name great, so that you will be a blessing. I will bless those who bless you, and him who dishonours you I will curse, and in you all the families of the earth shall be blessed.'

There are four distinct elements in this programmatic promise. First, land: 'Go to the land that I will show you.' Second, descendants: 'I will make of you a great nation.' Third, special relationship: 'I will bless those who bless you ...' and fourth, 'in you all the families of the earth shall be blessed.' There has been much discussion about the exact meaning of the blessing promised in the third and fourth promises, so we need to reflect briefly on this to see the importance of the promise of blessing to the nations.

Blessing is a key motif in the book of Genesis, and is especially associated with Abraham. His name contains two (b, r) of the three root consonants of 'bless' (b, r, k)

so that whenever Abraham is mentioned, blessing is suggested by the association of sounds. The special relationship with God means God will bless him, that is grant him success, in particular make his name great, that is make him famous. In fact, so famous will he be that he will become a blessing, in other words people will invoke his name in a blessing on themselves, 'May God make me as successful as Abraham.' Furthermore, those who do bless Abraham in this way are assured that they will be blessed in turn. 'I will bless those who bless you.' Just a few may think otherwise. The use of the singular 'him who dishonours you' almost implies that Abraham will only have one disparager. But however few, he who dishonours Abraham will be cursed.

Then comes the climax of the promises: 'in you all the families of the earth shall be blessed.' Commentators argue at length about the exact translation of the verb here: should it be 'be blessed', 'bless themselves' or 'find blessing'. Though the last rendering is probably best, it does not make much difference to the general gist of the passage, which is that through Abraham all the peoples of the world will be blessed. This then is the answer to the problem posed by Genesis 1—11. First, 'all flesh', i.e. man and the animals, proves so corrupt that God must destroy them all in the flood. After a new start with Noah and his family corruption sets in again, and things degenerate so much that another universal judgement on the human race is required, which is the dispersion of the nations at Babel. But the promise that all nations will find blessing in Abraham offers a glimmer of hope. As von Rad put it: 'the whole of Israel's saving history is properly to be understood with reference to the unsolved problem of Jahweh's relationship to the nations' (von Rad 1962, p.164) or in the words of Westermann: 'the promise of blessing to Abraham is aimed at a blessing which embraces mankind' (1985, p. 158).

The importance of this blessing is seen by its repetition in Genesis 22. After Abraham's demonstration of his total obedience by his readiness to sacrifice Isaac, the promises to Abraham are reiterated most dogmatically in the form of a divine oath. And once again they climax with the promise, 'in your offspring shall all the nations of the earth be blessed' (22:18). It is similarly reaffirmed to Isaac and Jacob at key moments in their careers (26:4; 28:14). There is thus no doubt about the importance of this promise as far as Genesis is concerned.

But on first reading there is little fulfilment of this promise apparent in the Pentateuch, so that it becomes difficult to see even its partial fulfilment. The Pentateuch ends with victories over the Amorites of Transjordan and the hope of conquest of Canaan, neither of which strikes the modern reader as a blessing to them! (Num. 21; Deut. 2—3). And this forces us to reflect to what extent we should talk in terms of fulfilment of the promises within the Pentateuch. It is a little too simple to talk of partial fulfilment. The degree of fulfilment seems to vary with the aspect of promise under consideration and the period within the

Pentateuchal time-frame being considered. It is also complicated by the way the scope of the promises is enlarged each time they are repeated, as we saw in our review of Genesis 12—50. For example, the promise of land is quite vague in 12:1 'the land I will show you'; it is a little more precise in 12:7 'this land'; it is more expansive still in 13:15 'all the land that you see'; and the promise reaches its maximum in 17:8 'all the land of Canaan for an everlasting possession.'

If one examines different aspects of the promises, it is clear that the gifts of the land and descendants make very slow progress in the book of Genesis. By the end of the book the only pieces of real estate owned by the Israelites in Canaan were a burial plot (Gen. 23), a few wells (26:22, 32–33) and a piece of ground near Shechem (33:19). And they were not living in Canaan but in Egypt. The rest of the Pentateuch tells of Israel's journey to the land, but they are still the wrong side of the Jordan as Deuteronomy closes. Moses sees the land and is reminded 'This is the land of which I swore to Abraham, to Isaac, and to Jacob, "I will give it to your offspring" ' (Deut. 34:4). Though the reader knows fulfilment of that promise is temporally much closer than it was in Abraham's day, it was just as unfulfilled for Moses as it was for Abraham. And the promise that the land would be Israel's 'everlasting possession' means that even when they are living in the land its fulfilment is incomplete.

The promise of descendants begins as a promise of nationhood, 'I will make of you a great nation' (Gen. 12:2), but like the other aspect of the promises it seems to grow as it is repeated. Abraham is assured his descendants will be as numerous as the dust of the earth and the stars of heaven (13:16; 15:5). In 17:5–6 he is promised 'I have made you the father of a multitude of nations. I will make you into nations, and kings shall come from you.'

In Genesis the fulfilment of this promise makes slow progress. But by the beginning of Exodus the Israelites are sufficiently numerous to be perceived as a threat to Egyptian security. They are big enough to invade Canaan, but they are insufficient to settle it all at once (Exod. 23:29–30; Deut. 7:22). One of Abraham's other grandsons, Esau, has become the nation of Edom (Num. 20:14–21; Deut. 2:4–8) by the end of the Pentateuch, but that hardly constitutes a multitude of nations. Nor has Israel at least appointed kings (cf. Deut. 17:14–20). So once again there is incomplete fulfilment of this aspect of the promise in the Pentateuch. Though partially realized, the hope remains of yet greater fulfilment.

On the other hand, the promise of a special relationship does seem to be fulfilled to a high degree within the narrative of the Pentateuch. Clines sees this relationship as essentially sealed at Sinai and embodied in the tabernacle, priesthood and sacrifice, which expressed and secured this special relationship. But even before this the LORD symbolized his protective presence with Israel in the flaming pot passing through the animal pieces (Gen. 15:17). And the covenant of

circumcision was a pledge of Israel's eternal covenant with God. A reading of the patriarchal stories suggests that the patriarchs lived a charmed life: even when they sinned (e.g. Gen. 12; 20; 27; 34) they are protected from the worst consequences of their folly. As Genesis puts it: God was with them (e.g. 28:15; 39:3, 21). In this respect the promise to Abraham seems to be fulfilled more or less immediately.

Above I observed that the final aspect of the patriarchal promises 'In you all the families of the earth shall be blessed' was also the climax. How is this fulfilled in the Pentateuch? In Genesis there are some partial fulfilments. Abraham rescues the property of the people of Sodom in Genesis 14:11–24, and prays for them in chapter 18. Though on this occasion his prayer for them is ultimately rejected, he does pray for the people of Gerar in 20:17 and they are healed. These are just minor examples of blessing to the nations through Abraham or his descendants. The great example is Joseph. Through his foresight grain stocks were built up in Egypt so that when famine struck, 'all the earth came to Egypt to Joseph to buy grain' (Gen. 41:57). Later on the Egyptians acknowledge 'you have saved our lives' (47:25). That this is not just polite conversation but a serious point is underlined by Joseph himself. Speaking to his fearful brothers he says: 'You meant evil against me, but God meant it for good, to bring it about that many people should be kept alive, as they are today' (50:20). Within the framework of Genesis then, there is evidence of some nations being blessed through Abraham and his descendants, even though most of the 70 nations listed in Genesis 10 are apparently unaffected.

But in the subsequent books there is very little sign of blessing to the nations. Egypt, which had benefited so much from Joseph's rule, suffers the plagues, and the peoples who oppose Israel on their journey to Canaan are defeated. Why should this be? In the first formulation of the promises blessing is promised to those who bless Abraham and a curse is pronounced on him who dishonours him. When the Pharaoh appointed Joseph to manage the food supplies of Egypt, he acknowledged 'God has shown you all this, there is none so discerning and wise as you are' (41:39). This was an implicit blessing on Joseph, so that it follows that Pharaoh's nation should be blessed. On the other hand the later Pharaoh's attempt to destroy all the Israelites was much more than 'dishonouring' Abraham and his descendants, so that divine judgement on Egypt was to be expected. Thus the absence of blessing on the nations in Exodus to Deuteronomy is not because it has been forgotten, rather it is because all the nations with whom Israel comes into contact oppose her. Like the promise of land, and the promise of a multitude of nations being fathered by Abraham and its concomitant hope of kings, the Pentateuch ends with this promise substantially unfulfilled but not forgotten.

Finally we need to address the place of Moses in the theme of the Pentateuch. He is the dominating human figure throughout Exodus to Deuteronomy, and I have argued that the Pentateuch is best understood as a biography of Moses. It does not necessarily follow that he needs to be mentioned in a definition of the theme. If it is right to define the theme as essentially about the fulfilment of the patriarchal promises, a definition could ignore him, but it would seem better to acknowledge his centrality. Perhaps a modification of Clines' definition might capture the theme more exactly.

The theme of the Pentateuch is the fulfilment of the promises to the patriarchs, which are a reaffirmation of God's original intentions for the human race, through God's mercy and the collaboration of Moses. To some degree these promises are fulfilled before Moses' death, but complete fulfilment awaits the future.

FURTHER READING

D. J. A. Clines *The Theme of the Pentateuch*. Sheffield: JSOT Press, 1978.

M. Noth *A History of Pentateuchal Traditions*. tr. by B. W. Anderson. Englewood Cliffs: Prentice-Hall, 1972 (German original 1948).

G. von Rad *The Problem of the Hexateuch and Other Essays*. tr. by E. W. Trueman Dicken. Edinburgh: Oliver and Boyd, 1966 (German original 1938).

G. von Rad *Old Testament Theology I*. tr. by D. M. G. Stalker. Edinburgh: Oliver and Boyd, 1962 (German original 1957).

C. Westermann *Genesis 12—36: A Commentary*. tr. by J. J. Scullion. London: SPCK, 1985.

P. R. Williamson *Abraham, Israel and the Nations: The Patriarchal Promise and its* | *Covenantal Development in Genesis*. Sheffield: Sheffield Academic Press, 2000.

Chapter 9

COMPOSITION OF THE PENTATEUCH

How was the Pentateuch written? In the last two centuries no question in Old Testament study has attracted more attention than this. But despite long and learned discussion scholars are far from reaching a consensus on this question. In this chapter I cannot hope to resolve the issues at stake, but simply outline the main scholarly options and track the ebb and flow of critical opinion. To do this I shall outline the history of the debate and point out how changing assumptions about the nature of revelation and the Bible have influenced the character of the critical debate.

The history of the debate falls into three main periods: up to about 1800 when traditional assumptions about the Mosaic authorship of the Pentateuch were all but universally accepted; roughly 1800–1975 when a documentary theory of the growth of the Pentateuch became critical orthodoxy; and finally from 1975 to the present, when the debate about the composition of the Pentateuch has become much more open and radically different positions are defended by different scholars.

THE TRADITIONAL ASCRIPTION OF THE PENTATEUCH TO MOSES

The Pentateuch may be described as a didactic biography of Moses: through recounting the life of Moses and what he taught, the Pentateuch instructs its readers in how they should live. But it nowhere says who wrote this biography. Certain passages are said to have been written down by Moses himself (Exod. 17:14; 24:4, 7; 34:27; Num. 33:2; Deut. 31:9, 24), though it is not clear just what is covered by these remarks. Furthermore, nearly every group of laws is introduced by a comment such as 'The LORD spoke to Moses' or something similar. If Moses received these laws from God, might he not also have written them down? And Deuteronomy of course consists of three sermons preached by Moses before he died: whether or not he wrote them down, they do profess to be by Moses.

In the light of these observations orthodox Jews from pre-Christian times to the present have understood the Pentateuch not simply to be a biography of Moses, but written by him. The way that the Pentateuch is referred to by other books of the Old Testament implies Mosaic authorship (e.g. Josh. 1:7–8; 1 Kgs 2:3; 2 Kgs 14:6; 2 Kgs 23:21, 25; 2 Chr. 8:13; 34:14; 35:12; Ezra 3:2; 6:18; Neh. 8:1; 13:1). This is the assumption of the New Testament too (e.g. Matt. 8:4; 19:8; Luke 2:22; 16:29, 31; John 5:46; 7:19–23; Acts 3:22; Rom. 10:5, 19; 1 Cor. 9:9; Heb. 7:14).

The last few verses of the Pentateuch describe Moses' death. Could they have been written by Moses? According to the first-century Jewish writers Philo and Josephus they were. Moses, as the greatest of all the prophets, was well able to describe his own death. However, this was not the usual Jewish view: the *Talmud* holds that Moses wrote the whole Pentateuch apart from the last eight verses, which may have been penned by Joshua.

The assumption of the Mosaic authorship of the Pentateuch continued to be the accepted view among Jews and Christians right up to the seventeenth century, but it was not often discussed. Occasional Jewish or fringe Christian groups questioned this view, and are dismissed by mainstream writers. Intrinsically it was not an important issue. The Bible, including the Pentateuch, was read for instruction in theology and ethics, not to answer historical and literary questions. In so far as the Church Fathers, medieval Jews or Christians, or the Reformers touch on Mosaic authorship, it is to underline the antiquity and authority of the teaching in the Pentateuch not to demonstrate who

wrote the books. The Reformers were so focused on hearing the Word of God in the Scriptures that they were not really concerned about the critical issues that were to dominate subsequent scholarship.

What do you think?
CLAIMS OF MOSAIC AUTHORSHIP

Read the following passages: Exodus 17:14; 24:4, 7; 34:27; Numbers 33:2; Deuteronomy 31:9, 24. For which parts of the Pentateuch do they appear to be claiming Mosaic authorship?

Read Matthew 8:4; 19:8; Luke 2:22; 16:29, 31; John 5:46; 7:19–23; Acts 3:22; Romans 10:5, 19; 1 Corinthians 9:9; Hebrews 7:14. Do you think they are teaching that Moses wrote the Pentateuch, or are they simply using his name as a convenient way of referring to the passages?

THE DOCUMENTARY HYPOTHESIS

The standard explanation of the development of the Pentateuch, the so-called documentary hypothesis, reached its definitive formulation in the late nineteenth century and dominated discussion for about a century. However, its origins may be traced back considerably earlier. The Renaissance of the fifteenth century, the Reformation in the sixteenth century and the Enlightenment in the seventeenth and eighteenth centuries all contributed to the change of intellectual climate that made the new approach to the Pentateuch appealing.

The Renaissance was characterized by a return to the ancient classical sources. People were fascinated to discover what the Romans and Greeks really believed and did. In particular the style of ancient Latin was revived, and people learned Greek and Hebrew. There was a belief that if one understood the origins of culture or ideas, one could understand that idea or culture better. This fostered an interest in the origin and dating of literature, including the books of the Bible. Issues that seemed to earlier generations hardly worth bothering about were now seen as important and worthwhile topics of discussion. Thus the Renaissance encouraged an interest in investigating the circumstances in which ancient works were written and establishing the best critical texts of these works.

The Bible was of course the most important ancient text for Christian Europe, but it became even more vital to theological discussion as a result of the Reformation. The Reformers appealed to the supreme authority of Scripture in their disputes with Rome, claiming that often the Bible was misinterpreted by the later Church. They argued that the Church must recover the original sense of Scripture and reorder itself in accordance with the principles of the Bible and the early Church. In this way the Reformation intensified scholarly interest in and debate about the meaning and origin of the biblical books.

The division of Europe into Catholic and Protestant countries that followed the Reformation also created space for freethinkers, who rejected the tenets of both forms of Christianity. Indeed, the wars of religion between Catholic and Protestant rulers created an atmosphere in which some people rejected all types of revealed religion, arguing that human reason must be the guide to life not the dictates of the Church, whether it be Catholic or Protestant.

It was in the late seventeenth and throughout the eighteenth century that this trust in reason blossomed and what is referred to as the Enlightenment occurred. Until this era Christians of all persuasions held that fundamental beliefs and morality were God given: they were revealed through Scripture and the teaching of the Church. But according to the Enlightenment view man, not God, was the measure of all things. Claims to truth, religious or otherwise, must be tested at the bar of human reason. Was there good evidence for the beliefs? Were the beliefs rational in themselves? Were the origins of these beliefs historically respectable and so on? Enlightenment thinkers therefore tended to be sceptical about miracles, prophecy and other alleged proofs of divine intervention in the world. And because the Bible contains many accounts of miracles and prophecy, and because it claims to be divine teaching, it was often subject to critical scrutiny. Indeed, many ideas that were later to be commonplaces of critical theory were first mooted among early Enlightenment thinkers.

Thomas Hobbes, the English political philosopher, included some observations on the Pentateuch in his work *Leviathan*

(1651). He pointed out some features that precluded Mosaic authorship of the present work, such as the description of the death of Moses and various anachronisms. He did not deny the whole Pentateuch to Moses: for example, he thought Deuteronomy 11—27 was by Moses and was the law book discovered in the temple by Hilkiah. Hobbes thought that Ezra was responsible for the final editing of the Pentateuch.

Benedict Spinoza was an unorthodox Jew, whose *Tractatus Theologico-Politicus* stirred up a storm of protest when it was published in 1670. He argued that the Pentateuch could not have been written by Moses, because it speaks about Moses in the third person, describes his death, and uses late names, e.g. Dan, for places visited by the patriarchs. He pointed to inconsistencies in the stories about Jacob and Joseph, which suggest that they have been put together from various sources. He suggested that the main editor of the Pentateuch was Ezra (fifth century BC), nearly nine hundred years after Moses. But Ezra did not quite complete his work, for there are still some duplications and contradictions in it.

The English deists often challenged traditional Christian beliefs. They believed in a creator god, who, having created the world, no longer interfered with it through miracles, prophecy or the incarnation. So in their works they question Christ's miracles, the predictions of Daniel, and traditional theories of biblical authorship. It was a deist, Samuel Parvish, who was apparently the first to

suggest that Deuteronomy was written to promote the reformation of Josiah recorded in 2 Kings 22—23. He thought the priests wrote it to feather their own nest as it were. 'I yet conclude that the whole [law] depends on Hilkiah: of whose ability and honesty we know nothing; but whose interest it was to have a law, either genuine or spurious' (Parvish 1746, p. 324).

These ideas were in their own time just straws in the wind; they were not taken up by the leading theologians and biblical scholars immediately. However, a new consensus about the composition of the Pentateuch gradually built during the nineteenth century, and this I shall now explain. It is based on three main pillars: first, the analysis of the Pentateuch into four main literary sources; second, the dating of Deuteronomy to the late seventh century BC; and third, the dating of the priestly material, i.e. the laws on worship in Exodus 25 to Numbers 30, to the post-exilic era, the fifth century BC.

Jean Astruc, a French doctor from a theological family, was much concerned by the denials of Mosaic authorship of the Pentateuch, which he described as 'the sickness of the last century'. He therefore put forward an explanation of the apparent inconsistencies in the Pentateuch entitled *Conjectures on the Original Memoirs that it Seems Moses Used to Compose the Book of Genesis* (1753). He observed that there are repetitions within Genesis, such as two accounts of the creation of man (Gen. 1 and Gen. 2), two accounts of Sarah being taken by a foreign king (Gen. 12:10–20 and Gen. 20) and so on. Second, there are

Digging deeper:
SOURCE ANALYSIS OF GENESIS 1—11

Using Astruc's criteria split up Genesis 1—11 into its sources. Start by assigning all passages using the name The LORD to one source, and all passages speaking of God to another. Then use the principle of non-duplication within a source to help sort out the rest of the material.

When you have finished, compare your results with Astruc's (see the table on page 164). Where do you disagree with him? What problems did you have in deciding which passages to assign to which source? Do you think that Astruc's criteria are valid ways of distinguishing between different sources? Compare Astruc's analysis with S. R. Driver's (1894) on p. 166.

different names for God in Genesis: sometimes he is called God, at others the LORD (Yahweh). Astruc argued that these names were not synonymous, but represented the preferences of different original authors. Using these two criteria Astruc split up Genesis into two long sources and two shorter ones. He suggested that when Moses wrote Genesis, he arranged it in four parallel columns rather like a synopsis of the Gospels. Later on, someone else combined the four sources into the present text, thereby creating the repetitions and inconsistencies that now characterize Genesis.

Astruc's theory about how Moses composed Genesis did not convince most people, but

his principles for analysing the book using doublets and changes in divine name became foundational in later discussion. It also became widely accepted that the Pentateuch was based on a variety of sources, which were combined by one or more editors to produce the present work. However, the nature of these sources and the process by which they came to be joined up was the subject of much debate. Three different models of the growth of the Pentateuch were advocated.

The simplest model of the composition of the Pentateuch is the fragmentary hypothesis. This posits one author or editor of the Pentateuch utilizing a variety of sources, some long, some short, and weaving them together into a coherent account. The author linked the various fragments together with his own comments. He may have felt free to alter the wording of the fragments to some extent, but not so much as to obscure their individuality. If he had changed the wording too much, scholars would not have been able to identify the fragments incorporated into the Pentateuch.

The two leading proponents of the fragmentary hypothesis at the beginning of the nineteenth century were a Scottish priest, Alexander Geddes, and a German academic, Johann Severin Vater. According to Geddes the Pentateuch was compiled from fragments dating back to the time of Moses or earlier, which were put together in the time of Solomon (tenth century BC). Vater developed Geddes' ideas further. He was not certain when the materials originated, but

ASTRUC'S ANALYSIS OF GENESIS 1—11

Column A	Column B	Column C	Column D
1:1—2:3	2:4—4:26		Nothing until Chapter 14
Chapter 5	6:1–8		
6:9–22; 7:6–10, 19, 22, 24	7:1–5, 11–18, 21, 24	7: 20, 23–24	
8:1–19	8:20–22		
9:1–10, 12, 16–17, 28–29	9:11, 13–15, 18–29		
11:10–26	10:1—11:9; 11:27–32		

suggested they may have been put together in Judah shortly before the fall of Jerusalem (587 BC).

Another way of explaining the different divine names, writing styles and duplications within the Pentateuch is the supplementary hypothesis. On this view, an original short work was expanded by later writers at different times. The headings in the book of Proverbs suggest this is how Proverbs was written (see Prov. 1:1; 10:1; 25:1; 30:1; 31:1). The different writers had different styles and interests, so each wrote in a different way. The supplementary hypothesis holds that the Pentateuch was successively revised, but that the different revisions did not eradicate or transform the previous work. It grew like a snowball getting bigger and bigger with time, rolling up material as it went along and preserving the distinctive character of the materials as they were combined together.

Supplementary hypotheses were popular in Germany in the 1830s and 1840s and endorsed by leading scholars of the time such as G. H. A. Ewald and W. M. L. de Wette. They suggested a series of layers could be detected. Earliest were the Decalogue and the laws in Exodus 21—23. They were incorporated into the next layer, the Elohim or God layer, i.e. all the material that referred to the deity as God. This was later supplemented by the Yahweh, the LORD, layer. Finally, the book of Deuteronomy was added. The supplementer who added Deuteronomy was also responsible for editing the whole Pentateuch.

But the fashion for supplementary hypotheses waned. In the second half of the nineteenth century debate crystallized around two rival documentary hypotheses. These reverted to the principles of Astruc, in that they held that the Pentateuch was composed of four main sources that often ran in parallel and had been subsequently combined to form the present narrative. These sources comprised two versions of world history that ran from creation to the conquest of

Canaan, a version of Israel's history from the time of Abraham to the conquest, and also the book of Deuteronomy as a fourth source. Whereas Astruc supposed that Moses had combined the sources together, the advocates of the documentary hypotheses supposed that a series of editors had worked on the Pentateuch integrating the sources one by one.

To understand the documentary theory that came to dominate Pentateuchal studies for most of the twentieth century, one must keep its two aspects separate. There is first the identification of the sources, whose principles of separation go back in essence to Astruc. Second, there is the dating of these sources, using the methods of historical criticism first proposed by early Enlightenment writers such as Spinoza and the English deists. The source analysis does not depend on the dating of the sources, so we shall examine this first.

THE IDENTIFICATION OF THE SOURCES

Four major sources were identified by Julius Wellhausen (1844–1918), the German scholar who established the documentary hypothesis as the accepted model for the growth of the Pentateuch. The oldest source was the Yahwistic source, which uses the name the LORD or Yahweh for God. Since Yahweh is spelled Jahweh in German it is usually called the J source. The J source consists of brilliantly told stories running through Genesis and the first half of Exodus. Small sections of

Numbers also are ascribed to this source. The next oldest source is called the Elohistic source, since it refers to God as Elohim or God. It again consists of vivid stories running in parallel with the J source for the most part: for example the Jacob and Joseph stories from Genesis 25—50 are split between J and E. However, unlike J, E has no account of the creation or the flood, because the narrative of the Elohistic source does not start until Genesis 15.

The third source is more or less the book of Deuteronomy. Its genre and style set it apart from the great narrative sources J and E. As we have said, Deuteronomy is a series of sermons about the law. It is full of exhortation to observe the law, urgent appeals to love the LORD with all one's heart, warnings about the dangers of disobedience and so on. Its characteristic designation for God is 'the LORD our/your God', which also sets it apart from the J and E sources, in which, as already mentioned, God is referred to by the names Yahweh and Elohim respectively.

The fourth source is the Priestly source, which roughly corresponds to Astruc's A source in Genesis, together with all those parts of Exodus, Leviticus and Numbers about worship and associated matters which priests would have been interested in. In Genesis the genealogies are ascribed to this source, as well as chapters 1, 17 and 23 because of their teaching about religious topics such as the Sabbath and circumcision.

Drastically simplifying the analysis we can sum it up in the following table:

IDENTIFICATION OF SOURCES

Source	Name of God	Character	Content
J Yahwist	The LORD = Yahweh	Narrative	50 per cent of Genesis to Exodus 24, fragments of Numbers
E Elohist	God = Elohim	Narrative	33 per cent of Genesis to Exodus 24, fragments of Numbers
D Deuteronomist	The LORD your/our God	Sermons	Deuteronomy
P Priestly	God = Elohim	Lists, laws on worship etc	17 per cent of Genesis; Exodus 25 to Numbers 36

In practice the documentary hypothesis dissects books into sources, which in the present Pentateuch are closely interwoven. In the English-speaking world the great advocate of the documentary hypothesis was S. R. Driver (1846–1914), professor of Hebrew at Oxford. Below is a simplified version of his analysis of Genesis 1—25.

The two basic criteria for source analysis are the divine names and the duplication of material (doublets). But it was pointed out that the different genres of material, lists, narratives, sermons, in the different sources also meant that the different sources had different styles. According to Driver, P's 'language is that of a jurist,

DOCUMENTARY HYPOTHESIS

Source	Name of God	Character	Content *indicates elements of other source included
J Yahwist	The LORD = Yahweh	Vivid narrative	2:4b—3:24; 4:1–26; 5:29; 6:1–8; 7:1–5, 7–10, 12, 16b–17, 22–23; 8:2b–3a, 6–12, 13b, 20–22; 9:18–27; 10:8–19, 21, 24–30; 11:1–9, 28–30; 12:1—13:18*; 16:1b–14*; 18:1—19:38*; 21:1a, 2a, 33; 22:15–18, 20–24; 24:1—25:6, 11b, 18, 21–26a, 27–34
E Elohist	God = Elohim	Vivid narrative	15:1–21; 20:1–18; 21:6–32, 34; 22:1–14, 19
P Priestly	God = Elohim	Lists, dates, religious issues	1:1—2:4a; 5:1–28, 30–32; 6:9–22; 7:6, 11, 13–16a, 18–21, 24; 8:1–2a, 3b–5, 13a, 14–19; 9:1–17, 28–29; 10:1–7, 20, 22–23, 31–32; 11:10–27, 31–32; 12:4b–5; 13:6, 11b–12a; 16:1a, 3, 15–16; 17:1–27; 19:29; 21:1b, 2b–5; 23:1–20; 25:7–11a, 12–17, 19–20, 26b

rather than a historian; it is circumstantial, formal, and precise; a subject is developed systematically; and completeness of detail, even at the cost of some repetition is regularly observed' (Driver 1894, p. 11). J's style is 'freer and more varied; the actions of God are described with some fulness and picturesqueness of detail' (Driver 1894, p. 7). But there is not much difference in style between J and E apart from their preference for different divine names. Deuteronomy by contrast 'has adopted a rhetorical style well suited to oral presentation. Its sentences are long and flowing. They are marked by assonance, key words, and stereotyped expressions' (Tigay 1996, p. xviii).

According to the documentary hypothesis these sources were originally independent. But they were not all amalgamated at one time by a single editor, but at different times by a succession of editors. The oldest source J was first combined with the next oldest source E to form the combined JE work. Then, some time later, JE was combined with D, Deuteronomy, to form JED. Finally JED was combined with the long priestly source P to form JEDP, i.e. the present Pentateuch. In a diagram it may be represented:

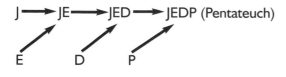

Figure 10: **THE DOCUMENTARY HYPOTHESIS**

When Astruc first put forward a documentary analysis of Genesis he

supposed he was recovering the documents used by Moses in about the thirteenth century BC. But according to the documentary hypothesis advocated by Wellhausen and Driver the documents originated very much later and had very little if any connection with Moses. The dates commonly associated with the documents are as follows:

DATING OF SOURCES

Document	Date BC
(Moses)	(1300)
J	950
E	850
JE	750
D	622
JED	600
P	500
JEDP	450

Except for the dating of Deuteronomy all the dates are approximate: different scholars would adjust them by half a century or so. But this is the least of the problems. Much more difficult to explain and justify are the raft of critical assumptions and historical arguments that lead to these dates for the Pentateuchal sources. It would confuse the exposition to mention all the qualifications and uncertainties that have been raised, so I shall just set out Wellhausen's views as he puts them in his *Prolegomena to the History of Israel* (1878), and later, when we look at the modern scholarly views, mention some of the problems with the documentary hypothesis.

Wellhausen examines the evolution of Israel's religion in five areas, and he tries to show that the developments described in the historical books match the different pictures of religion in the Pentateuchal sources. He looks at the place of worship, sacrifice, festivals, the priesthood, and priestly income. In each case he argues that at first things were rather disorganized and rules if any were simple, but that as time went on bureaucracy increased and laws became more detailed and demands more strenuous.

He begins with the place of worship. Reading the book of Judges one has the impression that sacrifice could be offered anywhere: Gideon offered sacrifice at Ophrah and Manoah in Zorah (Judg. 6:19; 13:2–23). This impression is confirmed by the books of Samuel, where the prophet offers sacrifice at various shrines (1 Sam. 7:10, 17; 9:13; 11:15). In 1 Kings 18 the prophet Elijah offers a huge sacrifice on Mount Carmel.

But the establishment of Jerusalem as Israel's capital and the building of the temple led to it becoming an important centre of worship as time passed. This trend reached its climax in the reformation of King Josiah described in 2 Kings 22—23 (c. 622 BC). He not only purified the temple in Jerusalem, but he destroyed all the places of worship outside Jerusalem and deposed all the priests of the rival shrines. In this way he made Jerusalem the exclusive place of worship for the whole nation.

However, as soon as Josiah died, the old shrines revived and people started worshipping at them again. But when the Jews were exiled to Babylon in 586 BC, the shrines were abandoned and forgotten. The Jews who returned from exile after 537 mostly settled in and around Jerusalem and never thought of worshipping outside Jerusalem. They just accepted that there was only one place to worship.

The historical books thus show a changing attitude to the place of worship. Originally people could worship anywhere. In the time of Josiah (622 BC) an attempt was made to limit worship to the temple in Jerusalem. This attempt at centralization of worship failed in the short term, but after the exile it was simply accepted. Wellhausen argued that these three stages in the development of religious practice are mirrored in the Pentateuchal sources. In J and E the patriarchs offer sacrifice and build altars in all sorts of places (Shechem, Bethel, Beersheba, Mount Moriah). The laws in JE also envisage sacrifice being offered wherever God makes his presence known (Exod. 20:24). J and E thus reflect common Israelite practice before Josiah's reformation.

But the book of Deuteronomy is insistent that Israel must only worship at 'the place which the LORD your God shall choose' and not at all the Canaanite shrines scattered through the land (12:4–6). This looks like a programme of centralization of worship such as Josiah implemented. Indeed 2 Kings 22:8–20 mentions that a law book was found in the temple which encouraged Josiah's reforms, so that

Wellhausen concluded that the law book in question must have been a version of Deuteronomy. (Here Wellhausen was building on the ideas of de Wette, who in a series of works from 1805 onwards had popularized this view of Deuteronomy.) The clear connection of Deuteronomy with Josiah's reform allows it to be dated much more precisely than all the other Pentateuchal sources.

Finally comes the Priestly source, which describes the tabernacle and its rituals in such detail. By describing sacrifice as taking place only in the tabernacle the Priestly source shows that it presupposes that there is only one place of worship. This corresponds to the situation after the exile, when the only place the Jews ever considered worshipping at was the rebuilt temple in Jerusalem. This implies that P's tabernacle far from being the prototype of the Jerusalem temple is but an echo of it. Because P's assumptions about the one place of worship match the historical reality of the post-exilic era, Wellhausen argues that it must be the latest of the Pentateuchal sources.

A similar development is discernible in the approach to sacrifice in the historical sources and the Pentateuch. In the early days Israelite sacrifice was little different from Canaanite practice: the Israelites simply offered their sacrifices to the LORD not to Baal. Worship was just part of life. Sacrifices were essentially joyful meals eaten at harvest times or when guests came (cf. Judg. 6:19–24). They were the equivalent of the meals served at baptisms, weddings or funerals today.

There were no rules defining sacrifice as a religious duty: this is why the prophets sometimes condemn sacrifices (Isa. 1:11–17; Mic. 6:6–8).

However, with the limitation of all worship to Jerusalem in Josiah's time the whole approach to sacrifice changed. Though the rites remained the same, the mood was transformed. 'To celebrate the vintage festival among one's native hills, and to celebrate it at Jerusalem, were two very different things.' No longer could you offer a sacrifice when you felt like it. Worship in the intimacy of the family circle was very different from worshipping in a huge crowd at Jerusalem. Centralization of worship led to 'a separation between it and the daily life ... A man lived in Hebron, but sacrificed in Jerusalem; life and worship fell apart' (Wellhausen, p. 77).

This segregation of worship from life was exacerbated by the exile. It was in this period that the priest-turned-prophet Ezekiel sketched out a vision of a restored temple in Jerusalem. The worship he describes is somewhat different from that prescribed in the Pentateuch so, Wellhausen argues, its detailed regulations did not yet exist. When the exile ended a tightly regulated system of worship was established in the second temple.

These changes in sacrificial practice Wellhausen correlates with the different sources of the Pentateuch. In J and E sacrifice and eating go together (e.g. Exod. 32:6): whenever meat was eaten, it came from a sacrifice. In these early sources there is little emphasis on the role of sacrifice in making atonement for sin: sacrifices are seen as occasions of thanksgiving and celebration.

Deuteronomy still sees sacrifice as an essentially joyous occasion, but it insists it must be offered only at the chosen place. This involves making the killing of animals outside the chosen place a purely secular slaughter: the only principle that matters is that the animal's blood should not be consumed (Deut. 12:15–19).

Much more information about sacrifice is found in the Priestly Code, which comprises most of Exodus 25 to Numbers 36. Its pedantic regulation of sacrificial procedures and its preoccupation with atonement annoy Wellhausen. He argues that it is P that introduced sin and guilt offerings, the

Day of Atonement, and incense in worship. This mood, he argues, represents the practice of the second temple.

Similar developments are traceable in the celebration of the festivals. Originally the festivals were closely connected with the cycle of nature: they celebrated the barley harvest, grape harvest or olive harvest. They took place in different towns on different dates determined by the progress of the harvest in different parts of the land. But with time came more attempts at regulation. The biggest change was making Passover a national festival in Jerusalem to celebrate the exodus. This began the disconnection of the festivals from nature and relating them to historic events in Israel's history. In post-exilic times this process went even further: the dates of the festivals were determined by

CHARACTERISTICS OF DIFFERENT ERAS AND SOURCES

	Early Monarchy / J E	Late Monarchy / D	Post-Exilic / P
Place of worship	Any holy place	Attempt to centralize all worship in Jerusalem	Jerusalem the only sanctuary
Sacrifice	Voluntary, joyful family occasions	Sacrifices only in Jerusalem. Secular slaughter elsewhere	Sacrifices highly regulated and expiatory
Festivals	Local harvest celebrations	Pilgrimage to Jerusalem required	Festivals fixed by calendar. Linked to history not harvest
Priesthood	Anyone could act as priest and sacrifice	Tribe of Levitical priests becoming important	Highly organized priesthood with great authority. Descended from Levi and Aaron
Priestly income	Parts of sacrifices voluntarily given by offerer	Shoulder, cheeks and stomach of sacrifices	Many sacrificial animals, tithes, firstlings

the calendar, not the weather, and all the great national festivals were linked with the exodus and wilderness experiences.

Once again Wellhausen argues that these changes are reflected in the different Pentateuchal strata. J and E reflect a largely unregulated approach to the festivals: they could be celebrated where one liked when one liked. Deuteronomy 16 links all the festivals to the chosen city and insists on their celebration there. But the agricultural aspect is still strong in its presentation. The Priestly Code (Num. 28—29), however, fixes all the festivals by the months of the year and is preoccupied by the number of sacrifices to be offered on the different festival days. The table on p. 170 sums up Wellhausen's view of the development of Israel's religious life and its relationship to the priestly sources.

The great innovation of Wellhausen's work was his sustained argument that the Priestly material was late. Earlier scholars, whether traditionalists who believed in Mosaic authorship or defenders of the old documentary hypothesis, believed that the priestly material was the oldest part of the Pentateuch and represented the official guide to approved divine worship from early times. The assertion that it was all a late fiction caused great controversy. Indeed Wellhausen was forced to give up his job as a professor of theology and teach Arabic instead.

However, by the early twentieth century the documentary hypothesis was widely accepted in secular universities and in mainstream Protestant denominations. By the mid-twentieth century the Catholic Church admitted the legitimacy of the documentary hypothesis, so that one could speak about it as an 'assured result of criticism'. The only people who rejected it outright were orthodox Jews and some conservative Christians who held that it undermined the inspiration and authority of the Bible. From time to time various modifications to the details of the documentary hypothesis were put forward by scholars, but by and large the hypothesis faced no serious challenge for the best part of a century.

TWENTIETH-CENTURY ADJUSTMENTS TO THE DOCUMENTARY HYPOTHESIS

But in certain ways the theory was softened, which probably made it more palatable to Church people and scholars who were sympathetic to the message of the Old Testament. In the previous chapter we noted the work of Noth and von Rad, who were both pupils of Albrecht Alt. Alt accepted the conclusions of the documentary hypothesis as far as the written sources were concerned, but he wanted to push back to the oral traditions that were eventually incorporated into the written texts. In his essay 'The God of the Fathers' (1929) Alt argued the religion of the patriarchs as portrayed in Genesis was typical of semi-nomads. Thus it is likely that some of the promises made to the patriarchs go back to the period in which they lived. So although the stories of the patriarchs were not written down in the J and E sources till a thousand years after the patriarchs, they still preserve grains of accurate historical reminiscence.

In his study of Israelite law Alt distinguished between the case law ('if a man does ...') and apodictic law ('thou shalt not ...'). He argued that case law had been borrowed from the Canaanites, but that apodictic law derived from covenantal settings such as Sinai. Though neither type of law originated with Moses, they were both very early forms of Israelite law, so the setting given them in the Pentateuch is not as misleading as the documentary hypothesis may suggest.

This attempt to demonstrate a real continuity between the earliest forms of Pentateuchal tradition and its final form was continued by Noth and von Rad. Both in their different ways tried to show that the message of the present Pentateuch was essentially a development of its earliest form. Von Rad argued that the present Pentateuch grew out of the ancient creed recorded in Deuteronomy 26:5–9. Noth posited a common source behind J and E, which was closer in time to the events it talks about. He also argued that the 12-tribe league, Israel's covenant organization and the central sanctuary all go back to the era of the Judges, that is within a century or so of the Israelite settlement in the land. The general drift of the Alt-Noth-von Rad modifications of the documentary hypothesis was that the Pentateuch was more credible than its late composition might have suggested.

The attempt to bolster the historical trustworthiness of the Pentateuch despite its late date was vigorously pursued in America by W. F. Albright and his school, and eminent fellow travellers such as E. A. Speiser and C. H. Gordon. They all appealed to comparative evidence from the ancient Near East to show that the texts of Genesis are very at home in the ancient world. The customs and laws presupposed by Genesis fit the early second millennium. This corroborates the historical accuracy of these stories of the patriarchs despite them not having been written down till many centuries after the events they record. On the basis of these parallels with Genesis, John Bright, in his standard *History of Israel* (1972, p. 91) wrote: 'We can assert with full confidence that Abraham, Isaac, and Jacob were actual historical individuals.' In this way the negative impression created by the documentary hypothesis was dispelled. By the mid-twentieth century the scholarly consensus seemed to be: the Pentateuch may have been written a very long time after the events it records, but further investigation shows that there is substantial continuity between what it affirms and what really happened.

THE COLLAPSE OF THE CONSENSUS SINCE 1975

But in the last decades of the twentieth century this cosy consensus disappeared, at least among scholars most engaged with Pentateuchal studies: inevitably many teachers of biblical studies still adhere to the theories they grew up with, which is the more understandable when there is no agreed alternative. At the moment the situation is highly confused. While many scholars are rejecting the documentary hypothesis in whole or in part, they often come to mutually contradictory conclusions. In order to clarify the central issues, I shall have to oversimplify the current debates. Those who want more detailed analysis should consult the bibliography at the end of the chapter.

The documentary hypothesis rests on two main pillars: the identification of the sources and their dating. Both pillars are being questioned today. On the one hand it is argued that the criteria for distinguishing sources are invalid, so that texts described by the documentary hypothesis as composite are in fact unities. On the other hand those who still identify separate sources within the Pentateuch dispute the conventional datings. There are those who would date the allegedly early J source late and others who would date the supposedly late P source early. Some even question the date of Deuteronomy. In an attempt to focus the issues clearly, I shall first look at issues of unity, and then proceed to review the questions of date.

THE TREND TOWARDS UNITARY READINGS

In recent study of the Bible there has been much more attention paid to the final form of the text. This is partly prompted by approaches in literary criticism and partly by the theology of canonical criticism, which observes that it is the final or canonical form of the Bible that is authoritative for the Church and therefore should be the focus of study. But some scholars who have argued for unitary readings seem to be driven by neither concern, simply what they see as logic and commonsense.

In the Pentateuch it is the book of Genesis that has been most carefully split into sources by the documentary hypothesis: in the later books lengthy blocks of material tend to be ascribed to one source, so the divisive reading of the text is not so evident. In Genesis, however, the material is split into three main sources, J, E and P, which are often interwoven. A prime example is the story of Joseph, where J and E tend to alternate with each other, with some blocks of material being ascribed to a different source, e.g. the story of Tamar in chapter 38.

The old documentary theorists tended to be very confident about the distinctiveness of P, whose contents set it apart from J and E so clearly, but they often expressed hesitation about differentiating between J and E. Driver (1894, p. 12) comments: 'In the *details* of the analysis of JE there is sometimes uncertainty, owing to the criteria being indecisive.' So it is perhaps not surprising that in recent work on Genesis the traditional analysis of the material into J and E has often been abandoned. The material assigned to E is now regarded as an integral part of J or in some cases as an expansion of J. In particular the Joseph story, once divided into two, now tends to be read as a unity. Even chapter 38, which on first inspection has little to do with the main story, is now held by many writers on Genesis to be integral to the Joseph story. Its motifs and interests both foreshadow and comment on the main story.

Digging deeper:
JOSEPH AND HIS BROTHERS, GENESIS 37

According to the documentary theory this chapter divides into two sources J and E as follows: Source 1 = 2b–11, 22–24, 28a, 28c–30, 36. Source 2 = 12–21, 25–27, 28b, 31–35. Can you work out which is J and which is E, and why?

C. Westermann in his big modern commentary on Genesis (1986) holds that it consists of four scenes vv. 3–11, 12–17, 18–30, and 31–35 from one author. He thinks vv. 25b–27, 28b represent a variant included by the author.

Which analysis do you prefer and why? How do you explain the similar actions of Reuben and Judah?

If the distinction between J and E is widely questioned, many scholars still think that J and P are clearly distinguishable sources. This is because P usually occurs in large chunks within the main narrative of Genesis. It is rarely intertwined with J as E is supposed to be. The main exception to this is the flood story, where a longer, fuller version usually ascribed to P has a number of additional features ascribed to J. It has been noted that the present version of the flood story is finely crafted as a palistrophe. (See discussion in Chapter 2 above.) But neither the J nor P versions by themselves form a palistrophe nor do they contain so many parallels with the Babylonian version of the flood as the final version does. There has therefore been fierce debate as to whether the flood story should be ascribed to two different sources or whether it is essentially the work of one author (see articles by Anderson (1978), Emerton (1987) and Wenham (1978, 1991)).

But are the principles of source analysis valid in themselves? This is the question raised by R. N. Whybray in *The Making of the Pentateuch* (1987). He points out that of the various models of the composition of the Pentateuch, fragmentary, supplementary, and documentary (for definitions see earlier in chapter), the documentary is the most difficult to demonstrate.

For whereas the fragmentary and supplementary hypotheses envisage relatively simple, and it would seem, logical processes and at the same time appear to account for the unevennesses of the completed Pentateuch, the documentary hypothesis is not only much more complicated but also very specific in its assumptions about the historical development of Israel's understanding of its origins (Whybray 1987, p. 48).

Whybray disagrees with the documentary hypothesis for two reasons: first, it is illogical and self-contradictory, and second there are better explanations of repetition and stylistic variation. First, the theory is illogical, and while professing to explain repetitions and contradictions, it fails to do so. The hypothesis says that the Pentateuch must be made up of different sources because it contains repetition and contradiction. However, the hypothesis supposes that the separate sources that make up the Pentateuch do not contain repetition or contradiction: that non-contradiction and non-repetition are the chief criteria for distinguishing a source. But when the sources were combined together, a repetitious and contradictory account was produced. But Whybray thinks this is odd. It presupposes that Hebrew writing practices changed drastically. Early writers did not tolerate contradiction or repetition, but later writers accepted it easily. But why did their attitudes change? If later writers did not mind repetition, why should we suppose earlier Hebrew writers did? But if the earlier writers, like the later ones, did not mind contradiction or repetition, how can we separate out the sources? He observes:

> Thus the hypothesis can only be maintained on the assumption that, while consistency was the hallmark of the various documents, *in*consistency was the hallmark of the redactors. (Whybray 1987, p. 49)

Second, Whybray maintains that there are better explanations of repetition and stylistic variation within texts than supposing that the changes reflect different sources. We accept repetition and variation in other literature without supposing that there is another source or author responsible for the change. For example, other religious texts use a variety of names for God, so why should a change of divine name in Genesis signal a change of source? Sometimes there could be a theological reason for change; at others the writer may just unconsciously feel the need of variety. Modern literary studies have led to a much deeper appreciation of repetition as a literary device. It does more than simply emphasize a point; it can give clues to the actors' attitudes and motives. This has been applied in detail to Old Testament storytelling in the works of Alter and Sternberg among many others.

What do you think?
IS WHYBRAY RIGHT?

What do you think about Whybray's criticisms of the documentary hypothesis? Look back at the description of the supplementary and fragmentary hypotheses at the beginning of the chapter. How far do Whybray's criticisms also apply to these hypotheses?

The second chapter of Whybray's book challenges the traditio-critical approach of Noth and more recent writers such as Blum and Rendtorff (for discussion of Noth see last chapter and this). Because they presuppose a documentary hypothesis, they are building their theories about the development of oral tradition on a shaky foundation. If the documentary hypothesis is illogical and self-contradictory, Noth's assumptions about oral traditions are even more speculative. Whybray thinks Noth's theories are arrived at by 'piling one speculation upon another' (Whybray, p. 194).

After this full-frontal assault on conventional criticism of the Pentateuch, Whybray finally states his own preferred approach. He wants a simple solution. Many recent studies have shown there is much more unity in the Pentateuch than the documentary hypothesis recognized. So why not recognize that there is a single author or editor responsible for its composition? Doubtless this editor used a variety of sources, so Whybray is endorsing a fragmentary hypothesis, even if the fragments cannot be exactly identified. He concludes:

> There appears to be no reason why (allowing for the possibility of a few additions) the first edition of the Pentateuch as a comprehensive work should not also have been the *final* edition, a work composed by a single historian. (Whybray 1987, pp. 232–33)

THE DATING OF THE SOURCES

While Whybray broke with the critical consensus when it came to the analysis of the sources, he stayed with it when it came to dating the composition of the Pentateuch. He argued that it was all put together in one fell swoop about 500 BC. This was much the same era as Wellhausen and his successors had proposed for the final editing of the Pentateuch when the early composite of JED was linked up with the late P source

to form the present Pentateuch. (See Figure 10, p. 167.)

John van Seters, a North American scholar, represents another more radical trend in Pentateuchal studies. In a series of books and articles over the last 20 years he has challenged both the source analysis and the dating of the Pentateuch. Whereas Whybray preferred a fragmentary hypothesis to explain the composition of the Pentateuch in one fell swoop, van Seters works with a supplementary model. He traces the growth of the Pentateuch over several centuries and believes it was completed about 300 BC.

Van Seters' key ideas are set out in his first book, *Abraham in History and Tradition* (1975). It begins with an assault on the view that archaeological discoveries have substantiated the historicity of Genesis. As mentioned above, the consensus-critical view especially in America was that, although the Pentateuch was written late, parallels between Genesis and ancient Near Eastern texts from the second millennium BC demonstrated that the stories had been faithfully transmitted over many centuries. Marriage customs, inheritance rules, names of people, the semi-nomadic lifestyle as known from Mesopotamian texts from the early second millennium seemed to match well the descriptions of patriarchal life found in Genesis. These parallels, it was argued, showed the authenticity and antiquity of the Genesis accounts. But van Seters argues that the closeness of the parallels has been exaggerated and that, where the parallels were strong, material from much later times should have been considered.

Having weakened the archaeological case for the historical reliability of Genesis, van Seters proceeds to develop his model for the growth of the Abraham stories in chapters 12—26. He regards many of the traditional criteria for distinguishing sources as flawed. Only real duplication of episodes warrants us detecting different sources. Repetition within sources may be merely stylistic, and variation of vocabulary or divine names need not indicate different sources.

The Abraham story in its earliest written form consisted of just three episodes, including 12:10–20, the account of Sarah's abduction into Pharaoh's harem. Later this was expanded by episodes now found in Genesis 20—21. One can see that this is expansion, because chapter 20, Sarah's second abduction, presupposes knowledge of the chapter 12 episode. Then came the work of the Yahwist, J, to whose hand van Seters ascribes most of Genesis 12—26 apart from the P material. To J he ascribes Genesis 15, which under conventional documentary theory had been ascribed to E, but he notes its affinity with Deuteronomic literature and Isaiah 40—55, which suggest it suits the exilic period better than any other. In other words van Seters is dating the Yahwist about 550 BC, about 400 years later than the conventional theory does.

Later additions to the book include the P material, that is the dates and other chronological data in Genesis and

chapters 17 and 23. Chapter 14, Abram's battle with the kings of the East, was added later still. Van Seters suggests that the kings of the East are really a coy way of referring to the Persians whose empire included Israel at this time. Finally came 14:18–20, the mention of Abraham's welcome by Melchizedek, which may be an attempt to justify the religious syncretism of the period. This would imply that Genesis reached its final present shape in about 300 BC.

In his later works van Seters applies his methods to the rest of the Pentateuch. In *Prologue to History* (1992) he argues that Genesis 1—11 shows acquaintance with both Greek historiography and Mesopotamian mythology. The Yahwist, he thinks, could have learned about these ideas while in exile in Babylon. In *The Life of Moses* (1994) he argues again that the JE material in Exodus is an essential unity from the hand of the Yahwist. It was written as an introduction to the historical books of Deuteronomy to Kings. Many of the ideas of the book of Exodus have been borrowed from the prophetic books. For example, the story of Moses' call is based on the calls of Isaiah and Ezekiel, and the idea of an exodus from Egypt is modelled on the idea of an exodus from Babylon, which Isaiah 40—55 proclaims.

Van Seters' conclusions are thus very radical. They turn traditional ideas of the composition of the Old Testament on their head. Instead of seeing the Pentateuch as the oldest part of the Hebrew Bible, he sees it as one of the youngest elements. Already Wellhausen had gone part of this way by arguing that the law came after the prophets. He meant that the laws in the Pentateuch came after the prophets, but in the van Seters' model, the law in the sense of the whole Pentateuch comes after the prophets. As yet the van Seters' paradigm has not swept the board as the documentary hypothesis did thanks to Wellhausen's advocacy, but a significant number of scholars do accept his late datings.

In Germany dissent from the documentary hypothesis has been led by Rolf Rendtorff and his pupil Erhard Blum. Like van Seters they prefer to think in terms of a supplementary model for the growth of the Pentateuch. Rendtorff believes that one must try and trace the growth of the Pentateuch from originally short and separate traditions into larger units. This happened through processes of accretion down the years and editors reworking older documents till eventually the present Pentateuch emerged. Rendtorff set out a programme for a new-look Pentateuchal criticism, which Blum has subsequently worked out in two lengthy books. At times the entities identified by Blum look similar to the traditional source documents. Though J and E have disappeared, the Deuteronomistic revision of the text that took place between 530 and 500 looks quite like van Seters' Yahwist. However, Blum does in general date material a little earlier than van Seters and he adopts a more positive approach to its historical value.

As in the English-speaking world, these new ideas have not been universally accepted in Germany. There have been plenty of studies presupposing the main lines of the documentary hypothesis and in some cases defending them. Nevertheless, there is more openness to new models than before Rendtorff wrote. He observed that 'we really do not possess reliable criteria for dating of the pentateuchal literature. Each dating of the pentateuchal "sources" relies on purely hypothetical assumptions which in the long run have their continued existence because of the consensus of scholars' (Rendtorff, pp. 201–2). When he wrote this in 1977 it sounded radical; today, a generation later, its truth would be widely acknowledged.

Most of the debate about source analysis and dating has focused on the book of Genesis and the early chapters of Exodus. Much less attention has been paid to the priestly material that dominates Exodus 25 to Numbers 36 and to the book of Deuteronomy. The neglect of the priestly material and its dating is perhaps surprising given the importance it has in Wellhausen's *Prolegomena*, whose chief thrust is to prove that P could not be early. Doubtless this lack of debate reflects Protestant scholars' lack of interest in and knowledge of the development of Old Testament worship. For in truth there is little in the *Prolegomena* to demonstrate that the worship described by the P material in Genesis actually corresponds to what happened in the post-exilic temple. The texts that describe this period, Ezra to Nehemiah and Haggai to Malachi, give us very little information about this period. It is true that, for example, there is no mention of the Day of Atonement being celebrated in pre-exilic times, but does that demand the conclusion that it must be a post-exilic festival as Wellhausen argued? It is nowhere mentioned in the post-exilic books either. Wellhausen's argument about the date of P is therefore essentially a negative one: P does not fit with his reading of pre-exilic worship texts, therefore it must be post-exilic.

It is particularly critical Jewish scholars who have objected to this line of argument. Long before the consensus in favour of the documentary broke down, Kaufmann argued in *The Religion of Israel* (1961) that the priestly material was pre-exilic not post-exilic. It reflected the practice of the first temple, not the second. Wellhausen sought to show that Israelite religion evolved from natural spontaneous worship rooted in family and agricultural custom into a highly organized and regulated system operated by priests. But in other ancient oriental cultures, such as Babylon and Egypt, there were well-organized systems of worship run by priests operating by fixed timetables and complicated rules. They are no proof of lateness.

Kaufmann's views have been elaborated in a series of major commentaries on Leviticus and Numbers by Milgrom, and linguistic studies by Hurvitz. They argue that Ezekiel seems to quote from Leviticus and Numbers, which would be strange if they were written after the exile, for Ezekiel was preaching at the beginning of the exile. The language and terminology

of Leviticus and Numbers is different from books definitely written after the exile, such as Ezra and Chronicles. In fact, the book of Ezekiel seems to be written in a kind of Hebrew intermediate between the early Hebrew of Leviticus/Numbers and the late Hebrew of Chronicles and Ezra or Nehemiah. Finally, though Wellhausen supposed that some of the practices regulated in the priestly material represented post-exilic custom, Jewish scholars have pointed out that there are often important differences between the practice of the second temple and the prescriptions of Leviticus/Numbers. For example, there were no animal tithes, the high priest was not anointed, and the Urim and Thummim were not in use. This is difficult to explain if the priestly material comes from post-exilic times.

More recently this discussion of the origin and date of the priestly material has been taken further. Israel Knohl's *The Sanctuary of Silence* (1995) has reversed another of Wellhausen's critical positions. Wellhausen thought that the bulk of the priestly material came from the fifth century, but that Leviticus 17—26 came from a century earlier. A careful analysis of all the material has convinced Knohl that really most of the priestly material is early and Leviticus 17—26 is somewhat later. He argues that the bulk of the priestly material comes from the time of Solomon, i.e. the tenth century BC, whereas Leviticus 17—26 and associated material probably originated in Hezekiah's time, the late eighth century.

These studies of the priestly material show that the debate about the priestly literature is still ongoing. Just as not everyone has been persuaded by van Seters' redefinition and redating of J, so not everyone is convinced by these arguments for redating P. Most scholars have not studied this part of the Old Testament in enough depth to be sure what to think. They recognize that the old arguments for a post-exilic date for P are not as strong as they once supposed, but they are not sure whether the case for an early date has been made either. With the collapse of the critical consensus people feel themselves being pulled in opposite directions: the radicals urge that the Pentateuch is all late fiction, while others argue that the supposedly late parts of the Pentateuch are relatively early.

These issues resurface with discussion of the book of Deuteronomy. It has in recent times been sidelined in the debate about Pentateuchal origins, yet for Wellhausen it was crucial. As he put it:

Deuteronomy is the starting point, not in the sense that without it, it would be impossible to accomplish anything, but only because, when its position has been historically ascertained, we cannot decline to go on, but must demand that the position of the Priestly Code must also be fixed by reference to history. (Wellhausen 1878, p. 13)

For Wellhausen the connection between Deuteronomy and the reformation of Josiah was his starting point. He believed he could show that JE, D and P showed a progression in their portrayal of Israelite religion and therefore allowed a relative dating: that is, scholars could, by comparing the content of these sources, establish in which order they were written. But it was Deuteronomy that allowed an absolute dating. And for most scholars this has remained the case: they accept a late-seventh-century origin for Deuteronomy and proceed to interpret it against that presumed background.

As we saw in Chapter 7 the book of Deuteronomy resembles in its shape legal documents from the second millennium,

DEUTERONOMY IN PARALLEL WITH HITTITE AND ASSYRIAN TREATIES

Hittite Treaties, Fourteenth Century BC	Deuteronomy, Date ??	Assyrian Treaties, Seventh Century BC
Preamble	Preamble 1:1–5	Preamble
Historical prologue	Historical prologue 1:6—4:49	Divine witnesses
Stipulations	Stipulations/Laws 5:1—26:19	Stipulations
Document clause	Document clause 27:1–8	
Divine witnesses		
Curses and blessings	Blessings and curses 28:1–68	Curses

such as ancient Hittite vassal treaties and law codes, such as Hammurabi's. Later Assyrian treaties from the first millennium have a different structure with the elements arranged in a different order and no historical prologue.

This was sufficient for the American scholar Meredith Kline and the British Egyptologist Kenneth Kitchen to argue that this supported the Mosaic origin of Deuteronomy. However, other scholars such as Weinfeld and Frankena observed the close parallel between the curses of Deuteronomy 28 and some Assyrian curses and concluded that this supported a seventh-century date for Deuteronomy after all.

The most sustained challenge to the seventh-century origin of Deuteronomy has come from Gordon McConville. In *Law and Theology in Deuteronomy* (1984) he argues that Deuteronomy is not so interested in legal precision as in encouraging people to keep the law. This explains many of the apparent differences from the priestly material, which he thinks precedes Deuteronomy. He thinks it wrong to connect the laws about worship at the chosen place, the feasts, and profane slaughter with Josiah's centralization of worship in Jerusalem. After all, Deuteronomy never mentions Jerusalem, and the only place it names where sacrifice must be offered is Mount Ebal (Deut. 27:1–8) about 40 miles from Jerusalem. Deuteronomy's regulations reflect a historical situation long before Josiah's reforms. In his recent commentary (2002) McConville has developed these ideas further. He suggests that the administrative arrangements

envisaged by Deuteronomy 16:18—18:22 with rule by priests, prophet, and a modest king reflects the constitutional ideals of the Judges period. That is not to rule out later additions to the book in later times, but they are difficult to demonstrate.

These are some of the very different approaches to Pentateuchal criticism that have been proposed in recent decades. I have selected a few key issues, rather than attempting an exhaustive coverage, as the whole modern debate is very complicated. But even when the issues have been simplified, it is apparent that they are very hard to resolve and that it will be difficult to reach a consensus to replace the documentary hypothesis.

It is necessary to ask why there are such divergent views, and why it is so difficult to come to rationally agreed conclusions. It partly depends on the quality of the arguments being deployed. In explaining different views I have set out to state them as fairly as possible, but what seems to be a strong argument to one scholar seems to be a weak argument to another. Repetition looks to one person to be a sure sign of multiple sources: to another it is a clever narrative device. Deuteronomy's similarity to Hittite treaties seems to some to be an indication it was written at a similar time to the treaties: to others it is mere coincidence.

Some progress towards agreement might be made if instead of counting arguments for a particular view, scholars weighed them. Ideally we could classify arguments into strong, moderate, and weak arguments, for and against a particular view. The weak arguments on either side could be disregarded and the strong and moderate arguments used to evaluate a particular critical stance. This procedure might thin the field somewhat, but still at the end of the day there will be elements of subjectivity: what one person regards as a strong argument will be dismissed by another as weak. For example, arguments based on the age of the language in different texts would be regarded by linguists as strong arguments for dating that text. Thus the argument that P must be pre-exilic because its vocabulary and style are earlier than Ezekiel's is essentially a powerful one. However, the validity of this argument does presuppose that the individual examples of P's antiquity are sufficient and compelling in themselves. If there are just a few, they could be archaisms. The argument also presupposes that the book of Ezekiel is an exilic work: if that premise is denied, P's pre-exilic age might also be questioned. Even allowing for some uncertainty in linguistic argument, it is noteworthy that professedly early works do not contain late features such as Aramaisms and Persian loan words found in obviously late works such as Chronicles and Ezra.

Because so few of the books of the Old Testament are dated beyond question, there is very little sure ground to build dating arguments on, especially when it comes to the Pentateuch. If the radicals are correct and the Pentateuch and most of the rest of the Old Testament is written in the late post-exilic period, although it purports to be describing life and events from a much earlier period, we must end up as historical agnostics. We can say very little about pre-exilic Israel and its history. The stories in the Old Testament are essentially wishful thinking by the post-exilic community trying to justify their existence in the land.

As far as the arguments for source analysis are concerned, outlook and predispositions are again very important in determining conclusions. Admiration for the skill of scholarship in unravelling intricately intertwined sources may lead one to look favourably on the traditional JEDP analysis. Others, however, may revel in the insights literary scholars find in repetition and variation and therefore incline to see texts as unities. It is partly a matter of taste.

But individual taste is influenced by fashion, and the last two centuries have been widely influenced by a hermeneutic of suspicion. Some of the most influential thinkers of these times, such as Nietzsche, Marx and Freud, have taught us that people have ulterior motives for much if not all they say and do. They are fighting to preserve their class privileges or avenge their harsh father or whatever. At the popular level we are suspicious of what those in authority say, whether they be politicians, police, journalists or clergy. It is a similar attitude that has infected much biblical study: texts are suspected of not being what they profess to be. They are propaganda on behalf of a particular viewpoint and therefore cannot be trusted. They pretend to be old only to make readers respect their authority. Such ideological criticism of texts has some validity: people do write or speak to put across their own ideas and we do not hear them properly if we do not pick up their message. But that is not the same as saying that they are lying. In fact, our usual presumption when listening to others is that they are telling the truth, not everything that could be said truly about a topic, but the relevant truth for the message they are conveying. Only when they say something very improbable or conflicting with something we already know, do we start to doubt them. Otherwise we believe them innocent until they prove themselves guilty.

Assyriologists and Egyptologists have observed that biblical scholars often are more suspicious about biblical texts than orientalists are about Babylonian or Egyptian texts. If orientalists demanded the level of proof that biblical scholars do before accepting the witness of an Assyrian or an Egyptian text we would know little about the ancient world. The present confusion in Pentateuchal studies should be an invitation to examine our assumptions and our methods. A return to uncritical naivety is not what is needed, but neither should we treat the biblical texts with more suspicion than we treat our friends and family.

FURTHER READING

BACKGROUND TO DISCUSSION

P. Gay *The Enlightenment*. London: Weidenfeld and Nicolson, 1966.

R. A. Harrisville and W. Sundberg *The Bible in Modern Culture: Theology and Historical-Critical Method from Spinoza to Käsemann*. Grand Rapids: Eerdmans, 1995.

P. Hazard *The European Mind 1680–1715*. tr. by J. L. May. London: Penguin Books, 1964.

T. Hobbes *Leviathan*. New York: Collier Books, 1967 (first published 1651).

S. Parvish *An Enquiry into the Jewish and Christian Revelation*. London, 1746.

J. W. Rogerson *W. M. L. de Wette, Founder of Modern Biblical Criticism: An Intellectual Biography*. Sheffield: JSOT Press, 1992.

CLASSIC STATEMENTS OF THE DOCUMENTARY HYPOTHESIS

S. R. Driver *An Introduction to the Literature of the Old Testament*. Edinburgh: T. & T. Clark, 1894.

A. Rofe *Introduction to the Composition of the Pentateuch*. Sheffield: Sheffield Academic Press, 1999. A modern restatement of the position.

J. Wellhausen *Prolegomena to the History of Ancient Israel*. Cleveland: Meridian Books, 1957 (German original 1878).

SURVEYS OF MODERN DEBATE

E. W. Nicholson *The Pentateuch in the Twentieth Century*. Oxford: Clarendon Press, 1998.

G. J. Wenham 'Pondering the Pentateuch: the Search for a New Paradigm', in *The Face of Old Testament Studies: A Survey of Contemporary Approaches*. ed. by D. W. Baker and B. T. Arnold. Grand Rapids: Baker Book House, 1999, pp. 116–44.

D. J. Wynn-Williams *The State of the Pentateuch*. Berlin: de Gruyter, 1997.

INFLUENTIAL TWENTIETH-CENTURY STUDIES

A. Alt *Essays on Old Testament History and*

Religion. tr. by R.A. Wilson. Garden City: Doubleday, 1968 (German originals from 1929 onwards).

M. Noth *A History of Pentateuchal Traditions*. tr. by B. W. Anderson. Englewood Cliffs: Prentice-Hall, 1972 (German original 1948).

G. von Rad *The Problem of the Hexateuch and Other Essays*. tr. by E. W. Trueman Dicken. Edinburgh: Oliver and Boyd, 1966 (German original 1938).

R. Rendtorff *The Problem of the Process of Transmission in the Pentateuch*. tr. by J. J. Scullion. Sheffield: JSOT Press, 1990 (German original 1977).

J. van Seters *Abraham in History and Tradition*. New Haven: Yale University Press, 1975.

J. van Seters *Prologue to History: The Yahwist as Historian in Genesis*. Louisville: Westminster/John Knox, 1992.

J. van Seters *The Life of Moses: The Yahwist as Historian in Exodus-Numbers*. Louisville: Westminster/John Knox, 1994.

SOURCE ANALYSIS

R. Alter *The Art of Biblical Narrative*. New York: Basic Books, 1981.

M. Sternberg *The Poetics of Biblical Narrative*. Bloomington: Indiana University Press, 1985.

R. N. Whybray *The Making of the Pentateuch: a Methodological Study*. Sheffield: JSOT Press, 1987.

The Joseph story

G. W. Coats *From Canaan to Egypt*. Washington: Catholic Biblical Association, 1976.

C. Westermann *Genesis 37—50*. London: SPCK, 1986.

The flood story

B. W. Anderson 'From Analysis to Synthesis: The Interpretation of Genesis 1—11' *JBL* 97, 1978 pp. 23–39.

J. A. Emerton 'An Examination of Some Attempts to Defend the Unity of the Flood Narrative in Genesis' *VT* 37, 1987 pp. 401–20; 38, 1988 pp. 1–21.

G. J. Wenham 'The Coherence of the Flood Narrative' *VT* 28, 1978 pp. 336–48.

G. J. Wenham 'Method in Pentateuchal Source Criticism' *VT* 41, 1991 pp. 84–109.

Priestly material

A. Hurvitz *A Linguistic Study of the Relationship between the Priestly Source and the Book of Ezekiel*. Paris: Gabalda, 1982.

Y. Kaufmann *The Religion of Israel: From Its Beginnings to the Babylonian Exile*. tr. by M. Greenberg. Chicago: University of Chicago Press, 1960.

I. Knohl *The Sanctuary of Silence*. Minneapolis: Fortress, 1995.

J. Milgrom *Leviticus*. (3 volumes) New York: Doubleday, 1991–2001.

G. J. Wenham 'The Priority of P' *VT* 49, 1999 pp. 240–58.

Deuteronomy

R. Frankena 'The Vassal Treaties of Esarhaddon and the Dating of Deuteronomy' *Oudtestamentische Studien* 14, 1965 pp. 122–54.

K. A. Kitchen *Ancient Orient and Old Testament*. London: Tyndale Press, 1966.

K. A. Kitchen *The Bible in Its World*. Exeter: Paternoster, 1977.

M. G. Kline *The Treaty of the Great King*. Grand Rapids: Eerdmans, 1972.

J. G. McConville *Law and Theology in Deuteronomy*. Sheffield: JSOT Press, 1984.

J. G. McConville *Deuteronomy*. Leicester: Apollos, 2002.

P. Pitkänen *Central Sanctuary and the Centralization of Worship in Ancient Israel*. Piscataway: Gorgias Press, 2003.

J. H. Tigay *The JPS Commentary:*

Deuteronomy. Philadelphia: Jewish Publication Society, 1996.

M. Weinfeld *Deuteronomy and the Deuteronomic School*. Oxford: Clarendon Press, 1972.

185

Chapter 10

THE RHETORIC OF THE PENTATEUCH

In Chapter 8 we discussed the theme of the Pentateuch and in Chapter 9 theories about its composition. Is it possible to bring these two approaches together and say what message the Pentateuch gave to different situations in the life of Israel? The importance of different historical backgrounds for the interpretation of the Pentateuch emerged quite clearly in the discussion of its own date of origin and that of its putative sources.

However, the discussion in Chapter 9 (Composition of the Pentateuch) indicated some of the major problems in this enterprise. Most obviously there is no consensus about the dating of the final form of the Pentateuch nor about its constituent sources, nor even about the definition of the sources. But the confusion and uncertainty are even worse than this. All the apparently historical books of the Old Testament are under a cloud. Scholars at one extreme take them more or less at face value; those at the other end of the spectrum regard them as little better than fiction. This uncertainty makes it impossible to write a history of Israel's life and literature that will command universal assent.

Instead of attempting to steer a middle course between the extremes of credulity and scepticism, I shall offer a variety of readings from the traditional to the radical. Some will regard this attempt at pluralism as misguided in a textbook designed to clarify issues not to muddy them. But hopefully it will allow every reader to think through some of the problems and recognize how important are the assumptions that determine our understanding of literary texts.

A traditional reading begins with the recognition that a work that is a biography of Moses cannot have been written within his lifetime, but accepts that it must have been composed some time after the hero's death, which it describes. But how long after that death is not clear. Though biographies are frequently written soon after their subject's demise, there is nothing to stop them being written centuries later if the biographer has access to appropriate sources.

Thus the earliest possible setting for the Pentateuch would be the time of Joshua or perhaps in the period of the judges who followed Joshua. What could the Pentateuch be saying to this situation? Is its theme relevant to that period, as it is portrayed in the books of Joshua and Judges?

GUARDED OPTIMISM – A TWELFTH-CENTURY SETTING

In Chapter 8 (Theme of the Pentateuch) we defined the theme of the Pentateuch as the fulfilment of the promises to the patriarchs, which are a reaffirmation of God's original intentions for the human race, through his mercy and the collaboration of Moses. To some degree these promises are fulfilled before Moses' death, but complete fulfilment awaits the future.

The age of Joshua saw a more complete fulfilment of the promises than the Mosaic era, in that Israel did at last capture the land and God evidently blessed the nation under Joshua's leadership. The long string of Canaanite defeats demonstrated that the promise that 'he who dishonours you I will curse' was effective. Furthermore, various lesser themes within the Pentateuch seem to be fulfilled in the person of Joshua himself. He first appeared as Moses' assistant near Sinai (Exod. 17:9–14), and went with Moses up Mount Sinai (24:13; 32:17). Subsequently he was chosen to be one of the 12 spies and toured the land of Canaan: among these spies only he and Caleb insisted that Israel would be able to conquer the land (Num. 13:8; 14:6–10, 38). Nearly 40 years later he was appointed as Moses' successor

to bring the nation into the land of promise (Num. 27:12–23; Deut. 3:23–28; 31:1–23; 32:44–52). Indeed, the Pentateuch ends with the observation that Joshua was accepted as Moses' successor, even though he was not the prophet who would succeed Moses (Deut. 34:9). In this respect the Pentateuch could be seen as endorsing Joshua's leadership. It shows he was well trained by Moses, faithful to his teacher and endorsed by God.

Another minor feature of the Pentateuchal story is the prominence of Joseph and his sons, Ephraim and Manasseh. Not only are Joseph's sons adopted by Jacob putting them on a par with their uncles (Gen. 48), but the tribe of Joseph, i.e. Ephraim plus Manasseh, is fulsomely blessed both in Genesis 49, the blessing of Jacob, and in Deuteronomy 33, the blessing of Moses. Then, under the land allocation to the different tribes described in the book of Joshua, the tribes of Ephraim and Manasseh received two of the largest territories. It may be that Ephraim enjoyed a primacy in this period as Joshua came from this tribe, something hinted at in Genesis 48:17–20. In this way the Pentateuch could be seen to be justifying the leading position of the tribes of Ephraim and Manasseh.

Read against the background of the latter days of Joshua's career the Pentateuch appears as an essentially up-beat book. The main promises of land, nationhood and blessing have been fulfilled. Israel has at last returned to the land promised to the patriarchs and has begun the process of subduing it. Even the minor promises made to the tribes of Manasseh and Ephraim and the divinely approved succession of Joshua have worked out well. God's power and goodwill towards Israel have been abundantly demonstrated.

But the Pentateuch is not pure optimism. Much of its story relates Israel's failures: indeed such failures often fall close on the heels of its triumphs. The law-giving at Sinai is immediately followed by the making of the golden calf; the spies' expedition to Canaan is followed by the rebellion at Qadesh and the postponement of the conquest; the apostasy at Baal Peor follows the blessings of Balaam. These stories illustrate the peril of success. Moses makes the same point again and again in his sermons in Deuteronomy. 'Take care lest you forget the Lord your God by not keeping his commandments and his rules ... when you have eaten and are full and have built good houses and live in them' (Deut. 8:11–12), for this will lead to the loss of the land.

Deuteronomy is pervaded by the fear that Israel will forget the Lord and worship other gods. Apostasy is the ever-present danger that they face, so they are urged to acknowledge the uniqueness of the Lord, and love him with all their heart, soul and might (Deut. 6:4–5). Joshua, in his farewell to the nation, makes a similar appeal. 'Now, therefore fear the Lord and serve him in sincerity and in faithfulness. Put away the gods that your fathers served beyond the River and in Egypt, and serve the Lord' (Josh. 24:14). In this respect the Pentateuch offers a very relevant message for the era depicted in the book of Joshua.

But if most of what the Pentateuch promises finds its fulfilment in Joshua, there are features that do not fit so comfortably. The climax of the patriarchal promises is that 'in you shall all the families of the earth be blessed' (Gen. 12:3), but apart from Rahab and the Gibeonites, there is very little sign of blessing being mediated to the nations in Joshua. Nor is there any sign of Abraham's descendants being ruled by kings (Gen. 17:6; Num. 24:7, 17) or of the prophet like Moses (Deut. 18:15; 34:10).

If then the Pentateuch is set in the settlement era as depicted in Joshua, it offers both reassurance and a warning to its readers, reassurance because so much of the patriarchal promises has been spectacularly fulfilled in the recent past and warning that these gains could be easily lost through infidelity to the Lord. In this setting too, the Pentateuch has a message for the future: there are divine promises yet to be experienced and enjoyed.

CELEBRATION AND PROTEST – A TENTH-CENTURY SETTING

It has often been suggested that the major narrative source in the Pentateuch dates from some time in the reigns of David or Solomon, that is the tenth century BC. If, as earlier critical scholars held, the priestly material antedates the main narrative source, it might be supposed that the whole Pentateuch reached its final form in the united monarchy era. In this period Israelite political power and wealth may have reached its zenith, as the usual great

189

powers of the ancient orient, Egypt and Assyria, were comparatively weak. According to 2 Samuel 8 David's empire, or at least his zone of influence, stretched from the border of Egypt in the south, through Syria to the river Euphrates in the north. This brought control of the trade routes linking the great cities of the Middle East, and encouraged rulers from beyond the empire, such as the Queen of Sheba, to pay their respects to the Israelite king (1 Kgs 10). David captured Jerusalem and made it the political and religious capital of the nation by bringing the ark of the covenant into the city. He planned to build a temple in Jerusalem, but he was dissuaded by the prophet Nathan from doing so. In the event it was built by his son King Solomon to the design of an architect from Tyre.

Much of the Pentateuch addresses the situation of this era very clearly. It could well be supposed that the promises of the land, nationhood and blessing had been abundantly fulfilled under the united monarchy. The king of Israel controlled much more than the promised land of Canaan, at least as its borders are defined in Numbers 34. Israel itself had become a great nation headed by significant kings, as promised by Genesis 17:6; 35:11. The prosperity and peace of the nation were a manifestation of divine blessing. Furthermore, imperial rule of the surrounding nations may well have been viewed, by Israelites at least, as a foretaste of blessing for all the families of the earth.

Other features of the Pentateuch could also reflect the concerns of the early monarchy.

The detailed prescriptions about building the tabernacle and the sacrifices to be held in it are clearly not a blueprint for Solomon's temple, whose design was different from that of the tabernacle, but the insistence that worship was prescribed at Sinai surely lent support to a campaign to build a temple. The importance of Judah in the book of Genesis and in particular the prediction by Jacob that 'the sceptre shall not depart from Judah' (Gen. 49:10) would surely have been read as endorsing the claims of the Davidic dynasty, which came from Judah and faced opposition from other tribes.

Read against the background of David and Solomon's reigns, the Pentateuch strikes an even more optimistic tone than when it is set in the settlement era of Joshua. Indeed if we ignored its negative notes, the Pentateuch could be construed as uncritical propaganda on behalf of the Davidic dynasty. But its constant warnings about the dangers of idolatry and forsaking the LORD for other gods suggest a great concern that present prosperity based on the fulfilment of the patriarchal promises could all be forfeit if the nation takes the wrong path. This is certainly the stance of the book of Kings, which accuses Solomon of worshipping many foreign gods (1 Kgs 11:2–8). The type of monarchy envisaged by Deuteronomy may be construed as prophetic condemnation of the rule exercised by Solomon. According to Deuteronomy the king 'must not acquire many horses for himself', but Solomon imported horses from Egypt, and built up a chariot force of 1400 chariots and 12,000 horsemen (Deut. 17:16; 1 Kgs

10:26–28). Deuteronomy insists: 'He shall not acquire many wives for himself, lest his heart turn away', but Solomon acquired 700 wives and 'his wives turned away his heart after other gods' (Deut. 17:17; 1 Kgs 11:3–4). Deuteronomy demands: 'Nor shall he acquire for himself excessive silver and gold', but Solomon received 666 talents (23 tons!) a year (Deut. 17:17; 1 Kgs 10:14). In this situation the warnings about judgement with which the later books of the Pentateuch abound have a peculiar urgency. Deuteronomy's warnings about intermarriage with pagan worshippers were flouted by Solomon, and instead of destroying altars belonging to foreign gods he built a high place to them (Deut. 7:3–5; 1 Kgs 11:2–8).

Set in the early monarchy era the Pentateuch leaves less to hope for, because the promises have been nearly completely fulfilled, but more to fear, in that the abuse of royal power makes it more likely that the warnings of judgement will be fulfilled too. From this perspective its message is no endorsement of the *status quo* but an alarm to the leaders of the nation about the dire prospects that their behaviour is opening up. In this setting it is not obvious why so much attention should be given to the place of Joshua and the importance of the Joseph tribes, but these features could be simply historical and without rhetorical significance.

REASSURANCE TO THE DISPIRITED – A SEVENTH-CENTURY SETTING

Since the work of de Wette in 1805 and especially since Wellhausen in 1878 (see

Chapter 9) it has often been asserted that the book of Deuteronomy must be connected with Josiah's great reformation in the southern kingdom of Judah, which culminated in the restoration of the temple in 622 BC. Deuteronomy concludes the Pentateuch, so that if the last book of the Pentateuch were composed about the time of Josiah, the whole work may have been produced then. To explore this possibility we need to sketch the political and religious circumstances of the time so far as they can be reconstructed.

As often in Old Testament history the biblical sources only give us glimpses of the period, so we need to set the reign of Josiah in a broader context. Israel's power declined markedly after the reign of Solomon, the nation splitting into two rival states, Israel in the north and Judah in the south. The larger of the two kingdoms, the northern kingdom of Israel, was conquered by the Assyrians in 722 BC and split up into Assyrian provinces. The southern kingdom, with its capital Jerusalem, retained its nominal independence, though its kings had to pay tribute to Assyria and demonstrate their loyalty by promoting Assyrian religion throughout the land.

But in 640 BC Josiah came to the throne in Jerusalem, while the empire of Assyria entered a period of decline that culminated in the fall of its capital Nineveh in 612 BC. Capitalizing on Assyria's weakness, in about 628 BC Josiah began a process of expansion and reform that embraced the territory of the old northern kingdom as well as his own southern kingdom of Judah. Historians surmise that Josiah wanted to resurrect the great kingdom of David. At any rate he incorporated much of northern Israel into his realm and began a great purge of worship in Jerusalem and in sanctuaries throughout the land. This involved destroying the altars and worship objects associated with Baal, Asherah and the stars and deposing the priests who officiated at sanctuaries outside Jerusalem.

There was also a drastic purge of the temple in Jerusalem, which involved the destruction of pagan altars and images introduced by his predecessor King Manasseh. Outside the city he destroyed shrines to Molech in the valley of Hinnom, and the high places Solomon had made for the deities of his foreign wives. In the course of the rehabilitation of the temple a book of the law was found there. This was read to the king and caused him great consternation, because of the threats it contained about foreign worship. Since Deuteronomy is so strong in its condemnation of Canaanite worship, this is one reason that it is often identified with Josiah's law book. In particular Deuteronomy's insistence that worship must be restricted to the place which the LORD shall choose is often taken to be a coded way of referring to Jerusalem (see Chapter 9). Indeed, it is commonly held that just the legal core of Deuteronomy (chs 12—28) was the part found in the temple.

But it could be much more; indeed, the natural way to understand the references to the book of the law in 2 Kings 22—23

would be to suppose the whole Pentateuch is meant. How does it read then as an address to the situation in Josiah's day?

If Josiah was a would-be second David trying to re-establish his predecessor's empire, much of the Pentateuch would be a great encouragement. The promises of land, nationhood and blessing could have fired his enthusiasm to take over the northern parts of the country again and incorporate them under Jerusalem's control. In particular the promise that the land would be Israel's for ever would have been reassuring after so many northerners had been deported by the Assyrians and foreigners settled in their place. Throughout the Pentateuch there are stories illustrating the perils of idolatry as well as the specific prohibition of foreign worship practices in the later books. This would have fuelled Josiah's campaign against pagan worship, while he evidently interpreted the restriction of worship to the LORD's chosen place as a justification for eliminating all places of worship outside Jerusalem.

In many ways then the message of the Pentateuch to the era of Josiah is very similar to the way it could address the time of David. In both cases it endorses Israel's claim to the land and nationhood under a great king. However, the experiences of the preceding century or two before Josiah were somewhat different from the circumstances of the rise of the Davidic-Solomonic empire. In that era the Pentateuch would have been read optimistically as all the promises seemed to have been fulfilled. But read in Josiah's time the promises would have seemed more problematic. It could hardly be claimed that all the nations were being blessed by latter-day Israel under Josiah. They were not the great nation they had been under David and Solomon. And their hold on the land was precarious. Certainly they were far from enjoying the comfortable security pictured by Jacob and Moses in their dying words of blessing (Gen. 49; Deut. 33). Furthermore the widespread adoption of pagan worship ran so contrary to the thrust of the Pentateuch's appeal for total allegiance to Yahweh, that the hope embedded in the promises is darkly shadowed by covenant curses found particularly in Leviticus 26 and Deuteronomy 28. In this setting then the Pentateuch offers a limited hope based on the patriarchal promises, but its main thrust must be a deadly warning of national catastrophe. Josiah, it is reported, reacted to the reading of the book of the law by tearing his clothes, a sign of mourning, and saying, 'Great is the wrath of the LORD that is kindled against us, because our fathers have not obeyed the words of this book' (2 Kgs 22:13). Such a reading of the Pentateuch seems to be demanded, if we situate it within the framework of Josiah's reign as described within the book of Kings.

The death of Josiah fighting an Egyptian pharaoh in 609 BC was followed, barely a generation later, by the sacking of Jerusalem and the deportation of the leading Jews to Babylon. There they stayed until, encouraged by the decree of Cyrus the Great in 538 BC, they started trickling back to Judah. The first attempt to rebuild the temple came to an abrupt halt as food shortages and economic difficulty forced the returned exiles to put their own needs first. But the prophets Haggai and Zechariah prodded the people into action, work restarted on the temple, and it was reopened in 516 BC.

HOPE IN DIFFICULT TIMES – A FIFTH-CENTURY SETTING

The fifth century BC saw the return to Jerusalem of two dynamic and fervent Jews, Ezra in 458 and Nehemiah in 445 BC. Ezra came with royal authority from the Persian court to promote obedience to the Jewish law and offer sacrifices in the temple. The latter was easy, but enforcing the law was more difficult. The major problem Ezra found was intermarriage between Jews and foreigners: even some of the priests and Levites had done this. Ezra led a national service of repentance in which the people pledged to put away their foreign wives.

Nehemiah, a Jewish official in the court of Artaxerxes the Persian king, was sent to be governor of Judah in 445 BC. He found the walls of Jerusalem still in disrepair and in 52 days completed the task of rebuilding them in the teeth of tough opposition from neighbouring Persian provinces. He found the rich enslaving the poor and taking over their land, but he enforced the release of the slaves and the return of the land. He expelled foreigners from the temple, banned trading on the Sabbath, and like Ezra fought against intermarriage.

On many scholarly scenarios the fifth century is the period in which the Pentateuch received its final editing and was published. Both Ezra and Nehemiah tried to enforce its regulations in ways they deemed appropriate for their situation, but how does the Pentateuch read if we hold that it was actually composed with the fifth century setting in mind?

In the fifth century the fulfilment of the promises must have seemed a distant prospect. Admittedly some of the Jews were in the land, but they occupied relatively little of the promised territory and their numbers, at least within the land, may have been a tenth of what they had been in monarchy times. Furthermore they were not independent, nor were they ruled by kings, nor were they economically prosperous. There was little sign of divine blessing either on the Jews or through them on the nations.

To compose and publish a work like the Pentateuch in such a situation must therefore be construed as an act of great faith. It is making the point that despite all appearances God will yet redeem his people Israel's situation and fulfil the promises to them. Abraham and Sarah had to wait 25 years for the birth of Isaac. Isaac and Rebekah had to wait 20 years for the birth of Jacob and Esau. If the patriarchs had to exercise patience for the fulfilment of the promises in their lifetime, should their descendants who have returned from exile not have to be patient too?

The Pentateuch says that obedience to God accelerated the fulfilment of the promises, whereas disobedience slowed down their fulfilment, indeed led to the covenant curses of bad harvests, few children and exile falling on the people. In the setting of the fifth century the recent Jewish experience of exile, and their current economic difficulties, could be viewed as demonstrating the validity of the negative message of the Pentateuch. On the other hand it also shows what Jews must do to escape their predicament. The detailed and lengthy attention to the rules about purity, worship and sacrifice, which fills the middle books of the Pentateuch, could be seen as backing up the mission of Ezra and the message of the prophets of that era on the importance of worship. The concern of both Ezra and Nehemiah about intermarriage between Jews and non-Jews coincides with Deuteronomy's ban on marrying Canaanites.

Read in this way the Pentateuch could be regarded as a great rallying call for fifth-century Jews to support the reforms promulgated by Ezra and Nehemiah. Only by avoiding mixing themselves with other races and by supporting worship in the rebuilt temple will the nation ever regain the glory and prosperity promised to the patriarchs and enjoyed by the nation under its great kings. To a dispirited people it recalls the great promises made to their forefathers, points out the fulfilment of Moses' warnings about the consequences of disobedience, and shows what the Jews must concentrate on doing if they are to flourish again in the promised land.

This setting of the Pentateuch in the fifth century has been widely accepted, but in

Digging deeper:
SETTINGS FOR THE PENTATEUCH

Which of these suggested settings for the Pentateuch appears most plausible to you? Why? Try to analyse your reasons. How important is tradition or scholarly consensus to you? Are you more attracted to the positive outlook of the author implied by an early date or by the great faith that must have motivated a late writer?

Read the relevant parts of the OT yourself (Joshua, 2 Samuel to 1 Kings 11, 2 Kings 21—25, Ezra and Nehemiah) and imagine what the Pentateuch could be saying to the different situations.

recent years some scholars have argued that it may have reached its final form a century or two later. Unfortunately we know very little about the situation of the Jews in Judah between the fifth and the second centuries BC, so that if the Pentateuch was addressing problems in that era, we can only guess at them from reading the Pentateuch itself. On this basis we would conclude that its message to that period was similar to that we have surmised for the fifth century BC, but further than that we can hardly go.

FURTHER READING

T. D. Alexander *From Paradise to the Promised Land*. Carlisle: Paternoster Press, 2002.

R. Albertz *A History of Israelite Religion*. (2 volumes) tr. by J. Bowden. London: SCM, 1994.

S. E. Balentine *The Torah's Vision of Worship*. Minneapolis: Fortress Press, 1999.

J. Bright *The History of Israel*. London: SCM Press, 1972.

V. P. Long, D. W. Baker and G. J. Wenham (eds) *Windows Into Old Testament History*. Grand Rapids: Eerdmans, 2002.

I. W. Provan *1 and 2 Kings*. Sheffield: Sheffield Academic Press, 1997.

G. von Rad *Old Testament Theology I–II*. tr. by D. M. G. Stalker. Edinburgh: Oliver and Boyd, 1962–65.

Chapter 11

EPILOGUE

The Pentateuch is the first section of both the Jewish and Christian Bible. Its position gives it a special status in Scripture, as it sets the tone and agenda for the rest of the Bible. Within the Old Testament the historical books, the prophets and the Psalms all look back to it and are inspired by it. The same is true of the New Testament, which frequently traces its teaching about God and ethics back to the Pentateuch. As Jesus put it, 'not an iota, not a dot will pass from the Law until all is accomplished.'

Each section of the Bible develops the theme of the Pentateuch further. If the original exposition of the theme is to be found in Genesis 12:1–3, it is restated with variations throughout Genesis and developed in the following books. The whole Old Testament revolves round the relationship of Abraham's descendants to the land, their growth into a nation, and their unique relationship with the LORD. Progress towards the fulfilment of the promises to Abraham does not all run in one direction. Setbacks are frequent, both within the Pentateuch and subsequently. The book of Numbers tells of the 40-year postponement of entry to the land as a result of the spies' lack of faith; the book of Kings tells of the fall of Jerusalem and the people's exile to Babylon because of their infidelity to God. Nevertheless, both episodes were followed by forgiveness and a new start that led eventually to a greater fulfilment of the promises.

But neither within the biblical period nor in the subsequent two millennia has complete fulfilment been achieved. If modern Jews look on their return to the land of Israel as fulfilling the promise to Abraham and an answer to their prayers, they do not enjoy the peace and security envisaged by the Pentateuch. Christians affirm that the coming of Jesus has brought nearer the day when in Abraham 'all the families shall be blessed'. But they too pray for God's kingdom to come and his will to be done on earth as it is in heaven. In this way the Pentateuch still speaks as much to the present as it does to the past.

GLOSSARY

* Refers to a further entry in the Glossary.

Akedah Literally 'binding': the Jewish term for the sacrifice of Isaac in Genesis 22.

Amalekites Nomadic inhabitants of the northern Sinai Peninsula and the Negeb.

Ammon A kingdom located east of the Jordan. According to Genesis 19:38 the Ammonites were descended from Lot, Abraham's nephew. Hence they were regarded as distant 'cousins' of Israel.

Amorites One of the indigenous peoples of Canaan.* Sihon and Og, kings of Transjordan,* are called Amorites. Deuteronomy 31:4.

Antediluvian 'Before the flood.'

Apodictic Laws expressed as absolute commands without specifying punishments if broken, e.g. 'Remember the Sabbath day.'

Ark of the covenant The gold-plated wooden box kept in the holy of holies.* It was the holiest item of furniture in the tabernacle* as it served as God's throne. It contained the Ten Commandments, some manna* and Aaron's staff.

Assyrian An inhabitant of northern Mesopotamia.* The dialect of Akkadian that Assyrians spoke.

Atrahasis The Babylonian name for Noah. The Atrahasis epic tells the story of the world from the creation of man to the flood.

Babel The Babylonian name for Babylon = gate of God.

Babylonian An inhabitant of southern Mesopotamia.* The dialect of Akkadian spoken by Babylonians. The Old Babylonian period is 1900–1600 BC.

Balaam A north Syrian diviner (prophet) who foretold Israel's future in Numbers 22—24.

Berossus Third-century Babylonian priest, who mentions the flood.

Booths The festival also called 'Tabernacles' commemorating Israel's wanderings in the wilderness, held in October. Leviticus 23:33–43.

Burnt offering An animal sacrifice in which the whole animal was burnt on the altar. Expressed dedication to God and secured general forgiveness. Described in Leviticus 1.

Canaan The promised land (Genesis 17:8), defined in Numbers 34. Roughly equivalent to modern Israel plus Lebanon and part of southern Syria.

Canonical criticism Study of the final form of the biblical text, because it is the authoritative (canonical) text for religious readers.

Canonization The process by which books of the Bible came to be recognized as authoritative.

Casuistic Sometimes called case laws, which deal with a specific problem and its remedy, e.g. 'If he knocks out the tooth of his slave, he shall let the slave go free.'

Cherubim Guardians of holy places such as Eden and the tabernacle.* There were two cherubim on top of the ark* of the covenant. They probably looked like winged bulls or lions with human heads.

Chiasm(us) A literary pattern in which a pair of items are repeated in reverse order, e.g. ABB'A'.

Circumcision The rite of removing the foreskin from eight-day-old baby boys to mark their entrance into the covenant.*

Clean(ness) Pure in the sense of 'fit to worship'. Some sins and ailments make a person unclean* and therefore unable to worship in the sanctuary.

Covenant An agreement between God and man, usually containing divine promises and obligations on the human side.

Cuneiform A method of writing on clay using wedge-shaped characters.

Day of Atonement The holiest day of the year (tenth day of seventh month), when ordinary Israelites had to rest, fast and confess their sins. The high priest offered special sacrifices and sent the scapegoat* into the wilderness (Leviticus 16).

Decalogue The Ten Commandments. Exodus 20.

Documentary hypothesis The view that the Pentateuch* consists of three or four main documents intertwined together. See Chapter 9.

E, Elohistic source The material in the Pentateuch* that uses the generic term for God, in Hebrew 'Elohim'. Often dated about 850 BC.

Ea The god of wisdom in Mesopotamia, who advised Atrahasis* (Noah) to build the ark.

Edom A kingdom located to the east and south of the Dead Sea. According to Genesis 36 the Edomites were descendants of Esau, which made them Israel's 'brothers'. See map 3, p. 119.

El The senior creator God of the Canaanites.

Elohim Hebrew for 'god'. It is a generic word for any divine being, but may be used instead of God's personal name, Yahweh* (the LORD).

Enlil The supreme god in the Mesopotamian pantheon.*

Enuma elish A Babylonian poem telling of a battle between the gods. It involves some acts of creation.

Epic A poem celebrating a hero's achievements.

Etiology A saying explaining a place name or custom, e.g. Genesis 28:17; 32:32.

Exile, exilic The period the Jews lived in Babylon, i.e. 587–537 BC.

Exodus The escape of the Israelites from Egypt led by Moses.

Fall The sin of Adam and Eve, which led to their exclusion from Eden.

Fragmentary hypothesis The view that the Pentateuch* is composed of a number of separate sources (fragments) assembled by a single author. See Chapter 9.

Genre A category of literature or art.

Gilgamesh epic A collection of poetic tales about the legendary king of Uruk called Gilgamesh.

Golden calf The gold-plated wooden calf made by Aaron. See Exodus 32.

Grace God's generosity to the undeserving.

Guilt offering An animal sacrifice offered when God's rights had been infringed. Described in Leviticus 5:14—6:7.

Hammurabi King of Babylon (1792–1750 BC) famed for his collection of laws.

Herodotus Greek historian of fifth century BC.

Holy of holies The innermost part of the tabernacle,* where the ark* was kept.

Holy place The outer part of the tabernacle* tent.

Holy/holiness Holiness is the essence of God's character, which Israelites were called to imitate. It entails moral and physical purity and fullness of life. It involves separation from uncleanness.

Hyksos The Semitic* Pharaohs who ruled Egypt *c.*1650–1540 BC.

Image of God According to Genesis man(kind) is the only being created in the image of God. He is thus God's representative on earth responsible for managing it (Genesis 1:26–27).

J see Yahwistic* source.

Jubilee A year of release when slaves were freed and land reverted to its original owners, held every 50 years. See Leviticus 25.

Kenites Nomadic inhabitants of the northern Sinai Peninsula.

Laver The large basin in the court of the tabernacle* for washing people and sacrifices. See Exodus 30:17–21 and figure 3 on p. 75.

Legend A story handed down by tradition, often fictitious.

Levi(tes) The tribe of Levi was the tribe dedicated to religious duties in the tabernacle.*

Lex talionis The legal principle of exact retribution, 'an eye for an eye', but not necessarily enforced literally.

Make atonement To re-establish relations between God and the worshipper. It is most commonly achieved by offering sacrifices.

Manetho Third-century BC Egyptian priest, whose works are quoted by Eusebius.

Manna The honey-like food that the Israelites ate in the wilderness (Exodus 16).

Mercy seat The lid of the ark* on which the blood was smeared on the Day of Atonement.* On it were mounted two cherubim* to serve as God's throne.

Mesopotamia The land between the rivers Tigris and Euphrates, roughly equal to Iraq.

Midian The name of a tribe of desert dwellers who lived in northern Arabia. According to Genesis 25:1–6 they were descended from Keturah, Abraham's second wife. Moses married a Midianite (Exodus 2:21).

Midianites Nomadic inhabitants of northern Arabia.

Moab A kingdom located northeast of the Dead Sea. According to Genesis 19:37 the Moabites were descended from Lot, Abraham's nephew. Hence they were regarded as distant 'cousins' of Israel.

Monarchy period Period when kings reigned in Israel and Judah *c*.1010–587 BC.

Monotheism The belief that there is only one god.

Myth A fictitious narrative usually involving supernatural persons giving a popular explanation of some phenomenon.

Nazirite A very holy* lay man or woman. They took a vow to abstain from wine, not to cut their hair and not to go near a human corpse. See Numbers 6.

Nephilim Ancient supermen, supposedly god-human hybrids, mentioned in Genesis 6:1–4 and Numbers 13:33.

Ordination The ceremony to make someone a priest described in Leviticus 8—9.

P, Priestly source The material in the Pentateuch* ascribed to priestly writers, often dated about 500 BC. See Chapter 9.

Palistrophe An extended chiasmus* in which many items are repeated in reverse order, e.g. ABCDED'C'B'A'.

Pantheon All the gods of a tribe or people.

Passover The festival celebrating the exodus* from Egypt, held at Easter (Exodus 12—13).

Peace offering Also translated 'fellowship' (NIV) 'well-being' (NRSV) or 'shared' (REB) offering is described in Leviticus 3. Usually a voluntary animal sacrifice and the only sacrifice the meat of which a worshipper could share.

Pentateuch The five books of Moses: Genesis, Exodus, Leviticus, Numbers, Deuteronomy.

Pillar of fire The manifestation of God's presence that led the Israelites in the wilderness.

Polytheism The belief that there are many gods.

Post-exilic The period after the Jewish exile* in Babylon, i.e. 537 BC onwards.

Protevangelium Literally 'the first gospel', i.e. Genesis 3:15 as traditionally understood by

Christians to predict the victory of mankind over evil in the person of Christ.

Protohistory A definition of the genre of Genesis 1—11. See Chapter 2.

Rubrics Instructions in a liturgical text about actions that should accompany the prescribed words.

Sabbath The seventh day of the week, on which Israelites had to rest from their usual work.

Scapegoat The goat chosen by lot on the Day of Atonement* to carry away the sins of Israel into the wilderness.

Semites Traditionally the peoples descended from Shem. Genesis 10:21–31. In modern usage people who speak Semitic* languages.

Semitic A group of languages including Hebrew, Arabic, Aramaic and Akkadian.

Septuagint The Greek translation of the Old Testament.

Sethites The descendants of Seth (see Genesis 5).

Sin offering An animal sacrifice to secure forgiveness of sins and purify the sanctuary. Its unique feature was the sprinkling or smearing of the blood on the altar or other sacred furniture. Described in Leviticus 4.

Sinai A mountain in the Sinai Peninsula where the law was given.

Sumerian The main language of southern Mesopotamia from about 4500 to 2000 BC. Sumerians are the first identifiable settlers in this area.

Supplementary hypothesis The view that the Pentateuch* grew by successive additions of material over a long period. See Chapter 9.

Surrogate marriage An arrangement in which an infertile wife provides a slave girl for her husband to produce a child. See Genesis 16.

Tabernacle The portable tent shrine carried through the wilderness by the Israelites.

Tabernacles, Feast of See Booths.*

Torah Hebrew for 'law, instruction'. Also refers to the Pentateuch.*

Traditio-historical criticism The attempt to trace the development of the oral sources of the Pentateuch.* See Chapters 8 and 9.

Transjordan The region east of the Jordan river.

Trinity The Christian doctrine that there are three persons in one God.

Twelve tribes Israel was divided into twelve tribes descended from the twelve sons of Jacob.

Type A type is an event or person that parallels an event or person in another era. See also typology.*

Typology A way of reading Scripture that sees events or people in one era foreshadowing or echoing events or people in another era.

Unclean(ness) The antithesis of holiness.* It is characterized by physical and moral disorder and associated with death. Skin disease, bodily secretions and certain sins make people unclean. The unclean are debarred from worship. See Leviticus 11—15.

Vizier The ruler of Egypt next in authority to the Pharaoh.

Weeks, Feast of The festival of Pentecost, marking the end of the grain harvest and commemorating the law-giving at Sinai. Leviticus 23:15–22.

Yahweh God's covenantal name revealed to Moses at Sinai (Exodus 6:2–3). In later times, in order not to break the third commandment (Exodus 20:7) inadvertently, the Jews refrained from using the name and said Adonai, the LORD, instead.

Yahwistic source, J The material in the Pentateuch* characterized by its use of the divine name Yahweh = the LORD. Often dated about 950 BC. See Chapter 9.

Ziggurat A stepped pyramid topped by a temple. Used in Mesopotamia.

INDEX

Note: Page references in **bold** type indicate panels in the text; those in *italics* indicate illustrations and tables.

Aaron 60–3, 73–4, 84, 113; challenges to 112; complaint against Moses 110; ordination 89–90

Abraham 35–6, 37–45, **106**, 110, 153; and blessing of the nations 40, 42, 44, 86, 116, 154–5, 156–7, 197; and covenant 42, 149; as foreshadowing Moses 3; and history 14, 146, 172, 176–7; and promise of descendants 40–5, 58, *106*, 110, 115, 149, 151, 153–6, 197

accusations, false 139

Adam 15, 20–1, 22, *46*, 152; Christ as second Adam 33–4; and Noah 21, 27, 31–2, 36, 40, 152

Akedah (binding) 43–4, **44**

Albright, W. F. 172

Alt, Albrecht 171–2

Alter, R. 175

animals, clean and unclean 85, 91–3, 92, 96, 98

apostasy: in Canaan 134–5, **137**; at Peor 116, 117, 129, 131, 189

ark of the covenant 76, 88, 95, 141

Astruc, Jean 162–3, 164–5, 167

atonement 29, 82, 85–7, 88, 111, 170

Atrahasis epic 10–11, 13–14, 15–16, 20, **86**

Baal Peor *see* Peor

Balaam: extra-biblical evidence **115**; prophecies 103, 114–16, 121, **130**, 147, 153

biography of Moses 110, 157; authorship 159–60; dating 187–8; death 103, 124, 127–8, 141–2, 160, 162; and Genesis 2–3, 142; and Leviticus 81, 89; and *Torah* 4, 36, 57, 145, 154

Blenkinsopp, J. 3

blessings: and curses 99, 126, 140, 181, 193; deathbed 47, 54–5, 141–2, 188, 193; priestly 107, **108**

blood: ban on eating 30, 93, 96, 134, 170; and sacrifice 74, 85, 88, 90, 95; and uncleanness 93, 94

Blum, Erhard 175, 178

Bodenheimer, F. S. 66

Booths, Feast *see* Tabernacles

Bright, John **38**, 172

burnt offering 77, 85–7, 89, 90, 91

Cain and Abel story 22, 24–5, 28, 152

Canaan: borders 118, *119*; conquest 105, 110-11, 113–14, 116, 118–19, 123–4, 127, 146, 149, 153, 155; as goal of narrative 151; Israelite claim 35, 42; religious practices **49**, 131–2, 134, 136, **137**, 141, 192

canonical criticism 173

cereal offering 87, 89

cherubim 15, 23, 69, 76, **76**

chiasmus 28

childbirth, and uncleanness 88, 93

circumcision 43, 60, 156, 165

Clines, D. J. A. 40–1, 150–3, 156–7

composition 159–83; circumstances 150; and dating of sources 167, 169, 171–2, 173, 176–83; documentary hypothesis 159, 160–75; fragmentary hypothesis 163–4, 174, 176; and Mosaic authorship 159–60, 162, 181; supplementary hypothesis 164, 174, 176–8; and unitary readings 173–6

covenant: with patriarchs 43, 148–9; renewal 125, 139–40, 147; at Sinai 2, 60, 67–71, 73–4, 77–8, 124, 130, 148–9

covetousness 70, 139

creation: and flood 21, 29–31, **30**, 152; in Genesis 16, 19–21, 22, 33, 149, 152, 165; and promises to patriarchs 153

Davidic dynasty 55, 190

Day of Atonement 76, 88, 91, 94–5, 98, 98, *117*, 170, 179

death, and uncleanness 93, 96, 97, 107, 108, 112, 118, 120

Deuteronomy 123–43; and blessing of Moses 141–2; and covenant renewal 125; dating 162, 167, 173, 180–1, 191–2; and documentary hypothesis

165, *166*, 167, 168–71, *170*; and exposition of the law 133–9; as farewell sermon 124–5, 159; first sermon 127–9; and genre 124, 165; and historical creed 148, 172; in Jewish worship **132**; as law-code and treaty 7, 125–6, 180–1, **180**; and love of God **130**; and love for God 85, 131, 189; and New Testament 123, 142–3; and promise of the land 128, 151–2; as prophetic book 123; and regulation of war 136–8, **137**; second sermon 129–40, *129*; structure 125–6, *125*; third sermon 140–1

discharges, as unclean 100–4

documentary hypothesis 159, 160–5; collapse of the consensus 172–3; dating of sources 167, 169, 173, 176–83; and identification of sources 165–71; twentieth-century adjustments 171–2; and unitary readings 173–6

Douglas, Mary 97

Driver, S. R. **163**, 166–7, 173

drunkenness 31, **32**

Egypt: in Joseph story **53**, 156–7; liberation from 63–6; and plagues 2, 61–3, **61**, 147, 157; slavery in 58–63

Elohistic (E) source 165, *166*, 167, 168–72, *170*, 173; and Yahwist source 173–4

Enlightenment 160–2

Enuma Elish 20

Esau, genealogy 37, 46, 51, 156

Eshnunna Laws 71

Ewald, G. H. A. 164

Exodus 57–79; and divine-human relationship 68, 74, 151; law-giving 67–74; New Testament use **64**, 69, **70**, 79; slavery in Egypt and liberation 58–67, 79; sources 165, 177, 178; structure 58;

Tabernacle 68, 74–9

exodus from Egypt: and God's promises 58, 59–61, 66, 73, 127–8; as theme of Pentateuch 146

Ezra 6, 162, 193–4

festivals, national 98, 103, 116–17, *117*, 135, 170–1

flood stories: Genesis 21–2, 27–31, 32, 152, 165, 174; Mesopotamian 10–12, 15–18, 27, **30**, 174

foods, unclean 91–3, 100, 135

forgiveness 88, 89, 111

Frankena, R. 181

Garden of Eden 15, 22–3, 33, 41, 76, 79

Geddes, Alexander 164

genealogies 18–19, 35–6, 165; Adam–Lamech 24–5, *25*; Adam–Noah 12, 14, 19, 22, 24–5, *25*; of Esau 37, 46, 51, 156; of Ishmael 37, 45; Shem–Abraham 12, 14, 19, 33

Genesis: dating **38**, 167, 177; and documentary hypothesis 165–7, 173–5; and genre 9, 12–15, 36–7; New Testament use 9, 33–4, **44**, 55–6; theme 40, 152–3

Genesis 1—11 9–34; ancient near Eastern parallels 3, 9–15, 172, 176, 177; family histories 18–19, 21–33; Greek parallels 3, 177; transformation of oriental origin stories 15–18, 27

Genesis 12—50 35–56; Abraham story 35–6, 37–45, 146, 149; Jacob and Esau story 36, 44, 45–51; Joseph stories 36, 51–5, 151, 156; and promise of descendants 40–4, 149, 151, 153–5, 197

genre 2, 145, 166; in Deuteronomy 124, 165; in Genesis 9, 12–15, 36–7

Gilgal, sanctuary 147

Gilgamesh epic 10, 13–14, 15, **30**, 37

golden calf story 2, 77–8, 79, **111**, 115, 131, 134, 189

Gordon, C. H. 172

grace, divine 69, 149, 152, 153

guilt offering 88, 89, 170

Hammurabi Law Code 6, 71, 126, 138, 187

Harel, 64

heart, in biblical thought **62**

Herodotus 3

Hexateuch 148, 153

historical criticism 165

history: ancient Near Eastern parallels 37, **38**, 176; family 37; and myth 12–14

Hittite Laws 71

Hobbes, Thomas 161–2

Hoffmeier, J. K. 64

holiness: of God 59, 68, 77, *91*; practical 89–90, 95–9

holy of holies 68, 75–6, 77, 95, 99–100

holy war 118

homicide 24, 31, 96, 120, **120**, 133, 136

Hort, Greta 63

humanitarianism, in Deuteronomy 135, **135**

Hurvitz, A. 179

Hyksos dynasty **53**, 58

idolatry, ban on 69–70, 71, 78, 96, 123, 129, 134, 190, 192

instruction, and *Torah* 4, 36, 57, 63, 145, 154

interest, ban on 138

Isaac, sacrifice 43–4, **44**, 86, 155

Ishmael, genealogy 37, 45

Jacob 36, 41, 44, 45–51, 52, 54–5, 141–2, 146–7, 188; and documentary hypothesis 165; as foreshadowing Moses 3

Jacobsen, T. 13, 17

Jerusalem, as national shrine **134**, 135, 168–71, 181, 190, 192

Jesus Christ: as second Adam 33–4; as second Moses 5, 121, 142–3

Joseph stories 36, 51–5, 151, 156, 188; and documentary hypothesis 165, 173–4, **174**

Josephus, Flavius 5, 160

Joshua 123, 127–8, 141, 149, 188–9, 191

Josiah, king 6, 162, 168–9, 180–1, 191–3

jubilee 98–9, **99**

Judah (brother of Joseph) 52, 54–5, **54**, 190

judges 136

Kaufman, S. A. 133

Kaufmann, Y. 179

kings 55, 116, 136, 189, 190–1

Kitchen, Kenneth A. 181

Kline, Meredith G. 181

Knohl, Israel 179

land, inheritance laws 116, 120, 176

Langton, Stephen, Archbishop of Canterbury 5

law: ancient Near Eastern 71, **72**, 125–6, 133, 172, 176; apodictic law 71–3, 172; case law 71, 172; and land inheritance 116, 120, 176; and narrative 4, 81, 103–4; and obedience 4, 68, 73, 113, 123, 128–31, 149, 194; of property 138–9; and prophets 123; and role of Moses 2, 70

Levites: cities 120; duties 81, 105–7, 108, 112

Leviticus 81–100; dating 179; and divine–human relationship 115, 151; New Testament use 92, 99–100; and practical holiness 89–90,

95–9; and priesthood 81, 89–91; problems of reading 82–4; and sacrifice 82, 84–9; structure 81–2; and uncleanness 91–9, 100

lex talionis 31, **72–3**

literary criticism 173

Lohfink, N. **137**

Louth, A. 34

love for God 85, 131, 189

love of God **130**

McConville, J. G. 181

Machpelah, ancestral grave 36, 39, 44, 46, 55

Maimonides, Moses **137**

mankind, in Genesis 16, 20–2, 34

manna 66–7, 110

marriage customs **38**, **48**, 120, 176; and intermarriage **137**, 138, 191, 193–4; Levirate marriage 19

Meribah 67, 103, 113, 127, 141

Mesopotamia: flood stories 10–12, 15–18, 27, **30**, 174; histories 3, 12–13, 37, 176

Mezuzah **132**

Middle Assyrian laws 71

Midianites 117–18

Milgrom, J. 179

Miriam 110, 113, 139

monotheism 15–16, **17**, 69, 126, 131

Moses: ascription of Pentateuch to 159–60, 162, 181; challenges to 112; Christ as second Moses 121; complaints against 59, 66–7, 109–10, 113; death 103, 124, 127–8, 141–2, 160, 162; and law 2, 67–74, 172; as mediator 2, 78, 108, 110–11, 130, 136; in Noth 147; and priesthood 89–90; as prophet 3, 123, 124, 142, 160; and tabernacle 75, 78, 98, 108; and theme of Pentateuch 153–4, 157, 188; *see also*

biography of Moses

murder 24, 70, 96, 120, **120**, 136

myth, meaning 12–14, **13**

names, significance 42, 50, 58–9

names of God **49**, 59, **60**, 61, 70; and documentary hypothesis 163, 164, 165–7, 175, 177

narrative 2, 29; in Deuteronomy 124; and law 4; in Leviticus 57, 81; in Numbers 103–4

Nazirites 88, 107

Nehemiah 6, 193–4

New Testament: and Mosaic authorship 160; and Pentateuch 197; and use of Deuteronomy 123, 142–3; and use of Exodus **64**, 69, **70**, 79; and use of Genesis 9, 33–4, **44**, 55–6; and use of Leviticus 82, 99–100; and use of Numbers 121

Noah stories: drunkenness 31–2, 40; and flood 16, 21, 27–31, 40, 86, 149, 152

Noth, Martin: and documentary hypothesis 171–2, 175–6; and theme of Pentateuch 145–7, 148, 150

Numbers 103–21; and Balaam 103, 114–16, 121, 147; and censuses 105, **106**, 116; complaints against Moses 109–10, 113; dating 179; journey from Kadesh to Moab 113–14; journey from Sinai to Kadesh 109–10, 114, 127; and national apostasy 116, 117; New Testament use 121; parallels with Exodus 109–10, *109*, 115, 115; and practical holiness 107–8; and promise of the land 115–16, 151; and sacrificial laws 111; sources 165; structure 103–4; and unbelieving spies 2, 103, 110–11, **111**, 127, 188, 197

obedience to law 4, 68, 73, 113,

123, 128–31, 149, 194; of
Abraham 43–4

Olson, D. T. 104, 121

origin stories: in Genesis 14,
15–18; Mesopotamian 9–18,
17, 24, 176

palistrophes 28, **28**, 39, 46, 51,
53, 174

Parvish, Samuel 162

Passover 60, 63–4, **64**, 66, 79, *98*,
108, *117*; and sacrifice 117, 135

patriarchs: as historical 14, 37,
38–9, 172, 176–7; religion **49**;
see also promises

peace offering 87, 89, 90, 134

Pentateuch: canonization 6–7;
dating 5, 167, 169, 171–2,
176–83, 187–9; division into
five books 5–6; as law 2, 4;
name 1, 2, 4; as national
history 1–2, 3, 35, **38**, 64, 145;
theme 145–57, 188, 197; *see
also* composition;
Deuteronomy; documentary
hypothesis; Exodus; Genesis;
Leviticus; Moses; Numbers

Pentecost (Weeks) festival *98*,
117, *117*, 135, 148, 170

people, chosen 1, 51, 93, 100,
135, 138

Peor (Baal Peor, Beth-Peor), and
national apostasy 116, 117,
129, 134, 189

Philo Judaeus 5, 160

phylacteries **132**, *133*

plagues of Egypt 2, 61–3, **61**,
147, 157

pollution: by sin 88, 94, 95–6,
134, 136; by uncleanness 94,
107, 112, 118, 120, 138

poor, care for 135, 139

Priestly (P) source 165–7, *166*,
169–71, *170*; dating 162, 171,
173, 177, 178–80, 182, 189;
and relationship with God 149

priests 81; institution of
priesthood 89–91; as

mediators 77, 88, 89–90;
ordination 77, 84, 88, 89–90;
and sacrifice 84, 85, 87, 88–9,
117; and uncleanness 89–90,
91–5, 112; *see also* Levites

promises **40**, 51–2, 114, 171–2;
of blessing to the nations 40,
42, 43, 52, 86, 116, 153–5,
156–7, 189–90, 192–4, 197; of
deliverance from Egypt 61; of
descendants 40–4, 58, *106*, 110,
115, 127, 149, 151, 153–6,
190, 192, 197; of divine–
human relationship 68, 74,
115, 129, 149, 151–2, 153–4,
156, 197; of land 40, 52, 55,
66, 73, 115–16, 128, 146,
148–9, 151–2, 153–5, 189–90,
192–4, 197; partial fulfilment
40–1, 149, 151–2, 153, 155–7;
as theme of Pentateuch 146–7,
148–9, 151–2, 153–7, 188, 197

prophets, and law 123

prostitution, sacred 27, 28–9, 94

Protevangelium **23**

Psalms, and the law 5

punishment, and sin 23–4, 31,
97, 111, 152

Rad, Gerhard von 147–9, 150,
151, 153, 155, 171–2

red cow rite 112

Red Sea, crossing 2, 64–6, 67, 79

Reformation, and the Bible 161

refuge, cities of 120, 136

Rendtorff, R. 175, 178

repetition **43**, 124, 162, 166,
174–5, 177, 181, 182

rhetoric of the Pentateuch
187–95; and Josiah's reform
191–3; and period of Joshua
and Judges 188–9; and period
of united monarchy 189–91,
192; and post-exilic period
193–5

ritual: interpretation 84;
significance 83–4

Rogerson, J. 15

Sabbath 14, 21, 67, 70, 77, 133,
165; and sacrifice *117*

sacrifice 6, 24, **44**, 74, 77, 111;
as act of generosity **86**, 139; as
atonement 29, 82, 85–7, 88,
111, 170; and central shrine
168–9, 181; of firstlings 135;
in Leviticus 82, 84–9; in
Numbers *117*; and Priestly
Code 170, 171

scapegoat 95

serpent, bronze **113**, 114, 121

Seters, J. van 3, 176–8, 180

sexuality, and uncleanness 68,
96–7, 138

Shema 69, 131, **132**, 142

shrines: local 71, 168; national
134, 147, 168–71, 181, 190,
192

sin: and atonement 29, 82, 86–7,
88–9, 94–5, 111, 170; and
flood 16–17, 21–2; in Genesis
16–17, 21–3, 27–8, 32–3,
41–2, 86, 152–3; and
punishment 23–4, 31, 97,
111, 152; and uncleanness
94–5, 96

sin offering 87–8, 89, 90, 95–6,
112, 170

Sinai: and law-giving 2, 67–74,
124, 142, 147, 148, 172;
location 64–5

skin diseases, and uncleanness
88, 93–4, 96, 100

slavery **72**, 99, 135

Smith, George 9–10

Song of Moses 141

Song of the Sea 65, 66

'sons of the gods' 25–7, 28

Speiser, E. A. 172

spies, unbelieving 2, 103,
110–11, **111**, 127, 188, 197

Spinoza, Benedict 162, 165

Sternberg, M. 175

Sumerian flood story 11–13, 17

Sumerian King List 12–13, **13**,
24, **26**

Tabernacle 68, 69, 74–9, *75*, 88, 156; and bread 76, 98; dedication 108; and Eden symbolism 23, 76, 79; and Levites 81, 105–6, 108, 112; and priesthood 90, 95, 97; and Priestly source 169; and temple 190; and uncleanness 94–5, 112

Tabernacles, Feast 98, *98*, 117, *117*, 125, 135, 141

Table of Nations 22, 32

tassels *111*, **112**

Tefillin **132**, *133*

temple: as central shrine 168–71, 190, 192; and Eden symbolism 23

Ten Commandments: and ancient treaties **126**; in Deuteronomy **126**, 130, *133*, 133; in Exodus 68–70, **70**, 71, 74, 76, 77–8; and Sabbath 21, 70, 133

theme of Pentateuch 36, 40; in Clines 40–1, 150–3, 156–7; and Moses 153–4, 157; in Noth 145–7, 148; as promise to patriarchs 146–7, 148–9, 151–2, 153–7, 188, 197; in von

Rad 147–9, 150, 151, 153, 155

Tigay, J. H. 167

Timnah temple, and copper snake **113**

tithes 112, 134, 135, 139, 179

Torah (law/instruction) 2, 4, 36, 57, 63, 145, 154

tower of Babel 17–18, 32–3, 40, 154

tradition, oral **38–9**, 145–6, 150, 171, 175

tribes of Israel: and allocation of land 116, 118, 120, 128, 146, 188; in camp *105*; Ephraim and Manasseh 48, 54–5, 120, 146, 188; equal standing 108, 188; and exodus from Egypt 146; on the march *106*, 107; and sons of Jacob 45; and wilderness stories 147

Trumpets, Feast 98, *98*, *117*

typology 36, **43**

uncleanness: in Leviticus 6, 91–9, 100–4; in Numbers 107–8; as polluting 94, 107, 112, 118, 120, 138

Vater, Johann Severin 163

Vaux, R. de **39**

violence, human 28–31, 152

vows 87, 99, 117, 138

war: holy war 118; regulations 136–8, **137**

Weeks, Feast *see* Pentecost

Weinfeld, M. 181

Wellhausen, Julius **38**, 165, 167–71, 176, 177–80, 191

Westbrook, R. 71, 138

Westermann, Claus 37, 155, **174**

Wette, W. M. L. de 164, 169, 191

Whybray, R. N. 3, 174–6

Wilson, Monica 83

worship, Jewish **132**

Yahwist (J) source 165, *166*, 167, 168–72, *170*; dating 148, 172, 173, 177, 180; and Elohistic source 173–4; and promise of the land 148–9

years, holy 98–9, 133